Commentary on 1 Timothy
and
Commentary on 2 Timothy

Commentary on 1 Timothy

and

Commentary on 2 Timothy

JOHANN GERHARD

Translated by Joshua J. Hayes

Edited by Benjamin T. G. Mayes and Joshua J. Hayes

CONCORDIA PUBLISHING HOUSE • SAINT LOUIS

Published by Concordia Publishing House
3558 S. Jefferson Ave., St. Louis, Missouri 63118-3968
1-800-325-3040 • www.cph.org

Cover Image: Depicting St Timothy, originally from Neuwiller (Lr. Rhine) (stained glass), French School, (12th century) / Musee National du Moyen Age et des Thermes de Cluny, Paris / Bridgeman Images

All quotations from Scripture and other authors in this work are translated from Johann Gerhard, *Adnotationes Ad Priorem D. Pauli Ad Timotheum Epistolam* (Erfurt: Saher, 1643) and *Adnotationes Ad Posteriorem D. Pauli Ad Timotheum Epistolam* (Erfurt: Saher, 1643).

This work uses the SBL Hebrew Unicode font developed by the Font Foundation, under the leadership of the Society of Biblical Literature. For further information on this font or on becoming a Font Foundation member, see http://www.sbl-site.org/educational/biblicalfonts.aspx.

Manufactured in the United States of America

4 5 6 7 8 9 10 30 29 28 27 26 25

Contents

Commentary on St. Paul's Second Epistle to Timothy

Dedication

> κήρυξον τὸν λόγον. ["Preach the Word."] The connection is that he is laying out his purpose for such a serious, grave charge—namely, that Timothy diligently discharge the office of preaching and the other duties of the ecclesiastical ministry.
>
> —*Johann Gerhard*

κήρυξον τὸν λόγον. This admonition is the motto of Concordia Theological Seminary, and so it is with great love that we—the Concordia Theological Seminary Master of Divinity Class of 2017 and Alternate Route Class of 2016—present these commentaries to our beloved seminary for the good of the Church and the glory of God as a token of our gratitude to the faculty and staff for faithfully forming and preparing us to meet this grave charge.

Patrons of This Translation

This translation of Johann Gerhard's *Commentaries on 1 and 2 Timothy* was commissioned by the Master of Divinity Class of 2017 and Alternate Route Class of 2016 of Concordia Theological Seminary, Fort Wayne, Indiana, as their class gift. In so doing, they have made available to all Christians throughout the world a theological treasure that will endure.

Bradley D. Akey
Phillip J. Allman
Adam P. E. Barkley
Kevin Belter
Phillip Beukema
Donald J. Bruce
Robert Q. Bruggeman
David D. Casey-Motley
René G. Castillero
Christopher Clark
Kurt Cochran
Thomas J. Cowell
Jacob Eichers
Eamonn M. Ferguson
George Fields
Phillip Fischaber
Kevin Foley
Alex C. Garber IV
Steven M. Hackman
Justin M. Hildebrand
Santi E. Keinbaum
Matthew C. Koterba
Kelly Krieg
Gabriel J. Martin
Nicholas D. Martinez
Kyle McBee
Adam M. McDowell
Thomas T. Presley
Dean G. Rager
James Rockhill
Eric M. Rudsenske
Scott A. Salo
Ryan B. Schneider
Aaron D. Spratt
Richard Craig Stephens
David J. Walsh
David M. Weirauch
Timothy J. Wilcoxen
Marcus A. Williams
Trenton Wollberg
Aaron E. Yaeger
Christopher James Yeager

Translator's Preface

The exegesis of Reformation-era and post-Reformation Lutheranism fills vast German and Latin volumes, but hitherto barely any of it has been translated into English. Lutherans in Germany in the sixteenth and seventeenth centuries wrote cursory explanations of biblical books; published commentaries that focused on the philology of the sacred text; preached through books of the Bible and Apocrypha at midweek worship services; published sermon studies and collections of sermons (postils) for the liturgical year; brought forth Bibles in parallel languages (Hebrew, Greek, Latin, and German); and even wrote rhymed paraphrases of entire biblical books.[1] The great dogmatic works of the era rest upon this exegetical literature, yet the vastness of the literature has perhaps daunted scholars and translators from making even a beginning of bringing this literature to English-speaking readers. The present volume makes a small contribution to this deficit.

Here we present Johann Gerhard's (1582–1637) commentaries on 1 and 2 Timothy, published posthumously by his son, Johann Ernst Gerhard (1621–68).[2] The elder Gerhard outlines the general pattern for these commentaries in *Method of Theological Study*.[3] There he describes how one should outline each chapter and make verse-by-verse notes on grammar, syntax, connections, interpretations of the church fathers,

1 See the extensive, though by no means exhaustive, bibliography provided by Johann Georg Walch, *Bibliotheca Theologica Selecta Litterariis Adnotationibus Instructa*, vol. 4 (Jenae: sumtu viduae Croeckeriane), 400–1050.

2 *Adnotationes Ad Priorem D. Pauli Ad Timotheum Epistolam* (Erfurt: Saher, 1643); *Adnotationes Ad Posteriorem D. Pauli Ad Timotheum Epistolam* (Erfurt: Saher, 1643).

3 Johann Gerhard, "Method of Theological Study," in *On Interpreting Sacred Scripture and Method of Theological Study*, trans. Joshua J. Hayes, Theological Commonplaces I–II (St. Louis: Concordia, 2017), part 3, section 1, ch. 4, "On the Meticulous Reading of Scripture."

the resolution of apparent contrarieties, noteworthy observations, etc. Therefore this volume helps us see how Gerhard practiced what he described in *Method of Theological Study*.

Gerhard's chief adversary in this volume is the Papist exegete Guilielmus Estius (Willem Hessels van Est, 1542–1613), whose commentaries on the New Testament Epistles ranked among the most dominant of their time. Clearly Gerhard wrote these commentaries, in part, as a response to Estius's work.

Throughout this commentary, Gerhard assumes proficiency in Greek and Latin. To make this volume accessible, we have included a literal translation of the Greek in [brackets] where Gerhard gave none. These translations aim to match Gerhard's interpretation but should not be considered the definitive way Gerhard would have translated the text. What of Gerhard's original Latin to include was somewhat a subjective decision, but we have generally included his Latin when it is a quotation from a Bible translation (e.g., the Vulgate) or is otherwise warranted to complete the sense. In his discussions on matters of textual criticism and translation, Gerhard sometimes draws on the Syriac translations of the New Testament.[4] We have transliterated the Syriac whereas Gerhard had it printed in standard Hebrew characters.

As the original publication title suggests, these are more notes (adnotationes) than an exhaustive commentary (enarratio), though the latter term was used in the title printed within each volume. Since Gerhard does not discuss or quote all of the Greek text, the reader was expected to read this commentary with an eye to his Greek New Testament. The concision of these commentaries, however, is appreciated and offers a useful pattern for the parish pastor who must prepare notes to teach on various books of the Bible.

The publication of this volume is directly the result of the patronage of the Concordia Theological Seminary (Fort Wayne, Indiana) Master of Divinity Class of 2017 and Alternate Route Class of 2016. They are to be commended for providing the church with such a lasting treasure. A commentary on the first two of St. Paul's "pastoral epistles" seemed an especially fitting gift from these future pastors to the church. Dawn Mirly Weinstock served as production editor for this volume. The Rev. Dr. Christopher W. Mitchell gave his expertise and attention to the Syriac in this volume. To God alone be the glory.

Joshua J. Hayes

4 For more information about the Syriac New Testament and its relation to textual criticism, see Peter J. Williams, "The Syriac Versions of the New Testament," in *The Text of the New Testament in Contemporary Research: Essays on the Status Quaestionis*, ed. Bart D. Ehrman and Michael W. Holmes, 2nd rev. ed. (Leiden: Brill, 2012), 143–66; and D. C. Parker, *An Introduction to the New Testament Manuscripts and Their Texts* (Cambridge: Cambridge University Press, 2008), 64–66, 121–22, 264–65.

Commentary on St. Paul's First Epistle to Timothy

Introduction

§ 1. The efficient cause[1] or principal author of this Epistle is the Holy Spirit, by whose inspiration Paul not only preached the Gospel orally but also put it down in the Scriptures (2 Pet. 1:21). Irenaeus (*Advers. haereses*, bk. 3, ch. 1, p. 169): "We have come to know the plan for our salvation through no others than through those by whom the Gospel came to us. Indeed, what they once preached, they later delivered to us by God's will in the Scriptures, which shall be the foundation and pillar of our faith."

The efficient, ministerial cause is the apostle Paul, as is clear from the very beginning of the Epistle. The Epistle begins: Παῦλος ἀπόστολος Ἰησοῦ χριστοῦ κατ᾽ ἐπιταγὴν θεοῦ ["Paul, an apostle of Jesus Christ by God's command"]. The Syriac paraphrase agrees with the Greek text here: *pawlos shliykha' dyeshu' mshikha'*.

§ 2. *Recipient.* Of Paul's fourteen Epistles,[2] four were given to individuals: two to Timothy, one to Titus, and one to Philemon. The rest were written to entire churches.

Timothy, to whom this Epistle was written, was born to a Jewish mother whose name was Eunice, the daughter of Lois (2 Tim. 1:5). His father was Greek. At Lystra in Lycaonia (Acts 16:1) Paul took him in as a permanent companion of his travels. Paul gives this outstanding testament to his faithfulness (Phil. 2:20): "I have no one like-minded, who is concerned for you with sincere affection" (so genuinely). He was circumcised because of the Jews (Acts 16:2–3). Petilianus the Donatist considered this Timothy, Paul's disciple, to be a layman (Augustine, *Contra lit. Petilian.*, bk. 3, ch. 106). However, it is clear from both of Paul's Epistles to him that Paul appointed him bishop of the church at Ephesus, and indeed he was the distinguished light of the eastern church. Eusebius (*Hist. eccles.*, bk. 3, ch. 4) and Jerome (*Catalog.*) testify to this. For fifteen years

1 Something by means of which something else happens and on which the effect of that happening depends; that which brings about an effect.

2 Gerhard included the Epistle to the Hebrews in the number of Paul's Epistles. See *On Scripture* (1625 *Exegesis*, Commonplace I), §§ 274–78.

(others say forty) he discharged this episcopal office with great renown and success, according to Eusebius (*Hist. eccles.*, bk. 3, ch. 4), who writes (bk. 11, ch. 20) that "this Timothy was Peter's successor at Alexandria." Some think he was the angel with whom Christ finds fault in Rev. 2:4. Nicephorus (*Hist.*, bk. 2, ch. 22) testifies that he was present with the apostles at the death of the God-bearing Virgin. As to his death, they say that he was stoned to death under Emperor Nero after he very harshly rebuked the idolatrous worship practices at the sacred feast of Diana.

§ 3. *The material or argument of this Epistle.* This entire Epistle is didactic and encompasses various admonitions regarding the duties of ministers of the church and other believers. Besides those admonitions, Paul also asserts his apostleship in this Epistle (chs. 1–2); he lays out the chief headings of the Gospel or Christian doctrine (at the end of ch. 3); and he predicts the apostasy to come in the last days through false teachers (at the beginning of ch. 4).

§ 4. *Form or arrangement.* In chapter 1 he reiterates the sum of Christian doctrine and convicts those who indulge in vain and useless questions.

In chapter 2 he lays out certain admonitions about the necessity of the public prayers, about the person and office of our Mediator, and about the adornment of women.

In chapter 3 he details the virtues and requirements for both bishops and deacons.

In chapter 4 he prophesies about the last days when many will abandon the faith.

In chapter 5 he passes on certain salutary teachings regarding the governing of church and state.

In chapter 6 he reminds servants of their duty, teaches about guarding against false teachers, and instructs the rich about the right use of wealth.

§ 5. *Purpose.* Estius (on this passage):

> When the apostle left Ephesus, he appointed Timothy bishop of that city and charged him tirelessly to keep watch against the Judaizers and other corrupters of the teaching of the Gospel. Some of these had already arisen, and some were going to arise, as he foresaw. Therefore the apostle instructs him not as just any Christian but as a bishop of the Christian people, though this Epistle was not written only for Timothy's sake but for all bishops, that they might have the precepts for rightly administering their office.

Cosmas Magalianus, a Jesuit, claims:

> The apostle wrote this First Epistle to Timothy chiefly on account of the school of Simon. Among his other errors, his most pernicious teaching was that the angels must be worshiped as sort of secondary gods and mediators without whom our prayers cannot reach the ears of God. Paul opposes this

error in chapter 2, saying, "There is one Mediator between God and man, the man Christ Jesus" [1 Tim. 2:5].

But it is more correct to say that the apostle's chief aim is that he wanted to use Timothy's person to instruct all faithful teachers of the church as to how [they] should conduct [themselves] in [their] office. Again, Magalianus warns that "in this Epistle the apostle teaches that faith must be joined to works," and he adds: "Would that the heretics of today grasped this teaching. Then with the curb of God's Law they would restrain the license to sin they brought upon us by their crooked opinions." I respond. It is one thing to separate faith from works; it is another thing to attribute justification to faith and not to works. The latter is our teaching; the former is Magalianus's false accusation. Magalianus casts baseless words to the winds when he blathers thus: "I am surprised that Luther and his ilk did not erase this Pauline Epistle from the sacred canon, for it so clearly upholds instructions that teach morality and demand purity of conscience, and it condemns every moral depravity." But we have no need for an eraser here because this apostolic teaching is in no way contrary to our teaching of justification.

§ 6. *Authorship.* The heretics who once either wholly rejected all of Paul's Epistles or at least corrupted them (Eusebius, *Hist. eccles.*, bk. 3, ch. 27; Nicephorus, bk. 4, ch. 4) also repudiated this Epistle. Marcion held to this heresy so that he rejected 1 and 2 Timothy, Titus, and Hebrews as unworthy of the apostle. But [the following points] confirm the canonical and truly divine authority of this Epistle and the rest of Paul's Epistles: (1) The author's name is clearly stated, that this was written by Paul as that chosen instrument of the Holy Spirit. (2) The nature of its teaching, which is truly divine. (3) Its most precise conformity with the rest of the undisputed books of Scripture in the canon. (4) Its majestic style and unique quality. (5) The attestation of the primitive church near to apostolic times. (6) The inner testimony in the heart of each believer by the Holy Spirit, who through this Epistle effectively teaches, persuades, and comforts.

§ 7. *Place of writing.* Athanasius (*Synop.*) and Theodoret (preface to the Pauline Epistles) claim that this Epistle was written in Macedonia. Baronius (*Annal.*, tom. 1, *anno Christi* 57) approves their opinion. They support this from the apostle's words in [1 Tim.] 1:3: "Just as I asked you to stay in Ephesus when I went to Macedonia." But the attached subscription contradicts this: "The first [Epistle] to Timothy, written from Laodicea, the metropolis of Phrygia Pacatiana." The Syriac also [speaks against this]: *shlmt 'egarta' dalwoth tiymathe'us qdmyth' de'tctbth mn ldiyqiya'* ("This concludes the First Epistle to Timothy which was written from Laodicea"). Therefore it is more correct to say that it was written in the town of Laodicea of Phrygia Pacatiana. Even Theodoret himself eventually accepts this opinion at the end of his commentary on this

Epistle: "The First Epistle to Timothy was written at Laodicea, which is the metropolis of Phrygia." Estius opposes this position on the grounds that the apostle asserts (Col. 2:1) that he has not appeared before the Laodiceans, and he thinks that this Epistle [to the Colossians] was written long after. But it has not yet been clearly demonstrated that Colossians was written long after 1 Timothy.

§ 8. *Time of writing*. Those who say that this Epistle was written in Macedonia think that it was written after Paul had left Ephesus and set out for Macedonia (Acts 20:1). They think this can be deduced from the opening words of this Epistle ([1 Tim.] 1:3): "Just as I asked you to stay at Ephesus when I went to Macedonia." But this is clearly an assumption, and the proof deduced for it is weak.

§ 9. *Worth and use*. Augustine (*De doctr. Christ.*, bk. 4, ch. 16) wanted "the man placed as a teacher of the church to carry before his eyes the three apostolic Epistles, two of which were written to Timothy and one to Titus." Tertullian (*Contra Marcion.*, bk. 5) teaches that "these three Epistles contain almost everything that belongs to the office, election, teaching, and virtues in which bishops and other ministers of the church should excel." Specifically regarding 1 Timothy, Nicephorus (*Eccl. hist.*, bk. 2, ch. 34) says that "in it Paul expresses an outline, so to speak, of a bishop's life."

Cosmas Magalianus, a Jesuit (preface to *Oper. hierarch.* or commentary on the Epistles to Timothy and Titus, sect. 8) writes: "Paul so earnestly and in so many Epistles dealt with the instruction of sacred ministers and episcopal discipline because he foresaw that there would be heretics such as Luther and [Matthias Flacius] Illyricus who taught that the sacred ordination of ministers of the church belongs to secular princes and lay magistrates."

I respond. (1) No one teaches that ordination belongs to secular princes and lay magistrates. Rather, we say that it uniquely belongs to ecclesiastical persons. (2) We grant the call to the Christian magistrate, but not to him alone but also to the other stations or orders of the church—namely, the ministers of the church and the Christian people.

Chapter I

[The parts of this chapter.]

Besides the inscription which comprises the first two verses, there are three parts to this chapter:

(1) An admonition (νουθετική), wherein he urges Timothy to restrain certain perverse teachers of the Law (vv. 3–11).

(2) A defense, wherein he asserts his apostleship (vv. 12–17).

(3) An encouragement (προτρεπτική), wherein he encourages Timothy bravely to keep up the fight in his ministry against all impediments. He connects [having] a good conscience to sound teaching (vv. 18–20).

Verse 1.

Παῦλος ἀπόστολος Ἰησοῦ χριστοῦ. ["Paul, an apostle of Jesus Christ."] First, he gives the usual subscription, inscription, and greeting. *But why does he call himself an apostle right from the start of the Epistle?* I respond. He does this: (1) To gain authority for his teaching, which the false apostles were disparaging. (2) To show the dignity of his office. Although he had no need to assert his apostolic authority for the sake of the letter's recipient, it was still necessary for the sake of those under Timothy's charge, so that they would not despise the teachings of their bishop which were supported by the apostle's authority. (3) To expose the perversity of the false apostles.

Chrysostom (tom. 3, homil. ult.) reminds us that the noun "apostle" is so completely attached to Paul that his epithet is "the apostle." "When you say 'the apostle,'" he says, "everyone thinks of Paul."

κατ' ἐπιταγὴν θεοῦ σωτῆρος ἡμῶν καὶ κυριόυ Ἰησοῦ χριστοῦ τῆς ἐλπίδος ἡμῶν. ["By command of God our Savior and of the Lord Jesus Christ our hope."] This is how the oldest copies read, with the conjunction καὶ ["and"] coming after σωτῆρος ["Savior"]. However, in the *Editio Complutensis* it reads thus: κατ' ἐπιταγὴν θεοῦ πατρὸς καὶ σωτῆρος ἡμῶν Ἰησοῦ χριστοῦ ["By command of God the Father and our Savior Jesus Christ"], where the conjunction comes before the word σωτῆρος ["Savior"]. Those who altered the first, usual reading (which even blessed Luther followed) undoubtedly thought it unusual for God the Father to be called "our Savior," since elsewhere this title is attributed to Christ. But since salvation is a work [God does] outside [of Himself] [*opus ad extra*], it is common to the entire Trinity with the order and distinction of persons still maintained. The Father is our Savior because He sent the Son into the flesh to accomplish the work of redemption. Hence, Titus 3:4 expressly gives Him the title "Savior." The Son is our Savior because He redeemed us by His blood and gained salvation for us. The Holy Spirit is our Savior because He brings the benefits of Christ our Redeemer to us in the Word of the Gospel and applies them to us through faith, which He works in our hearts.

Ἐπιταγὴν ["command"] (from ἐπιτάσσω, "I enjoin, I command") is an order or command. The Syriac has *bepuqdana*, "by command," which is also how Theophylact's translator rendered it. Chrysostom and Theophylact rightly highlight that ἐπιταγὴν is more forceful than κλῆσιν ["a calling"]; ἐπιταγὴν not only means "command" but also an injunction and delegation. In his other Epistles he says "by the will of God," but here he says it "by the command and delegation of God." This authoritative command [*imperium*] to which Paul appeals he received from the Son (Acts 9:6; Gal. 1:1). And yet here he ascribes it to the Father because it is a work the Trinity does outwardly (cf. Theophylact, Oecumenius).

τῆς ἐλπίδος ἡμῶν. "Who is our hope." The article has an expository force. Moreover, Christ is called "our hope" (1) because we hope and believe in Him; (2) because He is the sole foundation of our hope, for through Him alone we hope for eternal life. (3) Some add that "Christ is called our 'greatest hope' because He Himself works faith in our hearts." This is in reference to the Judaizers who put their hope of salvation in the Law and the ceremonies, though Christ alone is and should be our hope. For by His merit alone can we hope for and obtain forgiveness and eternal life.

Reproof. From the fact that Christ is called our "greatest hope," Tertullian (*De Trinit.*) rightly concludes that Christ is true God: "If Christ were only a man, then why put hope in Him since Jer. 17[:5] curses hope that is put in a man?"

It is also worth noting that here the Father is called "Savior" [and] the Son, "our hope," but in 1 Tim. 4:10 and Titus 2:13 Christ is called "Savior"; also, Rom. 15:13 calls the Father "the God of hope." From this Theodoret also infers the ὁμοοὐσία ["consubstantiality"] of the Father and the Son, and thus Christ's true divinity. He says: "He joined the Lord Christ to God, showing the equality of honor. He calls God 'salvation' and Christ 'hope,' neither dividing nor attributing one thing to the other, but he understands that both belong to each person (Ps. 65:5)."

A defense. Estius (on this passage):

> It does not contradict this teaching—that Christ is our hope—for Christians sometimes to call the saints who reign with Christ their hope, for they trust that they are helped by their prayers and merits. For all the help they expect from them, whatever it finally is, they expect only by the merit of Christ. So also even Paul himself sometimes asks for the prayers of those to whom he writes. Surely he could not have done this without the hope and trust he had in them—not to mention that he calls the Thessalonians his "hope" (1 Thess. 2:19).

I respond. (1) Scripture teaches in six hundred places that we are to trust in God alone and put our hope in Him; that they are blessed who trust in God, but they are cursed who make something other than God the object of their trust and hope. (Cf. *On Death* [Commonplace XXIX], § 366.) (2) There is no command, promise, or good example that anyone trusted in dead saints. Therefore faith and trust are not to be divvied up among Christ and the saints. (3) It is one thing to hope well about a man; it is another thing to put hope and trust of the heart in him. The former belongs to love; the latter, to unbelief. (4) The passage in 1 Thess. 2:19 has this meaning: "You are our hope," that is, the reason for our hope that we shall receive the promised reward of grace in heaven as faithful ministers of Christ and the Gospel.

Verse 2.

Τιμοθέῳ γνησίῳ τέκνῳ ἐν πίστει. ["To Timothy, true son in faith."] He calls him "son": (1) Because he had instructed him in the Christian faith. (2) Because he held him in fatherly love (1 Cor. 4:17). (3) Because Timothy in turn held him in filial love. Therefore he calls him "son" with respect to instruction and mutual love.

The Vulgate rendered this *dilecto* ["beloved"], but the Greek more signifies "true son"—that is, with respect to teaching and imitation, not merely age, as Erasmus thinks. Therefore he calls him his "true son"—that is, genuine, sincere, *sharira'* ("true," as the Syriac rendered it)—in that beyond others and as close as possible he approached similarity to Paul in faith, confession, and life (Phil. 2:20).

χάρις, ἔλεος, εἰρήνη. ["Grace, mercy, peace."] These three are combined only in the Epistles to Timothy and Titus, as Theophylact noted. They are distinguished as cause and effect. Χάρις ("grace") means the undeserved kindness and favor of God toward us, which is the source of all good things He bestows upon us.

Ἔλεος ("mercy") means the undeserved forgiveness of sins and the restoration of the image of God.

Εἰρήνη ("peace") denotes a peaceful conscience, joy from knowing the favor of God, and true blessedness. Mercy comes from grace, for it is graciously given to us who are in need of mercy; and peace of conscience comes from mercy (Rom. 5:1). In other places he connects grace and peace, but here he inserts mercy as the source of grace and peace and of all God's benefits.

ἀπὸ θεοῦ πατρὸς ἡμῶν καὶ χριστοῦ Ἰησοῦ τοῦ κυρίου ἡμῶν. ["From God our Father and Christ Jesus our Lord."] In some copies the word κυρίου is repeated twice: καὶ κυρίου Ἰησοῦ χριστοῦ τοῦ κυρίου ἡμῶν ["and from the Lord Jesus Christ, our Lord"]. Erasmus translates it *a Domino Iesu Christo, qui est Dominus noster* ["from the Lord Jesus Christ, who is our Lord"], as if in the one instance He is Lord of all and in the other the Lord of the faithful (1 Tim. 4:10).

However, the Greek copies of Robertus [Stephanus], and also Oecumenius, only read the word κυρίου once, which is also how the Syriac and the Latin translation read it.

Verse 3.

Καθὼς παρεκάλεσά σε. ["Just as I asked you."] The Syriac omitted the particle καθὼς and rendered it simply *b'yt hwyt menak* ("I implored, or asked, you"), possibly because there is no apodosis[1] in the text. Some copies read οὕτως ("thus, so"), which Faber Stapulensis thinks is what should be translated: "Thus I asked you." But Erasmus rightly rebukes this on the grounds that οὕτως is never the same as ὡς ["as"]. In this elliptical construction something must be repeated from what is common (ἀπὸ τοῦ κοινοῦ): "Just as I asked you to stay in Ephesus, so do" or "so I now repeat my same request in writing." Cajetan hangs the meaning of this part of the verse until v. 18, but this would be an excessively awkward hyperbaton.[2]

Παρεκάλεσά means "to beseech, urge, or ask in persuasive words." Elsewhere it also means "to console and advise." Chrysostom and Theophylact ask us to note that Paul does not use the tone of a teacher but of a suppliant, and in this respect they commend Paul's modesty. Erasmus claims that "the verb παρεκάλεσά in this passage obtains the meaning of urging, since it better fits Paul's person to urge Timothy, whom he calls his son, than to ask him." But in his *Paraphrasis* he expressed it in the sense of asking, which is also what the Syriac translator did.

προσμεῖναι ἐν Ἐφέσῳ. ["To stay/Stay in Ephesus."] Προσμεῖναι, as Erasmus notes, can be in either the infinitive or imperative mood. Some Papists draw proof from these words that the residence of bishops is by divine right, and accordingly there can be no dispensation by the pope in it. To these

1 The main clause of a conditional sentence.

2 An inversion of the normal order of words, especially for the sake of emphasis.

Cosmas Magalianus (commentary on this passage) responds quite in favor of [papal] authority: "As if in things that are by divine right the supreme pontiff cannot grant a dispensation, as in a [monastic] vow, an oath, or even in a ratified marriage."

πορευόμενος εἰς Μακεδονίαν. ["As I was going to Macedonia."] This is an anastrophe[3] in the Greek text: Πορευόμενος εἰς Μακεδονίαν παρεκάλεσά σε προσμεῖναι ἐν Ἐφέσῳ ["As I was going to Macedonia I asked you to stay in Ephesus"]. Paul's departure for Macedonia is mentioned in Acts 20:1: "After the" (Ephesian) "riot died down, Paul summoned his disciples, exhorted them, said good-bye, and set out to go into Macedonia." Timothy was chief among those disciples, and so in saying good-bye he asked him to stay in Ephesus and made him bishop of the presbytery with the laying on of hands.

Apparent contrariety. *In this passage it says that Paul asked Timothy to stay in Ephesus. But, to the contrary, in Acts 20:4 Timothy is listed among those who accompanied Paul on his journey from Ephesus.* I respond. After Paul could not return to Ephesus as quickly as he had hoped (1 Tim. 3:14), Timothy went to him when he was still in Macedonia, and then was with him for a while (as 2 Cor. 1:1 implies).

ἵνα παραγγείλῃς τισὶν. "That you might command certain people." Luther rendered it *und gebötest* ["and might charge"], but this seems to introduce something of a disconnect. By τισὶν he means those who had committed themselves to Christ but were teaching certain useless, false, and harmful things under this guise. Some understand him to mean the Jews. Luther understands them to be the false disciples of the apostles.

μὴ ἑτεροδιδασκαλεῖν. "Not to teach different things," that is, things different from the teaching of the apostles. The verb ἑτεροδιδασκαλεῖν properly signifies to use these teachers at this time and those teachers at another. Here, however, we—along with Chrysostom, Theodoret, Primasius, Ambrosius, and Theophylact—rightly confine it to the false apostles, whose teaching was not only different and foreign but also adulterated the true doctrine. Ἕτερος is used in this way in Acts 2:4 and 1 Cor. 14:21, from which Theophylact rightly teaches that ἑτεροδιδασκαλεῖν is to introduce other teachings or a different doctrine. Moreover, with this word the apostle has in view not only a kind of teaching but also a way of teaching. You see, he wants to maintain both the purity of teaching and the ὑποτύπωσιν ὑγιαινόντων λόγων ["pattern of sound words"] (2 Tim. 1:13).

Estius (commentary on this passage): "It means another teaching that excludes the first. Therefore this passage cannot be opposed to traditions."

3 The inversion of the usual order of words or clauses.

I respond. (1) Not only must nothing contrary to the Gospel be taught in the church, nothing except the Gospel is to be taught (Gal. 1:8). (2) The false apostles were not denying justification through faith in Christ, but they were adding works to faith in the act of justification.

Note that the primary, chief concern for the apostle was to preserve purity of doctrine, for it is the foundation of all religion.

Verse 4.

μηδὲ προσέχειν μύθοις καὶ γενεαλογίαις ἀπεράντοις. ["Nor to pay attention to myths and endless genealogies."] The apostle uses a specific example to illustrate the above general command about being wary of "other teaching" [v. 3]. It can happen that someone is not teaching falsehood but empty and useless things that have no bearing on piety.

Some take "myths" generally to mean false and fictitious things which are therefore also useless. Tertullian (*De praescript.*, ch. 33) understands the Valentinians' disputations about infinite eons. Others understand the astrologers and magicians of Ephesus (Acts 19:19). Others understand the fables of the heathen. But it is more correct to understand it specifically as the Jewish fables and human traditions called *deuterosis*. (Cf. Athanasius and Augustine.)

ἀπεράντοις. "Having no end." Ambrose has "infinite"; Tertullian, "indeterminable."

Apparent contrariety. *In the Old Testament there are some genealogies (1 Chronicles 1). In the New Testament the genealogy of Christ is in Matthew 1 and Luke [3:23–38]. The genealogies of princes have been recorded by many.*

I respond. (1) There were various reasons why it was necessary to keep track of genealogies in the Old Testament. First, to distinguish the tribes and their inheritances, the confusing of which God had forbidden (Num. 36:7). Second, because of the priestly office, to which no one was to be appointed except those from the tribe of Levi. Third, because of the rights of the firstborn, who were owed a double portion of the inheritance. Fourth, and most important, for knowing the Messiah's birth from the tribe of David. All of these reasons have ceased in the New Testament. (2) The apostle does not forbid genealogies in the state or church, but Jewish ones, the misuse of genealogies in the church, and false genealogies of Christ. (3) The Jews sinned with regard to genealogies in that they were obsessed with these thorny, useless questions, which is why the apostle expressly adds "endless genealogies." It takes an endless amount of work to explain all the questions and difficulties that usually arise in searching out and drawing up genealogies.

αἵτινες ζητήσεις παρέχουσιν μᾶλλον ἢ οἰκονομίαν θεοῦ τὴν ἐν πίστει. ["Which occasion questions rather than the plan of God in faith."] This is a comparison of impropriety, where one thing is affirmed and another is denied:

"which occasion questions, not the edification of the church." Genealogies provide the material for innumerable questions, but they do nothing at all for piety, which brings men to God.

By ζητήσεις the apostle understands not just any questions but those that are useless, unnecessary, indeterminable, such that he calls them ἀπεράντοις ["endless"] earlier in the verse.

There is a variant reading here. Some codices read οἰκοδομὴν while others read οἰκονομίαν. The Greek fathers mostly follow the latter reading. Οἰκοδομὴν means "edification," which is how the Vulgate translated it. Οἰκονομίαν means "providence over management and arrangement," especially that of household affairs. Here it means the arrangement of God, which He ordered and ordained, that the mysteries of religion be received by faith since they are incomprehensible. Those who promote useless questions resist His plan.

Estius (commentary on this passage): "He means 'faith clothed and dressed in love,' that is, faith which works through love. For 'love builds up' (1 Cor. 8[:1]). Therefore faith does not edify except through love."

I respond. (1) We concede that true, living faith is inseparably joined with love, but we deny that faith is formed through love. (2) Faith does not get its efficacy to edify from love; rather, it makes us partakers of the Holy Spirit who is effective in us for edification.

Verse 5.

τὸ δὲ τέλος τῆς παραγγελίας ἐστὶν ἀγάπη. ["But the goal of the command is love."] Some think the particle δὲ here is connective ["and"], but it can keep its usual meaning ["but"]. For the apostle is setting the true treatment of theology in opposition to these "useless and endless questions." Here love serves as the goal; and godliness, the foundation. Those idle questions were rousing up contentions (1 Tim. 6:4) and thus were opposed to love.

τέλος τῆς παραγγελίας. The "aim" and "goal" of God's commands, or Law, is love—both with respect to the one commanding, since God so exalted the Law that it should be the norm of love and the other affections and acts of men, and with respect to the one obeying, to whom the τελείωσις ("perfection") prescribed in the Law applies (Augustine, *Enchir.*, penultimate ch.; *De doctr. Christ.*, bk. 1, ch. 35). Thomas (commentary on this passage) gives this reason: "Because all the commands of the Law come down to love." The most fitting explanation comes from Rom. 13:10: "Love is the fulfillment of the Law," because τέλος means "perfection and fulfillment." Therefore the meaning is: "The Law is fulfilled by love, not by airing meddlesome questions."

παραγγελίας. ["Command."] Theophylact applies this only to the apostle's command. Ambrose more correctly thinks it should be related by synecdoche[4]

4 A figure of speech in which a part is made to represent the whole or vice versa.

to all the commands of the Law. "Law" is understood by the word "command" since it is comprised of many commands.

ἐκ καθαρᾶς καρδίας. ["From a pure heart."] Love is "from a pure heart" when it not only shows itself in words but also flows forth from the heart. Augustine (*De civ. Dei*, bk. 1, ch. 35): "The heart is pure which is free from lust and love of self and loves nothing but what should be loved."

καὶ συνειδήσεως ἀγαθῆς. ["And a good conscience."] A conscience is good when it is free from pretense and hidden hate. Ambrose translates "good conscience" as *vitam bonam* ["good life"]. This follows from the former, because a pure heart is the source of a good conscience. Augustine (*De doctr. Christ.*, bk. 1, last ch.) thinks this was said "because of hope, which is the effect of a good conscience. For the stimulus of a bad conscience resides in him who has no hope of reaching what he believes and loves."

καὶ πίστεως ἀνυποκρίτου. ["And a sincere faith."] For faith that is true and living is the root of love and all good works. A faith that is ἀνυποκρίτου is that by which one believes in Christ from the heart without hypocrisy (2 Tim. 1:5).

Apparent contrariety. (1) *It says here that love is the goal of the Law. But Rom. 10:4 says that Christ is the goal of the Law.* I respond. Τέλος has two preferred meanings. First, it denotes the "end" or "completion of a thing." Hence in Demosthenes it is τὸ τέλος ἔχειν ["having completion"].[5] Second, [it denotes] a "payment owed" or "tribute," from which comes τελωνία ["tax office"] (cf. Matt. 17:25; Rom. 13:7). Christ is called the "end of the Law" according to both meanings; but love [is called the "end of the Law"] only according to the former.

(2) *"From sincere faith." But how can faith be faked?* I respond. It can be faked to the eyes of men, but not to the eyes of God "who knows the heart" [Acts 15:8].

(3) *"From a pure heart." But who can say, "My heart is pure" (Prov. 20:9)?* The heart is not pure by nature, and even within the reborn it is not yet pure from every stain of sin. Still, the reborn are said to have a "pure heart" because Christ dwells in their hearts through faith, and they are purified by faith (Eph. 3:17; Acts 15:9).

Verse 6.

ὧν τινες ἀστοχήσαντες ἐξετράπησαν εἰς ματαιολογίαν. ["Some, having wandered from these, have turned aside to idle speech."] He now adds a confirmation for his prior statement from the contrary.

Ὧν, that is, from the three things just listed: a pure heart, a good conscience, and a sincere faith.

5 Demosthenes, *Oration* 58 (LCL 351 [1939], p. 326).

ἀστοχήσαντες. "Wandering from the mark." The Vulgate has *aberrantes* ["wandering away"], but in Greek the participle is past tense: "from which things, after some wandered away." According to Chrysostom, Theophylact, and Oecumenius, this is a metaphor taken from poor javelin throwers.

ἐξετράπησαν. The Vulgate rendered it *conversi sunt* ["turned"], but it is better rendered as *deflexerunt* ["turned aside"], which is more emphatic. This is to be related, first, to a wandering from the faith and, second, from morality.

εἰς ματαιολογίαν. "To idle speech." Luther has *zu vnnützem Geschwetz* ["to useless talk"]. They have turned aside to useless and fruitless studies, teachings, and disputations—such as "myths and genealogies" (v. 4). Erasmus (commentary on this passage) rightly recalls how "the Scholastic teachers have turned aside to idle speech." Because of this, Cosmas Magalianus and Guilielmus Estius berate him, though they still admit that "sometimes some sinned from being excessively curious or superfluous."

Verse 7.

θέλοντες εἶναι νομοδιδάσκαλοι. ["Wanting to be teachers of the Law."] He is explaining who those men are who wander from the true aim. By this charge he is ascribing significant ignorance to them.

They want to be "teachers of the Law." Luther has *Wollen der schrifft Meister sein*. Matt. 23:7: "They love to be called 'rabbi' by men." Rom. 2:19–20: "You trust that you are a guide for the blind, a light for those who are in darkness, an instructor of the foolish, διδάσκαλον ['a teacher'] of infants."

μὴ νοοῦντες μήτε ἃ λέγουσι, μήτε περὶ τίνων διαβεβαιοῦνται. "They know neither what they are saying nor about the things they are speaking." They do not understand the principles of their teaching nor the conclusions they derive from them.

Theophylact (on this passage): "Through ambition they themselves became the authors of this ignorance and error of theirs."

Verse 8.

Οἴδαμεν δὲ ὅτι καλὸς ὁ νόμος, ἐάν τις αὐτῷ νομίμως χρῆται. ["But we know that the Law is good if one uses it lawfully."] This is an anthypophora[6] by which he shows that he is not attacking the Law itself but the crooked teachers of the Law. By this charge he, at the same time, inculcates the true use of the Law.

"But we know," that is, we believers in Christ, the true and sincere teachers.

"The Law is good" (1) because it comes from God, who is good; (2) because it teaches and commands nothing but good; (3) because when kept it leads to the infinite good.

6 A figure of speech in which one reasons aloud, usually by raising and answering one's own question.

There is a nice pun in the apostle's words. "The Law is good, if one uses it legally" or "lawfully," that is, according to the nature of the Law and the mind of the Lawgiver.

By "the Law" Ambrose understands "the ceremonial law," but what follows shows that Paul is talking about the moral Law, for the sins he lists as being contrary to "the Law" are committed against the moral Law.

Apparent contrariety. *"The Law is good." To the contrary, Ezek. 20:25: "I gave them precepts which were not good."* I respond. (1) Some take the statement in Ezekiel as about the ceremonial law, which is not good after its abrogation. (2) Cassianus (*Collat.* 23, ch. 4) takes it as "about the moral Law compared to the Gospel of perfection." (3) Jerome thinks they should be called "not good, that is, indifferent, because it does not say 'bad' but 'not good.'" (4) Lyranus thinks this should be taken "with respect to its outcome, because they were not good for them on account of their transgression." (5) The meaning of this prophetic saying is this: "In My just judgment I allow them to follow such a religion that gave them neither peace of conscience nor salvation of their souls." (See Luther, marginal notes on this passage.)

Observation. Because in this life we cannot perfectly fulfill the Law and become fellows of eternal life by it, he "lawfully uses the Law" who uses it as a pedagogue leading to Christ (Gal. 3:24).

Verse 9.

Connection. The legitimate purpose of the Law is explained, that through it behavior and vices are corrected and amended.

εἰδὼς τοῦτο. ["Knowing this."] In v. 8 he had spoken in the plural, but here he speaks in the singular. This change of person is not infrequent for Hebrews. But more correctly this relates to what immediately precedes: "If one uses it lawfully." The meaning, therefore, is that it belongs to the legitimate use of the Law that one knows that it was not established for the righteous.

ὅτι δικαίῳ νόμος οὐ κεῖται. "The Law is not established for the righteous."

(1) Not because the righteous man is not obligated by the Law or is not bound to keep the Law or has been utterly released from laws.

(2) Rather, this must be understood in three respects. First, with respect to justification. The Law is not established for the righteous so that it can hinder him from the gracious justification through faith in Christ. "For Christ is the end of the Law for righteousness for all who believe" (Rom. 10:4). "The Law is our pedagogue to Christ, so that we may be justified from faith" (Gal. 3:24). Second, with respect to compulsion. You see, since the one who has been justified and regenerated through faith in Christ freely obeys the Law and does what is pleasing to God by the leading and impulse of the Holy Spirit, there is no need to pull him back and deter him from sinning by the threats of the Law.

Philo: "The righteous need neither commands nor prohibitions." So the Law is no longer established in a way that harms the reborn, but to them it is the norm and rule of good living (Gal. 5:23). Nor does it concern the righteous man as coercive but as guiding. Third, with respect to condemnation. The Law does not exercise its proper office against the righteous man, accusing, terrifying, and condemning him. It is not established for the righteous so as to condemn him, for he has been justified through faith in Christ and has been regenerated through His Spirit unto a holy life. You see, the verb κεῖται denotes "the burden of the curse" which weighs heavy upon transgressors of the Law. Thus in Matt. 3:10 the ax is said to be κεῖται against the base of the tree, that is, it stands ready to fell the tree. Augustine: "The Law is not imposed on the righteous as a burden that oppresses him with the fear of punishment." Thomas speaks the same way. Augustine again (*De Spiritu et lit.*, ch. 9): "A boy has no need for a pedagogue or guide after he arrives at his teacher. He does not need conveyance who has already arrived at his destination." From this one can easily determine how to respond to this apparent contrariety based on Psalm 119: "Put the Law on me, O Lord" [v. 33]. (Cf. Augustine, *Contra Faust.*, bk. 15, ch. 8; on John, tract. 3; Letter 19 *ad Hieron.*; *De nat. et grat.*, ch. 57; *De grat. et lib. arb.*, ch. 12; and Sermon 11 on Psalm 118.) By the word "righteous" the apostle means the one who truly believes in Christ, is reborn, pious, and committed to righteousness, as can be understood from the antithesis.

ἀνόμοις δὲ, etc. ["But for the lawless."] The apostle begins the antithesis [moving] from the general to the specific, and in the specific he follows the order of the Decalogue.

ἀνόμοις δὲ καὶ ἀνυποτάκτοις. The Vulgate has *iniustis et non subditis* ["for the unrighteous and insubordinate"]. Ambrose has *exlegibus et inobsequentibus* ["for the lawless and disobedient"]. Theophylact's translator has *iniquis et inoboedientibus* ["for the iniquitous and disobedient"]. By these two words he signifies unrighteousness in general, but with the following words he signifies specific and chief aspects of unrighteousness. The ἀνυποτάκτοις are those who refuse to be subordinated, nor do they tolerate authority; they are rebellious and disobedient people.

ἀσεβέσιν. ["For the ungodly."] Those who do not give God due worship.

ἁμαρτωλοῖς. ["For sinners."] Those beholden to notorious sins, the infamous.

ἀνοσίοις. "Profane." Those not held back from sins by any scruples.

βεβήλοις. "Impure, worldly, tainted by sin."

πατραλῴαις καὶ μητραλῴαις. ["For those who strike father and mother."] These words not only denote parricides but also those who strike parents without killing them.

ἀνδροφόνοις. "For murderers." In the Hebrew way of speaking, the word "man" [*vir*] often also includes woman.[7]

Verse 10.

πόρνοις. "Fornicators." Those who lie with women outside of marriage.

ἀρσενοκοίταις. Those who lie with a man "as if with a woman" (Lev. 18:22; 20:13).

ἀνδραποδισταῖς. The Vulgate renders it *plagiariis* ["enslavers"], "those who steal and sell free men or the servants of others." They are called ἀνδραποδισταῖς who are ἀνδραπόδων ποδισταί ("stealers of slaves") or who derive profit from slave trading.

Lawyers generally define enslavers as "robbers of men," that is, those who abduct men (be they slave or free), hold them, and sell them. This even includes those who buy people for slavery when they know that they are free.

Lyranus puts it humorously: "Enslavers [*plagiarii*] are those accustomed to inflicting blows [*plagas*] and beatings on others."

ψεύσταις. ["For liars."] Those who promote lies maliciously (Rev. 21:27; 22:15).

ἐπιόρκοις. "Those who commit perjury."

καὶ εἴ τι ἕτερον, etc. ["And if anything else."] The particle εἴ ["if"] here does not express doubt but addition (cf. Rom. 13:9). Because it was too long to list one by one all the kinds of sins for which the Law was established, he comprehends them in the generic clause "whatever else."

τῇ ὑγιαινούσῃ διδασκαλίᾳ. ["To sound teaching."] Heavenly teaching is called ["sound"] through metaphor—because it is not afflicted by sicknesses of errors—and through metonymy—because it brings true health to the soul. A parallel passage is 2 Tim. 1:13: Ὑποτύπωσιν ἔχε ὑγιαινόντων λόγων ["Hold to the pattern of sound words"]. Specifically, however, the Gospel is called "sound teaching" because it cures consciences wounded by the terrors of the Law by showing them Christ as their Savior and Physician.

Estius concludes from this passage that "all these kinds of sins are mortal, that is, one does not become righteous through them but unrighteous." Hence the logical conclusion, he claims, is that "there are some sins that do not hinder one from truly being called and being righteous. Accordingly, he truly keeps the Law and fulfills it, and this not merely by imputation. There are sins which are called venial, and it is impossible for even the righteous to live life without them." I respond. (1) We do not deny or remove the distinction between mortal and venial sins. (2) We do deny, however, that some sins are venial by their very nature, for all sins are committed against the Law. (3) The reborn do not stop

7 Gerhard is referring to how this Greek word is cognate to ἀνήρ, which means a man and not a woman, but here the murder of women is also included.

being righteous through venial sins since through faith they are in Christ and under grace. At the same time, however, their venial sins keep their inherent and actual[8] righteousness from being perfect so that by it they could stand up before the judgment of God. (4) For the righteousness that stands up before the judgment of God must be perfect and pure. Such is the righteousness of Christ alone which has been imputed through faith, not our habitually inherent and actual righteousness.

Verse 11.

Connection. He commends the Gospel both because of its effect and because of its efficient cause[9] and principal author.

"Which is according to the Gospel of glory." The "which is" is not in the Greek, but Theophylact rightly advises that it needs to be supplied. For this is the explanation of the aforesaid "sound teaching."

τὸ εὐαγγέλιον τῆς δόξης. That is, "the glorious Gospel." This is a common Hebraism. He calls it this because:

(1) It teaches how Christ gloriously rose from death, ascended into heaven, and brought back a glorious triumphal procession of men.

(2) In it God manifests His glory, because through it He manifests His wisdom, goodness, truthfulness, power, etc. (2 Cor. 4:4). Therefore it is called "the Gospel of the glory of God" because God is glorified and praised through it.

(3) At the same time it shows the way to reach heavenly glory.

ὃ ἐπιστεύθην ἐγώ. This was poorly translated by Faber [Stapulensis] as *cui creditus sum ego* ["to which I was entrusted"]. Erasmus put it more correctly as *quod concreditum*, that is, "which was entrusted to me." This is also how the Vulgate rendered it. [The sense is:] "The preaching of which was assigned to me by God" (cf. Rom. 3:2).

Verse 12.

Connection. Paul illustrates the teaching of the Gospel by his own example and tells of his calling to be an apostle. Lest he seem to be saying that it was because of his own merits that the Gospel was entrusted to him, he thanks Christ not only for entrusting the office of preaching the Gospel to him but also for having him administer it fruitfully and bravely despite so many persecutions.

Καὶ χάριν ἔχω τῷ ἐνδυναμώσαντί με χριστῷ, etc. ["And I thank Him who strengthened me, Christ," etc.] In some Latin copies the particle "in" is added: *Gratias ago ei, qui me confortavit in Christo Iesu* ["I thank Him who strengthened me in Christ Jesus."] However, that "in" is not in the Greek copies.

---

8 "Actual" in the sense of a righteousness that comes from acts and works as opposed to the righteousness that comes through faith.

9 See above, p. 3 n. 1.

ὅτι πιστόν με ἡγήσατο. ["Because He considered me faithful."] Ambrose limits this to salvific faith. But Chrysostom, Theodoret, Theophylact, and Oecumenius more correctly claim that "faithful" here does not mean "one who believes in Christ" but "one who diligently and assiduously persists in the things entrusted to his trustworthiness" (1 Cor. 4:2). Therefore the sense is, "afterward He granted me that faithfulness by grace." 1 Cor. 7:25: "As one who received mercy from the Lord that I may be faithful."

θέμενος εἰς διακονίαν. "[Appointing me] into ministry." The Vulgate puts it less aptly *in ministerio* ["in ministry"].

Estius (on this passage) correctly notes:

> When he says "because He considered me faithful," this is not to be understood as if God found Paul faithful but did not make him faithful. Rather, in saying less he wanted more to be understood. For men, of course, entrust the management of their goods to those whom they consider faithful (even though they do not make them to be faithful), but God, on the other hand, judges no one to be faithful unless He makes him faithful. That this was the apostle's intention is proved by his thanksgiving.

Verse 13.

Connection. He amplifies and highlights both his own fault and God's grace.

τὸν πρότερον ὄντα βλάσφημον, etc. ["Who formerly was a blasphemer," etc.] The accusative refers to the pronoun με in the previous verse.

The amplification[10] *of fault.* He lists three grades of malice. First, he says that prior to his call to the apostolate he was a βλάσφημον ["blasphemer"], for he publicly ridiculed the teaching of the Gospel as the most pestilent heresy, and he called Christ a deceiver. Second, he says that he was a διώκτην ["persecutor"] of the Christian church (Acts 9:13–14, 21) and that he has persecuted Him in His members. Third, he says that he was ὑβριστήν ["an insolent man"], because he not only inflicted violent persecution on the Christians, but he also ridiculed them with false accusations and mocked them as they suffered persecutions. You see, ὑβριστήν signifies both a "reviler" and a "violent aggressor." Augustine (*Contra Donatist.*, bk. 4, ch. 5) reads *iniuriosum* ["hurtful"] based on Cyprian.

Therefore the first grade of sin was blasphemy or cursing. The second was persecution, which is a greater sin than cursing. The third was violence, which is the greatest sin of all since it adds cruelty to persecution.

Some Greek copies read with an added conjunction καὶ, but this pleonasm[11] is not in the other copies.

---

10 The use of rhetorical tropes (of thought) or schema (of words) to create emphasis.

11 The use of more words than are necessary to convey meaning, either as a fault of style or for emphasis.

The amplification of grace is set forth by the word ἠλεήθην ["mercy was had on me"]. For mercy is more than condoning or pardoning since these only bring the forgiveness of sin. But mercy also includes the calling to the noble office of apostle.

ὅτι ἀγνοῶν ἐποίησα. ["Because I acted ignorantly."] *But how can ignorance be the cause of pardon?* I respond. (1) Augustine, Thomas, and the *Glossa ordinaria* claim that the mention of ignorance increases Paul's sin. (2) According to their hypothesis, one must say that here the particle ὅτι corresponds to the Hebrew *ci*, which should be taken not *causally* ["because"] but *adversatively* ["though"]. It is used in this sense in Acts 3:17. "I obtained mercy, for though I acted ignorantly, that grace superabounded with faith." (3) This explanation is proven from the fact that if the particle ὅτι is taken causally, then ignorance and unbelief will be the cause of the forgiveness of sins; and therefore everyone who sins out of ignorance and unbelief (like the Jews in Acts 3:17; 13:27; 1 Cor. 2:8) would obtain grace. (4) To the contrary, Theophylact and others state that "the mention of ignorance mitigates Paul's sin since he did not wage war against the saints out of hatred but he fought for the Law." Those are Theophylact's words. You see, though ignorance cannot be the direct cause of pardon, it can still be the indirect cause—that which removes prohibition, that is, deliberate malice. For if that were present, then it would be a massive hindrance and would prohibit the showing of mercy so long as it remained. (5) Cyprian (Letter *ad Iubaianum*), Tertullian (*De pudicitia*), Augustine (on Psalm 50; *Contra Donatist.*, bk. 4, ch. 5), Gregory (*Homil. 21 inter 50*) or whoever the author is on the third penitential psalm, and Bernard (*De conversion S. Pauli*, sermon 1) interpret this ignorance as a circumstance extenuating sin. (6) The simplest answer is that Paul is not excusing or extenuating his sin but distinguishing it from the sin against the Holy Spirit.[12] "I acted ἀγνοῶν"—not knowing that the Christian religion was true, out of a certain blind zeal for God's Law; that sin of mine did not proceed from a malicious opposition to known truth.

Parallel passages. Acts 3:17: "And now, brethren, I know that you acted through ignorance, as did your rulers." Luke 23:34: "Father, forgive them, for they know not what they do." Estius states that

> he cites ignorance neither to increase his sin nor to mitigate it, for to some degree it is common for all sins to be done out of ignorance. Instead, he cites ignorance as the reason that he is a very fitting object for God to exercise His mercy upon. For the object or material of mercy is misery; hence the greater the misery, the more it is apt to provoke mercy.

12 See *On Actual Sins* [Commonplace XIII], §§ 107–109.

ἐν ἀπιστίᾳ. ["In unbelief."] Either the preposition ἐν is being used for διά ["through, on account of"] as a Hebraism, or we are to understand the participle ὢν ["being"]. Moreover, these words intimate his status prior to his conversion.

Apparent contrariety. *"I obtained mercy because I acted ignorantly." But in Ps. 59:5 David prays: "Do not have mercy on all," that is, "to none of them who work iniquity."* I respond. The Davidic oracle has to do with those who remain hardened to the end.

Verse 14.

ὑπερεπλεόνασεν δὲ ἡ χάρις τοῦ κυρίου ἡμῶν. ["And the grace of our Lord superabounded."] He again highlights the grace of God as a confirmation. There is great emphasis in the verb ὑπερεπλεόνασεν ("superabounded"): "God's grace more than abounded." "God's grace showed itself abundantly toward me, was effective in me." He is preaching home the immense, incomprehensible treasury of God's grace.

He says that mercy overflowed its bounds toward him both because the gift God gave him through His grace was entirely free (especially as compared to his unworthiness) and because it was great and rich. For not only did it erase his sins, but it also gave him the adoption of sons [cf. Rom. 8:15; Eph. 1:5] and then added the dignity of the apostolic office on top of that.

μετὰ πίστεως. ["With faith."] Chrysostom, Theophylact, Oecumenius, and Primasius explain the preposition μετὰ here causally: "by faith." This is a common Hebraism in the Old and New Testaments.

καὶ ἀγάπης τῆς ἐν χριστῷ Ἰησοῦ. ["And love which are in Christ Jesus."] "By the love with which I love Christ and all believers in Christ." He sets faith in opposition to his former unbelief, love in opposition to his former cruelty which he had directed against the church.

To God's grace he adds its main effects: faith and Christian love, which, he says, superabounded in him by grace.

Estius teaches that "love is joined to faith because without love faith is not enough for salvation." I respond. (1) We concede this about dead faith, or the bare profession of faith, but not at all about true and living faith. (2) Love is joined to faith because true faith "is effectual through love" (Gal. 5:6).

He moves from the grace given to him to the common gift of redemption and salvation given through Christ to mankind.

Verse 15.

Πιστὸς ὁ λόγος. ["The word is trustworthy."] He is applying the specific to the general. Ambrose and Augustine render πιστὸς as "a human word, pleasing and welcome." Jerome (Letter 102 *ad Marcellam*) opposes this on the grounds that "if it were human and not divine, then it would not be worthy of all acceptance." However, they called this λόγος "human" in a different sense than that.

Erasmus suspects that this Latin reading came from some Greek copies that read χρηστός ("pleasant") instead of πιστὸς.

"The word is trustworthy," that is, certain and undoubted. For the apostle this word has the same force as *n'm* ["oracle, prophecy"] for the Hebrews. Theodoret describes it as "sure and free of all deceit." This manner of speaking is frequent for the apostle (1 Tim. 3:1; 4:9; 2 Tim. 2:11; Titus 3:8).

καὶ πάσης ἀποδοχῆς ἄξιος. ["And worthy of all acceptance."] Ἀποδοχῆς denotes acceptance and approval, which is how the Syriac rendered it *mhaymna' hy melta' wshawya' hy lamqabalwth* ("The word is trustworthy and worthy of being received"). Paul Fagius (*Annotat. ad paraph. Chaldaic.*, Deut. 5:27) claims not absurdly that the apostle has in mind the Jewish *Cabala* with the word ἀποδοχῆς:

> The verb *qibel* does not mean simply "to receive," but "to receive something for sure and without doubt, to assent, to have faith." The word "cabala" is derived from this, whereby the Hebrews understood "something authentic, certain, and undoubted." The *Cabala* arose from this because the sacred mysteries—especially those about the reign of Christ—were once handed down through oral succession from the fathers, one receiving them from another. Hence they were called *Cabala*, "reception," (etc.). The apostle alludes to this cabalistic way in 1 Tim. 1[:15] where he also uses the word "reception." For he writes thus: "The word is trustworthy and worthy of all acceptance," that is, "cabala, that Christ Jesus came into this world to save sinners." In other words: "If anyone wants to hear cabala, I will make known the true, certain, and undoubted one. It is this: that Christ Jesus came into this world to save sinners. This is the true cabalistic teaching, and nothing of it need be rejected at all."

Here the question arises: *Why does the apostle use this earnest entreaty?* I respond. Because it seems paradoxical and unbelievable to human thinking that God justifies the ungodly.

ὅτι χριστὸς Ἰησοῦς ἦλθεν εἰς τὸν κόσμον. ["That Christ Jesus came into the world."] Although we do not simply prove Christ's divinity from His coming into the world (as Ostorodus falsely claims, *Instit.*, ch. 16, § 1) since we know that this language is also used of mere men in John 1:9, nevertheless we can prove this with complete confidence based on the parallel passages that connect His coming forth from the Father, His coming down from heaven, and His being sent into the world.

Therefore it says that Christ came into the world because, though He was already in the world beforehand through His divinity, yet according to His assumed nature He began to be among men (who are meant by the word "world") after He became incarnate (John 1:14).

ἁμαρτωλοὺς σῶσαι. ["To save sinners."] Understood here are sinners who come to their senses, for Christ came to call sinners to repentance (Matt. 9:13).

He is alluding to the name "Jesus," which means "Savior" (Matt. 1:21). From the apostle's words here one may gather: (1) That the Son of God would not have had to become incarnate had man not sinned. (2) Even infants are sinners, since Christ is the Savior of sinners (Augustine, Sermons 9 and 10 *de verb. apost.*).

ὧν πρῶτός εἰμι ἐγώ. ["Of whom I am first."] "First," that is, "worst," as Augustine interprets it (Sermon 10 *de verb. apost.*). Chrysostom and Theophylact take it as a reference to the time of his conversion, but that is hardly appropriate. Augustine puts it more correctly (commentary on Psalm 70): "Therefore that which is first excels everyone not in time but in wickedness." This is to be set in opposition to the early heretics who (according to Thomas, commentary on this chapter, lect. 4) imagined that "the sinful soul of Adam was infused into Paul, and because of this he was truly called the first sinner." Such μετεμψύχωσις ("transmigration of souls from body to body") has long since been repudiated in the church as a heretical error.

Estius notes that Paul does not say "of whom I was first," but "am first." "Indeed everyone," he says, "should always hold before his eyes the sinful state from which he has been rescued by God's grace and in which he would still persist if left to himself."

Apparent contrariety. *He says that he is the first sinner. But surely among those whom Christ saved there were some greater sinners. If no one else, then at least Adam, who ensnared the entire human race by his fall.* I respond. He says he is the greatest sinner either because he was one of the chief, more notorious sinners, since he persecuted the church with great zeal, or because he was the greatest sinner of all in his own estimation, which is a mark of humility.

Verse 16.

πᾶσαν μακροθυμίαν. ["All patience,"] that is, "complete patience," whereby He awaits the conversion of the ungodly. There is a similar Hebraism in 1 Cor. 13:2.

Earlier he gave the reason for the mercy God showed him with respect to its object, that is, his misery. Now he gives the reason with respect to the final cause: to show a certain, unique leniency of God. The apostle means that Christ acted as doctors tend to, for they invite all men to themselves by giving a display of their skill in perfectly curing someone who is desperately sick.

εἰς ὑποτύπωσιν. "To express a form and example." Christ not only gave Paul to the church as a famous preacher of God's grace, but [He] also [gave Paul] to all men as the chief example showing that same grace.

Verse 17.

Connection. He begins to give thanks and heaps up some marvelous epithets of God so as to rouse our spirits to Him from whom descends such great mercy.

After considering the great gift given to him and all mankind through Christ, he bursts into doxology.

Τῷ βασιλεῖ τῶν αἰώνων. ["To the King of the ages,"] that is, "to the eternal king who lives through all ages." This is a Hebraism.

By τῶν αἰώνων he means "the created ages" (Heb. 1:2). Therefore he calls God "King of the ages," that is, "the King of the universe," because by the word "ages" the apostle includes whatever is measured by the ages or times—that is, all creation.

ἀφθάρτῳ, ἀοράτῳ. ["Immortal, invisible."] The former stands opposite to mortality and corruptibility; the latter, to visibility and corporeality. (Cf. 1 Tim. 6:16.)

μόνῳ σοφῷ. God is called "alone wise" because, of Himself, He is perfectly and unchangingly wise. The Latin and Syriac translations omit the word σοφῷ ["wise"], but the Greek fathers read it consistently. ([Cf.] Theophylact, commentary; Cyril, *Thesaur.*, bk. 12, ch. 10.)

Estius suspects that some Greeks, confused about the different passages, moved the word σοφῷ here from the end of Romans because "(1) The Latin copies and commentaries do not have it, nor does the Syriac; (2) Chrysostom, Theodoret, and Oecumenius do not discuss it in their commentaries." But this evidence is not forceful enough to dissuade us from the reading of the Greek text, nor should it.

Apparent contrariety. *God is called "invisible," but in Gen. 32:30 and Isa. 6:1 the patriarch Jacob and the prophet Isaiah claim to have seen God.* I respond. (1) One must distinguish between a comprehensive and a simple seeing, (2) and between seeing the bare Essence and contemplating some visible figure.

Theodoret notes that "the apostle gives this doxology not only to one person but to the very undivided Trinity" (inasmuch as [praise] given to one is given to all [three]). Still, this refers uniquely to the Father because He is the source of the Trinity alone, of Himself. The Greek fathers take this with reference to the First Person of the Godhead.

Ἀμήν. ["Amen."] This is a sort of particle of approval and confirmation, Hebrew in origin. Some render it *fiat* ["may it be so"]. Aquila translated it πιστομένως ("faithfully" or "truly"). In the primitive church the custom arose from this in which the faithful would answer the spoken prayers with "amen" (1 Cor. 14:16), and this practice continues to this day. (On this word, see Jerome, on Galatians 1; and Augustine on John, tract. 41.) The apostle appends this particle here as a sort of seal to confirm and, insofar as it is in him, to ratify what he just said.

Verse 18.

Ταύτην τὴν παραγγελίαν παρατίθεμαί σοι. ["I entrust this command to you."] "I entrust it to you and deposit it with you as a valuable treasure."

The question arises: *But what command does he mean?* Ambrosiaster and the Greek fathers refer it to what immediately follows: "that in them you war the good warfare." Others claim that the apostle has his earlier words in mind, and specifically the command in v. 3. Hence Cajetan thinks that "the apostle is just now finishing his speech which he there left unfinished." Some want the "command" to mean not that by which he commands Timothy anything but that by which Timothy should enjoin others. He calls Timothy his "son," lest he seem to command him as a master but as a father.

κατὰ τὰς προαγούσας ἐπὶ σὲ προφητείας. ["According to the prophecies made earlier upon you."] Chrysostom and Theophylact comment that at the beginning of the church God was in the habit of ratifying the election of distinguished men to be bishops and presbyters through manifest prophecy (Acts 13:2). For there were prophets in the church at that time who could predict what future things ministers of the church would have to bear or what God was going to accomplish through their ministry (Acts 11:28). Hence by "prophecies" (1) some understand a sign that happened in the heavens when Timothy was elected. (2) Some understand them to be prophecies of the future, given when Timothy was elected, or revelations from God about Timothy that indicated that he would be a useful minister to the church. These prophecies came partly from Paul as he ordained [him] and partly from other believers who had the gift of prophecy. (3) Some [think they refer to] unique gifts of the Holy Spirit. (4) Ambrose takes them with reference to the admonitions and counsel of the apostles.

ἵνα στρατεύῃ ἐν αὐταῖς. ["That you war in them."] "In them," that is, in the prophecies—which is to say, according to them as well as by their power. This is an elegant metaphor which Chrysostom, Theophylact (commentary on this passage), and Augustine (*De civ. Dei*, bk. 1, ch. 1) explain.

τὴν καλὴν στρατείαν. "The good warfare," one that is strenuous, faithful, and lawful (2 Tim. 2:3). In other words, it is against false teachers and the persecution of the world for the defense of the Gospel. "That you present yourself strenuous and strong in opposing the reign of Satan and spreading the reign of Christ. That you strenuously and manfully carry out your office." As in war, so also in the episcopacy there is perpetual fighting, vigilance, labor, and danger in the face of the enemies.

Verse 19.

ἔχων πίστιν καὶ ἀγαθὴν συνείδησιν. ["Having faith and good conscience."] Faith and a good conscience are inseparably intertwined. He is showing what things are most necessary for one who is about to war the good warfare. From the effect he has in mind the cause, for the cause of a good conscience is an upright life.

ἥν τινες ἀπωσάμενοι. ["Which some having rejected."] The Vulgate has *quam quidam repellentes* ["which some rejecting"]. But it is past tense: "Having rejected; after they rejected this."

περὶ τὴν πίστιν ἐναυάγησαν. "They made a shipwreck as regards the faith." The Vulgate puts it barbarously as *naufragaverunt* ["they shipwrecked"]. The metaphor is taken from merchants whose goods are lost in a shipwreck—or, rather, from sailors who drowned in a shipwreck. Anselm (on this passage): "They suffered shipwreck as regards the faith as if by going around the truth, neither abandoning the faith wholeheartedly nor yet remaining within it." This explanation gains support from the fact that the subject here is heretics who do not throw out the whole teaching of the Christian faith but only part of it.

A defense. The Calvinists understand this shipwreck merely as "apostasy from the truth of the Gospel," because they foster the preconceived notion that "once one has saving faith it cannot be lost again." But the antithesis shows that it is to be taken as about apostasy from saving faith through depraved living. The shoals and rocks against which the ship of faith crashes are both heresies and the morals of a corrupt life.

Estius (on this passage): "The apostle does not think that, when one has lost a good conscience, faith is subsequently lost, but that generally it happens that if one receives the faith but does not live according to it, he also loses his faith." I respond.. Estius's supposition, that Paul is discussing a faith that is merely historical, is false. Rather, he is talking about true, saving faith which does not coexist with sins against conscience.

Connection. The apostle strengthens his earlier admonition by the examples of Hymenaeus and Alexander.

Verse 20.

ὧν ἐστιν. ["Of whom are."] The Vulgate has *ex quibus* ["of whom"]. The meaning more to the original is "of whose number." The Syriac has the particle *ayk* ("just as").

Hymenaeus made shipwreck concerning the faith in the days of Domitius Nero, about AD 56. He became an apostate and heretic and turned away many from the truth by teaching that the resurrection had already happened (2 Tim. 2:[17–]18): "Hymenaeus taught that the resurrection had already happened." It is thought that this is the same heresy as Alexander's. It seems that he fell into heresy in pursuit of pleasures, as his very name implies, for to the Greeks "Hymenaeus" is both a god and a wedding song.

Alexander is called ὁ χαλκεὺς ["the coppersmith"] (2 Tim. 4:14). Hoping for glory and chasing after popularity, he became the sworn enemy of Paul.

Baronius suspects that "this Alexander is the same one whose speech, as Luke reports (Acts 19:33[–41]), hushed the rioting crowd in Ephesus." Estius, however, rightly refutes this, for he was the town clerk, and who would believe that a Jew was the town clerk of Ephesus?

οὓς παρέδωκα τῷ Σατανᾷ. ["Whom I delivered to Satan."] Tertullian (*Apol.*, ch. 39) calls this excommunication "divine judgment." Cyprian (Letter 62) calls it "the spiritual sword." Jerome (Letter 1) calls it "the spiritual lance" and (Letter 13) "the iron rod." Chrysostom thinks that those excommunicated by Paul were also tormented bodily by Satan (1 Cor. 5:5).

ἵνα παιδευθῶσιν μὴ βλασφημεῖν. "So that" (through this chastisement) "they may learn no longer to blaspheme."

The church's intent when it excommunicates is that the sinner may return to a sound mind.

Chapter II

Connection. Having set forth a summary of Christian teaching in chapter 1, the apostle instructs Timothy with various ecclesiastical precepts, beginning with the prayers which are the foundation of the church's εὐταξία ["good order"] and εὐτυχία ["well-being"].

Summary of the chapter.

Διαταγὴ περὶ εὐχῶν ("apostolic arrangement on prayers").

(1) On the object of prayers—or for whom to pray—and the driving cause for prayer (vv. 1–7).

(2) On the place and manner of prayers (v. 8).

(3) On women's apparel in the prayers and their duty (vv. 9–15).

Verse 1.

Παρακαλῶ οὖν πρῶτον πάντων ποιεῖσθαι δεήσεις, προσευχάς, ἐντεύξεις, εὐχαριστίας. ["I urge, therefore, that first of all be made supplications, prayers, petitions, thanksgivings."]

Πρῶτον ["first"] denotes not an order of time but of dignity, that concern for the prayers should be chief.

Some apply the genitive πάντων ["of all"] to persons: "I urge, therefore, that there be made of all," that is, "by all supplications." But it is more correct to relate this to the subject: "I urge that first of all," that is, "before all supplications be made." Luther rendered it *für allen dingen* ["before all things" or "above all"].

Some establish the distinction between these four species of prayer: that δεήσεις are supplications made to God for the averting of evils; προσευχάς are prayers which ask God for things and goods necessary for salvation. Both of these species of prayer have mostly to do with only our concerns. Ἐντεύξεις are intercessions commending the well-being of others to God; εὐχαριστίας thank God for His gifts.

Others distinguish them a little differently, so that in δεήσεις we are asking for ὧν δεῖ ("what we need or lack"); προσευχάς are prayers to

God for something for which we hope. (Cf. Hilary on Psalm 140; Ambrose, *De sacram.*, bk. 5, ch. 5; Augustine, Letter 59 *ad Paulin.*, q. 5; Prosper, *De vocat. gent.*, bk. 1, ch. 12.)

ὑπὲρ πάντων ἀνθρώπων. ["On behalf of all people."] Beza (*Gloss. margin.* and *Resp. ad colloq. Mampelg.*, part 2, p. 195) says that "one must not understand a universality of individuals but only of kinds, since one should pray only for the predestined." But the apostle commands prayer for whomever God wants to be saved and whoever have Christ as their Mediator. But now, God wants entirely all men to be saved, and Christ is the Mediator entirely of all men [1 Tim. 2:3–4]. Therefore. Hence the church also prays and indeed should pray not only for [all] kinds of individuals but also for [all] individuals of [all] kinds, and she desires everyone to be saved, not only some from each kind of people. (Cf. Acts 20:31.)

A defense. Estius says, "This passage shows that the sectarians are talking nonsense when they say that it detracts from the office of the sole Mediator if the saints intercede for us or are asked to intercede."

I respond. (1) We do not deny that the departed saints intercede for the church in a general way. (2) We do say that they should not be invoked religiously on account of this [general] intercession. (3) For the saints living on earth are not invoked on account of their intercession. Accordingly, we invert Estius's argument.

Verse 2.

ὑπὲρ βασιλέων. ["On behalf of kings."] Oecumenius (commentary on this passage): "He wants there to be prayers on behalf of kings that they may conquer and endure, for he knows that peace with barbarians lends much to the peace we ought to have among ourselves."

καὶ πάντων τῶν ἐν ὑπεροχῇ ὄντων. ["And all who are in authority."] He means any magistrates distinct from kings, those who are subject to kings yet who rule the people.

Christians in the primitive church diligently observed this. Tertullian (*Apolog.*, ch. 39): "We pray even for the emperors and their servants and authorities, for the state of the world, for tranquility in the state."

ἵνα ἤρεμον καὶ ἡσύχιον βίον διάγωμεν. ["That we may lead a quiet and peaceful life."] This should be the purpose and aim set forth for public office in the government.

ἐν πάσῃ εὐσεβείᾳ καὶ σεμνότητι. ["In all piety and dignity."] Εὐσεβείᾳ pertains to the First Table of the Law [Exod. 20:3–8]; σεμνότητι, to the Second [Table] [Exod. 20:12–17]. Ambrose (commentary attributed to him) reminds us that "peaceful and tranquil times are very serviceable for piety, which gives due worship to God, and also for honorable morals, which shine forth in social virtues."

Verse 3.

τοῦτο γὰρ καλὸν καὶ ἀπόδεκτον ἐνώπιον τοῦ σωτῆρος ἡμῶν θεοῦ. ["For this is noble and acceptable in the sight of God our Savior."] He is adding the reason why he wants prayers to be offered to God on behalf of all people.

Verse 4.

ὃς πάντας ἀνθρώπους θέλει σωθῆναι. ["Who wants all people to be saved."] The Calvinists explain this as being about kinds of individuals, not about individuals of kinds. They take dividedly (διαιρετικῶς) what should be taken as a whole (συμπληρωματικῶς). But they contradict the passages that bear witness to God's universal mercy (Ezek. 33:11; Rom. 11:32; 1 Tim. 4:10; 2 Pet. 3:9).

Estius lists eight explanations, and though he calls them all probable, he especially approves the seventh. The sixth is that "God wants all people to be saved insofar as He wants and makes godly people to want and desire the salvation of all people." The seventh is that "God wants all people to be saved because He commands action from us that all may be saved." But it is clear that the apostle is not talking about what God wants us to want or to do, but what He Himself wants. Therefore the genuine explanation is that which Estius lists third, from Damascenus (*Orth. fid.*, bk. 2, ch. 29), that "God in His antecedent or merciful will wants all to be saved." Against this explanation Estius objects that "God's will for salvation does not extend too far. For if this is talking about His antecedent will, then one will have to say that God wants even the demons and the souls of the damned to be saved. Neither will a reason be given by the apostle as to why we should pray for all people unless we grant that prayer is also to be said for the damned (far be it!)." I respond. (1) Nowhere does Scripture say of the demons that God wants all or some of them to be saved. But this passage speaks of men, for whom alone He sent Christ as Mediator and offers them the benefits of Christ in the Word of the Gospel. (2) It is right to say of the damned that they were not condemned by some absolute[1] hatred but that God also offered them the means of salvation. Accordingly, in His antecedent will He wanted them to be saved, but in His consequent or judicial will He condemned them.[2] (3) The apostle is talking about prayers for the living. Therefore even the additional reason is to be taken as being about people who live on this earth.

1 Not having any relation to anything else, relationless, independent, or unconditional.

2 See *On Election and Reprobation* [Commonplace X], §§ 57–80 (antecedent will), and §§ 93–94, 149, 154, 187, 205–6 (consequent will).

εἰς ἐπίγνωσιν ἀληθείας ἐλθεῖν. ["To come to knowledge of the truth."] That is, the truth about salvation given through Christ. Salvation is the purpose; knowledge of the truth is the means that leads to the purpose. Elsewhere in Scripture this knowledge of the truth of salvation is called "faith."

Verse 5.

Εἷς γὰρ θεός, εἷς καὶ μεσίτης, etc. ["For there is one God, and one Mediator," etc.] This is the reason for the previous statement. As the oneness of God excludes all false gods, so the oneness of the Mediator excludes all false mediators.

Estius comments on this passage truthfully and catholically:

> Note that just as he understands one God to the exclusion of many, so he also understands one Mediator between God and men, who is Christ Jesus. Therefore we should also recognize from the mind of the apostle that this office is unique to Christ, lest it be ascribed to anyone else, whether man or angel. For it says that the Mediator of God and men is the one who immediately approaches God by His very own merit which does not depend on the merit of another and placates God to men and acquires all the gifts of salvation from God for men.

What, then, of the saints whom some Papists make to be mediators also?

But Estius later adds what is hardly catholic: "Now this office does not belong to Christ according to His divine nature (for in this way He is also the other of the two extremes) but according to His human nature. Hence the apostle explicitly says, 'The man Christ Jesus.'" The answer to be given to Estius's argument here has been fully expounded in *Conf. Cath.* (art. *de persona Christi*).

Neither is it truly catholic when Estius adds that "there are some who are mediators in an imperfect way, that is, our intercessors to God, such as anyone who commends our salvation to God by pouring out prayers to Him." I respond. (1) The apostle's exclusive language does not admit other gods nor other mediators, properly so called. (2) As to the office of Mediator, not only is intercession required but also merit, which is why the Papists attribute both to the saints. (3) Intercession does not yet imply a religious invocation, which Estius wants to prove from it. Otherwise even the living saints on earth could be invoked religiously.

The universal signifier πάντων ["of all"] from the next verse should also be supplied here in each part: "There is one God of all and one Mediator of all."

Verse 6.

ὁ δοὺς ἑαυτὸν ἀντίλυτρον. ["Who gave Himself as a ransom."] He is showing why the office of mediator befits Christ alone, namely, with respect to redemption. A λύτρον has a place in every liberation or redemption, but an ἀντίλυτρον properly has its place in war, when the head and life of one man is redeemed by another's death. This is very aptly used of the redemption provided through Christ. (Cf. 1 Pet. 1:18–19.)

[ὑπὲρ πάντων. "For all."] After Estius discusses the universal redemption piously enough from Prosper, he then adds: "This 'for all' can suitably be understood according to the usage of Scripture as 'for people of all nations.'"

τὸ μαρτύριον καιροῖς ἰδίοις. ["The testimony at the proper time."] The coherence of this word [μαρτύριον] with the preceding is obscure. If it relates to Christ through apposition, then it will be metonymy. But it is more correct to relate it to the whole preceding sentence, the sense being: "(which is) the testimony (the sum of the entire Gospel in which God testifies of His will toward us) which at its proper time (had to be manifested and preached)" (Eph. 1:9–10; 3:5). Luther has *Das solches zu seiner zeit geprediget würde* ["that this would be preached at its time"]. The Syriac fills it out thus: *sahduta de'tat bzabnah* ("the testimony that came about at its time"). Chrysostom, Theophylact, and Oecumenius interpret it that "Christ gave testimony to the truth through His suffering by which He gave Himself as a ransom for all, for He had been sent by the Father for the preaching of this grace. You see, He underwent suffering and death for speaking the truth that He was the Son of God sent from the Father for the salvation of the world." (Cf. 1 Tim. 6:13.)

Verse 7.

εἰς ὃ ἐτέθην ἐγὼ κῆρυξ καὶ ἀπόστολος. ["For which I myself was appointed a herald and apostle."] Namely, "for this testimony," which is to say, "I was appointed a herald, a teacher of the Gentiles, to proclaim the truth for which Christ gave His testimony unto death." (Cf. Acts 15:3, 12; Gal. 2:8.)

ἀλήθειαν λέγω, etc. ["I am speaking the truth," etc.] Some take this with the preceding "for which I was appointed a herald." But it is more correct to take it with what follows, namely, "I was appointed teacher of the Gentiles." The Jews themselves were enraged by this term.

ἐν πίστει καὶ ἀληθείᾳ. ["In faith and truth."] That is, "faithfully and candidly" or "that I may preach the faith and truth of the Gospel." Thus it can be applied either to the apostle who preaches the Gospel or to the Gentiles to whom the Gospel is preached.

Connection. He returns to the exhortation he started earlier regarding the prayers. He had mentioned for whom there should be prayer. Now he goes on to teach in what place there should be prayer.

Verse 8.

προσεύχεσθαι τοὺς ἄνδρας. ["The men to pray."] Tossanus interprets "men" [*viros*] to be those "who have been consecrated unto the ecclesiastical ministry, since the apostle is speaking about maintaining churchly good order in the public prayers." According to this assumption, this specification "in every place" should be explained as "in all the places where the church assembles." But because "women" in general are contrasted to "men" a little later on, it is more correct to say that the apostle is talking about Christian men in general.

ἐν παντὶ τόπῳ. ["In every place."] Not only in the Jerusalem temple but in whatever place. There is a parallel in John 4:21.

Estius thinks that "the apostle added this so that no one would think that there should be no public prayers outside of the Jewish synagogues—or, at the least, that there should be only one, definite place [of prayer] for each city. Because of persecution this would have been difficult to observe."

ἐπαίροντας ὁσίους χεῖρας. ["Lifting up holy hands."] In Exod. 9:33 and 17:11, Moses stretched out his palms to the Lord. "Holy hands" are those which have not been contaminated by blood and common things (Isa. 1:15).

This purity of hands should be joined to purity of the heart, for it means hands that are pure from murder, theft, greed, and lust.

The lifting up of hands signifies (1) that one's mind is lifted up to God (2) and that help is being sought from God on high.

χωρὶς ὀργῆς καὶ διαλογισμοῦ. ["Without anger or doubting."] Where there is anger, there love is exiled. Where love is exiled, there faith, too, has no place. But without faith, prayers have no weight.

διαλογισμοῦ. "Debating, doubting," which also militate against faith (James 1:6).

Ambrose (*De sacram.*, bk. 6, ch. 5; and *De Abel et Cain*, bk. 1, ch. 9) understands "debate" to mean "cogitating; dreaming about other things while praying and spoiling prayer." But it is more correct to understand it with reference to doubt that fights against the promise of surely being heard.

Verse 9.

Ὡσαύτως καὶ τὰς γυναῖκας. ["Likewise also the women."] Understand from the previous verse βούλομαι προσεύχεσθαι ["I want them to pray"].

He gives commands appropriate to both sexes. He removes from the men those vices which tend to [beset] men, and from women he removes womanly vices. In general, this sex sins by excessive bodily ornamentation when it comes to the public assemblies. And yet both commands are appropriate to both sexes in a certain way.

ἐν καταστολῇ κοσμίῳ. ["In modest attire."] Theophylact and Oecumenius teach that the καταστολῇ is a longish garment that covers everything since it gets its shape from the στολή ["stola"], which was a kind of woman's robe that went down to the ankles. Κοσμίῳ not only signifies "ornamented" but also "respectable, moderate, modest."

μετὰ αἰδοῦς καὶ σωφροσύνης. ["With modesty and restraint."] Chrysostom and Oecumenius take this as a reference to "chastity," but the Greek word signifies "restraint" or "moderation" in general. And this pertains to the spirit as well as to the body.

The Latins explain it "that women are commanded to adorn themselves with modesty and chastity, because these are the true ornaments of this sex." The Greeks explain it "that women should adorn their body with fitting apparel," modestly and chastely, not provocatively or shamelessly. This is also how the Syriac rendered it.

μὴ ἐν πλέγμασιν. "Not in braided hair." (Cf. 1 Pet. 3:3.) Some understand it to mean netlike caps worn on the hair, but the former interpretation is more apt.

Ἱματισμῷ πολυτελεῖ is a sumptuous garment of great price.

Apparent contrariety. Prov. 31:22: "Fine linen and purple is her clothing." Necklaces, bracelets, earrings, and similar women's jewelry are listed among the gifts of God (Ezek. 16:12–13; Hosea 2:13; Isa. 3:18). Also, Eliezer gave them to Rebekah (Gen. 24:22).

I respond. The apostle's prohibition should not be taken simply but with qualification—namely, if women conduct themselves with sumptuous apparel beyond their condition and station, unconcerned for the inner cultivation of the soul. The apostle's statement is opposed to luxury, vanity, levity, and sumptuous excess.

Verse 10.

ἐπαγγελλομέναις θεοσέβειαν. "Who allow room for divine worship," that is, who want to be seen as pious matrons. Luther has *die Gottseligkeit beweisen* ["who show godliness"]. In this passage, piety is worship of God, as is clear from the Greek.

δι' ἔργων ἀγαθῶν. ["Through good works."] This can be understood in two ways: either that truly pious women testify to their piety with good works or that women who want to be considered pious should adorn themselves with good works. Theophylact mentions both constructions and meanings as good and acceptable.

Connection. Of women he had said: ὃ πρέπει γυναιξὶν ἐπαγγελλομέναις θεοσέβειαν ["what is fitting for women professing divine worship"]. Now he adds that to a woman is not given any kind of preaching, but preaching with actions, that is, that she preach piety though her good works. She should, however, refrain from verbal preaching in the public gatherings of the church.

Verse 11.

ἐν ἡσυχίᾳ. "Quietly," without contradiction and contention. There is a parallel in 1 Cor. 14:34.

ἐν πάσῃ ὑποταγῇ. "With all subordination," to which it applies that she silently listen and learn in the public gathering of men, especially the ecclesiastical gathering.

Verse 12.

αὐθεντεῖν ἀνδρός. "To be lord over a man." "To take to herself power and authority over men."

The meaning is: "I do not allow a woman to teach publicly in the church, but privately she may teach those of her household. I do not forbid this even among those of hers who are male if she is better instructed in the faith (Acts 18:26). But on this occasion she should not arrogate to herself authority over a man."

διδάσκειν. ["To teach,"] namely, in the church, in church assemblies. This specifier should also be read into the previous verse.

Observation. The office of teaching, therefore, is not common to all Christians, nor does it belong to all who are led by the Holy Spirit. Although it is undeniable that some women have unique gifts of the Holy Spirit, they are still excluded from the office of teaching.

ἀλλ' εἶναι ἐν ἡσυχίᾳ. ["But to be in quietness."] That is, in the church. He is restating what he already had said in v. 11.

The question arises: *Why does the apostle drive home this teaching so diligently not only here but also in 1 Cor. 14:34?* I respond. Because at the time of the apostles some women had been endowed with the gift of prophecy and interpretation of Scripture (Joel 2:28; Acts 21:9). Using this gift inordinately, therefore, they wanted to speak in the church, which by apostolic authority was to be forbidden.

Verse 13.

Ἀδὰμ γὰρ πρῶτος ἐπλάσθη, εἶτα Εὔα. ["For Adam was formed first, then Eve."] He proves what he said, that authority over a man is not given to a woman, (1) from the order of creation; (2) from the order of deception, which shows that man has the greater mental vigor. One could also say that the apostle is proving both of his statements. He proves from the order of creation that a woman should not have authority over a man; and from the order of seduction, that a woman should not teach in the church.

Apparent contrariety. *The apostle proves that man is above the woman from the fact that he was created first. But animals were created before mankind, and yet they are not above mankind.* I respond. Animals were created for mankind, but man was not created for woman, but woman for man (1 Cor. 11:9).

Verse 14.

"Adam was not led astray," etc., namely, first and immediately by the devil. The Greek ἠπατήθη properly means *seductus* ["led astray"].

Estius says otherwise: "Even though the woman convinced the man of falsehood, she did not deceive him, properly speaking, for she did not act with the intent to deceive. She thought what she was urging him to believe was true." However, though Adam was not immediately led astray by the serpent, he was still immediately led astray.

ἐν παραβάσει γέγονεν. "Fell into transgression." She became guilty of transgression, that is, she was the first to transgress God's command and persuaded Adam to commit the same transgression himself. It could also be rendered "was the cause of transgression," that is, "for Adam." Luther has *Sie hat die Vbertretung eingefüret* ["she brought the transgression in"].

Connection. Although a woman must not be permitted to teach in the church, she is not lacking something to do to please God.

Verse 15.

διὰ τῆς τεκνογονίας. ["Through childbearing."] Estius thinks this should be understood as rearing children—a figure of speech in which the latter is understood from the former (cf. 1 Tim. 5:10: εἰ ἐτεκνοτρόφησεν ["if she reared children"]; [1 Tim.] 5:14: "I desire younger widows τεκνογονεῖν ['to bear children']"). But childbearing and child-rearing are two different things.

On the basis of this passage, Salmeron concludes that "the natural works of believers done in faith are meritorious for eternal life." I respond.

(1) The apostle's aim is to comfort women over against the subordination imposed on the female sex as a punishment and also against the other part of that punishment, namely, their vexation and torment in bearing and rearing children: their eternal salvation is not hindered by these punishments.

(2) The sense, therefore, is: "God made and called the woman to bear children and to rear them in the fear of God, not to teach in the church. If she remains in this, her vocation, and perseveres in faith and love, she is saved, even though pain in childbirth has been imposed on her as a punishment."

(3) The preposition διὰ ["through"] is used for ἐν ["in"], a usage that occurs in other statements of Scripture as well. Acts 14:22: διὰ πολλῶν θλίψεων, "through many tribulations" (among many tribulations) "we must enter the kingdom of heaven." That is to say, the variety of tribulations does not hinder our entrance into the kingdom of heaven. 2 Cor. 6:7–8: ἐν λόγῳ ἀληθείας, ἐν δυνάμει θεοῦ, διὰ τῶν ὅπλων τῆς δικαιοσύνης τῶν δεξιῶν καὶ ἀριστερῶν, διὰ δόξης καὶ ἀτιμίας, διὰ δυσφημίας καὶ εὐφημίας. ["In the word of truth, in the power of God, through the weapons of righteousness for the right hand and the left, through glory and dishonor, through cursing and praise."] Gal. 4:13: δι'

ἀσθένειαν τῆς σαρκὸς εὐηγγελισάμην. ["Through the weakness of the flesh I preached the Gospel."] 1 Pet. 3:20: "Eight souls were saved δι' ὕδατος ('through water')," that is, "the water of the flood notwithstanding."

(4) Therefore the apostle is not talking about the cause, merit, or means of salvation—nor even about a needed quality of those to be saved—but about a condition and state that does not hinder salvation.

(5) Hence Thomas (commentary on this passage): "The vocable 'through' does not signify the merit but the condition. That is to say, the woman will be saved even though she is not a virgin but marries and goes through the marital estate and the bearing of children." Vatablus: "The woman subjected to bearing children will be saved, so that διὰ τεκνογονίας is a Greek idiom for τεκνογονοῦσα ('bearing children')." Cornelius à Lapide takes it in the same way (commentary on Rom. 2:27): "She will be saved through the bearing of children, that is, she will be saved bearing children, if she remains in faith." Even Bellarmine (*De sacram. matrim.*, ch. 2) writes this way:

> The apostle does not mean to signify that the bearing of children is a cause of salvation, but that the woman in the state of bearing children will be saved, if she remains in faith. Therefore "through childbearing" stands for "in bearing children." This is a very common way of speaking in the Scriptures. Acts 15:21: "Through every Sabbath Moses is read." (The Greek has κατὰ ["according to"].) Acts 26:11: "Through all the synagogues I was punishing them." (Again, the Greek has κατὰ.) Rom. 4:11: "That he be the father of all believers through uncircumcision." (This fits here, for the Greek has δι' ἀκροβυστίας, which stands for ἐν ἀκροβυστίᾳ, as can be deduced from the preceding v. 10.) For uncircumcision is not the cause because of which Abraham was the father of all believers, but being in the state of uncircumcision he was made the father of all through faith.

ἐὰν μείνωσιν ἐν πίστει. ["If they remain in faith."] Some Latin copies have the singular *permanserit* ["she remains"]. However: (1) The Greek copies consistently read in the plural. (2) The Syriac does as well. (3) Ambrose (commentary on this passage) and Jerome (*Contra Jovinian.*) do also. (4) The best accepted Latin copies have the plural.

(1) Jerome (*Adversus Jovinian.*) relates this to her children: "Then she will be saved if she bears children who will remain virgins." Chrysostom speaks to the same opinion: "The woman can be saved if she bears children and diligently sees to their instruction in faith in Christ and chaste morals." Ambrose does not dissent from this reading and interpretation. Estius likewise applies this to children, so that the sense is: "The woman will be saved through the virtuous and holy rearing of the children she has received from her husband, if she works steadfastly so that her children remain in faith and holy living." From this he concludes that "salvation is not from faith alone but also from works."

(2) Jacobus Faber Stapulensis and Cardinal Cajetan take the verb "remain" with reference to the woman and also the man: "She will be saved though bearing children if they remain, that is, if she with her husband remain in faith and love." However, it does not in any way detract from the salvation of pious women if neither the children she bore nor her husband from whom she received children remain in faith and love. And really, who believes that Paul means to make the salvation of a spouse depend on the husband's or the children's perseverance in faith? (3) Therefore it is more correct to say that this applies to the women themselves and not to the children so that there is a synthesis to the apostle's words. For he is not talking about one, individual woman but about womankind, about the entire feminine sex, with respect to Christian women. This change of number is common with the apostle. [1 Tim. 1:]9: "Likewise also women in ornate attire." Then v. 11: "Let a woman learn in silence." Gal. 6:1: "You [pl.] who are spiritual, instruct such a one, keeping watch on yourself [sing.]."[3] (3) Therefore the meaning is: "If they remain," that is, "if each one of them remains in faith." (4) Some Jesuits approve our interpretation, including Salmeron. Moreover, this is not slipshod language, for the word "woman" does double duty as a collective noun which includes under it many individual women. It is similar to words such as "the crowd run" or "the forum shout," etc. Besides, it is nothing strange in the prophets and Paul to go from one number to another. Bellarmine ([*De sacram. matrimon.*], on this passage) reminds us that "in the Greek copies and some Latin ones 'if she remains' is plural: 'if they remain.' Therefore several fathers related this verb to the children and not to their mothers, so that the sense is: 'Woman will be saved through childbearing if her children remain.'" But it is much better to take the verb with reference to the mothers, and this can be done whether we read "if she remains" (as Augustine reads it, on Psalm 83; and, based on him, Bede, commentary on this passage) or if we read "they remain" with the majority of copies. For, as Sedulius [Scotus] and Primasius have noted, the apostle often goes from one number to another, as he does in this very chapter.

μετὰ σωφροσύνης. ["With self-control."] Jerome (*Contra Jovin.*) renders this *pudicitia* ["modesty"]; and Erasmus, *castitas* ["chastity"]. Theophylact seems to understand it as honorableness or temperance in general, the chief parts of which are chastity and sobriety. "Chastity" was already expressed by the word ἁγιασμῷ ["holiness"].

Observation. Love, holiness, and chastity are joined to faith because true faith is not separate from these virtues.

3 In this sentence, the first two verbs are in the second person plural while "keeping watch on yourself" is all second person singular.

Chapter III

Connection. After Paul has instructed Timothy about the public prayers, now he proceeds to describe the qualities of those to be chosen for the ecclesiastical ministry.

This chapter has two parts.

(1) In the first part he describes how bishops (vv. 1–7) and deacons (vv. 8–13) should conduct themselves and with what virtues they should be endowed.

(2) In the second part he gives the reason why he prescribed such admonitions to Timothy (vv. 14–16).

Verse 1.

Πιστὸς ὁ λόγος. ["The word is trustworthy."] Some claim that it is more correct to join this asseveration to the previous statement because it is in more need of asseveration than the following statement. Thus think most Greek commentators. Ambrose (*De dignit. sacerdot.*, ch. 4) takes it as a commendation of the teaching that follows.

εἴ τις ἐπισκοπῆς ὀρέγεται. "If anyone strives for the episcopacy." This word has a more emphatic signification than the following ἐπιθυμεῖ ["desires"], because the same thing is more fervently desired by the name "episcopacy" than it is by the name "work" and "office."

καλοῦ ἔργου ἐπιθυμεῖ. ["He desires a noble work."] He who desires the episcopacy does not desire honor but work. Jerome (Letter 83 *ad Oceanum*): "He who desires the episcopacy desires work not dignity, labor not pleasures—a work through which he decreases in humility, not puffs up in haughtiness." The word itself signifies this, for ἐπισκοπῆς comes from ἐπίσκεψις ("inspecting, overseeing, visiting"). Augustine (*De civ. Dei*, bk. 19, ch. 19): "Episcopacy is a name for the work, not honor." So ἐπισκοπῆς signifies oversight [*superintendentiam*], not idle preeminence.

A καλοῦ ἔργου is an honorable, noble, and good work, all of which befit the office of bishop.

The question arises: *Why does the apostle teach here what sort of man should be a bishop?* I respond. (1) So that Timothy may have a norm and pattern by which to examine and evaluate those who seek the episcopacy. The well-being of the church depends in large measure on [having] faithful, suitable ministers of the church. (2) Lest any unworthy man strive for or be taken into the holy ministry. (3) So as to repress an inordinate desire for this office in the hearts of glory-seeking men.

Verse 2.

ἀνεπίληπτον. ["Beyond reproach."] Augustine (commentary on John, tr. 41; *Contra duas epist. Pelagi.*, bk. 1, ch. 14) explains that this is "one who is not guilty of grave, deadly sin." Chrysostom (on Titus, homil. 2) explains through [the word] ἀνέγκλητος ["beyond reproach"] (Titus 1:6) that men are called ἐπίληπτοι ["reproachable"] when they are so corrupted by illnesses that they cannot move any of their members and, second, when they are guilty of a crime. Therefore ἀνεπίληπτον refers to [one] whom no one can justly reproach for some severe crime. In this passage οὖν ["now"] is not illative but expletive.[1]

μιᾶς γυναικὸς ἄνδρα. ["The husband of one wife."] Eusebius (*Demonstrat. evang.*, bk. 1, ch. 9) recalls that "some crossed out the word εἶναι ['be'] and substituted the past tense γεγονέναι ['have been'] to prove that a man can be admitted into the episcopacy who used to have a wife but does not have one now." But this corruption is refuted by the fact that a little later it says of deacons (v. 12): Διάκονοι ἔστωσαν μιᾶς γυναικὸς ἄνδρες. ["Let deacons be husbands of one wife."]

The apostle does not say: Δεῖ οὖν τὸν ἐπίσκοπον γεγονέναι μιᾶς γυναικὸς ἄνδρα. ["Now the bishop must have been the husband of one wife."] Neither does he say δεῖ γενέσθαι μιᾶς γυναικὸς ἄνδρα ("must become the husband of one wife"), as if no man can be bishop unless he lives in the marital estate. Rather, he is referring to the man who lives in marriage now. He speaks in the present tense: "A bishop must be the husband of one wife." You see, everything else listed here is required of a bishop simply. But to be the husband of one wife and to have modest, moral children is not required simply but only if he lives in marriage. Then he ought to be the husband of one wife, and if he has children, then they ought to be moral.

Moreover, "the husband of one wife" is not to be polygamous, the husband of many wives, as were many men at that time. Justin (*Dial. cum Tryphone*, p. 285): "Even to this day your rabbis allow each of you to have four or five wives."

1 Illative words introduce an inference or conclusion (e.g., "therefore," "then," etc.) while expletive words are used for filler (e.g., "now," "as I was saying," etc.). The Greek οὖν can denote either sense.

Estius claims that we teach that "the apostle commands every bishop to have a wife, but only one." However, this is not what we think. We do say (1) that the apostle allows a bishop to have a wife, (2) but that he forbids polygamy and thus requires that if he wants to be married he must be the husband of only one wife. This is our explanation, and it is Cajetan's as well, but Estius objects to it, saying: "The Jews had already nearly ceased the practice of polygamy, and under Roman law, which ruled even in Asia [Minor], the Gentiles were not allowed to have multiple wives at once. Therefore there was no reason for giving this prohibition to the bishops." But we have set forth the response to be given to these objections in *On the Ecclesiastical Ministry* [Commonplace XXVI], § 365. Scaliger (*Notis ad N. T.*):

> At that time the Jews, as we learn from Josephus, either married several wives or took concubines in addition to one wife, as do the Jews today who live under the Turkish Empire. If I were to expend effort in demonstrating that the pagans took concubines in addition to a wife, I would be wasting my time. Moreover, they did not send them away after they had dedicated themselves to Christ, so that the oldest Greek canons, published by Tilius, do not admit into the diaconate a Christian who kept a concubine at home. Therefore Paul prohibits one from ecclesiastical office who either has two wives, such as Jewish converts, or has a wife and a concubine, such as former pagans who confessed Christ.

νηφάλεον. ["Sober."] The Vulgate has *sobrium* ["sober"]. Some translate it "vigilant, one who tends to the flock diligently." Both meanings fit.

νηφάλεον, σώφρονα, κόσμιον. ["Sober, prudent, collected."] Some Latin copies have three words—"sober, prudent, prepared"—while others have four words—"sober, prudent, prepared, chaste." But the Greek and Syriac have only three, and so the first Latin reading should be preferred.

Some have rendered σώφρονα "prudent"; others, "chaste"; others, "temperate"—for the Greek signifies all these things, and there is no virtue that is not desirable in a bishop.

κόσμιον. "Well and decently collected in countenance, gait, speech, and one's entire bodily demeanor."

φιλόξενον. ["Hospitable."] Such a one who freely shows hospitality and support to Christians arriving on a journey, especially ministers of the church.

διδακτικόν. "Endowed with gifts for teaching." One who has at hand both the will and the capacity to communicate teaching to others.

Verse 3.

"Full of wine," that is to say, "addicted to wine," to guzzle it. Chrysostom and those who follow him take this not about drunkenness but about its attendant vice. You see, they think the command is "that the bishop not be a savage or a reviler in imitation of those who, full of wine, rage against others." But this should be taken in its proper sense, as is clear from v. 8. Ambrose renders it "not addicted to wine." The apostle adds this because the Asians were infamous for debauchery and drunkenness.

πλήκτην. ["Striker."] Jerome and Chrysostom say that "this is not about violence with the hands but bitterness of the tongue, that he not be a ruthless, unjust chider, just as he says ([1 Tim.] 5:1): πρεσβυτέρῳ μὴ ἐπιπλήξῃς ['Do not harshly rebuke an older man']." The Syriac has *la' rahta' 'ideh lmemkha'* ("whose hand should not be quick to strike"). Anselm, Thomas, and Cajetan take it literally. Therefore both explanations can be combined, because intoxication and violence are related vices.

αἰσχροκερδῆ. "One who pursues shameful gain."

Estius conjectures that "this item was transferred here from the Epistle to Titus (1) because neither Chrysostom nor any other ancient Greek or Latin commentator discusses it here, and (2) because he adds a little later ἀφιλάργυρον ['not a lover of money']." But these are not forceful reasons because (1) judgment about the text should not be made on the basis of commentators, and (2) αἰσχροκερδῆ is one vice, but ἀφιλάργυρον [is] another.

ἐπιεικῆ. "Fair, kind, gentle, one who adapts himself to the ways and moods of others." The word comes from εἴκων ("he who yields or concedes his rights for the sake of peace"). Hence the next item is ἄμαχον ["not quarrelsome"]. For whoever inflexibly maintains his own rights often comes to fighting and brawling.

ἄμαχον. "Not one to fight." Jerome (*Contra Pelag.*, bk. 1): "Without quarrel." For the Greeks, litigation and quarreling are called μαχαί.

ἀφιλάργυρον. "Free from the love of money or greed." The Vulgate has *non cupidum* ["not desirous"]. However, the Greek word here does not speak against just any desire, but against the desire and love of money. Jerome renders it "without greed."

Verse 4.

τοῦ ἰδίου οἴκου καλῶς προϊστάμενον. ["Governing his own house well."] This should be taken more as about training his household in the fear of the Lord than as about earthly support.

The man who will be elevated to the episcopacy should in fact first have demonstrated that he knows how to rule his house so that he may go from ruling the smaller house to the greater house, that is, the church.

τέκνα ἔχοντα ἐν ὑποταγῇ. ["Having children in submission."] This clarification belongs to the previous part. "Having children who are accustomed to paternal subjection, to obeying his command."

μετὰ πάσης σεμνότητος. ["With all respectability."] The Vulgate rendered it *cum omni castitate* ["with all chastity"]. Erasmus has "reverence." The Greek word signifies gravity and respectability of conduct generally, and modesty and temperance specifically. Titus 1:6: "Having faithful sons, not under the charge of excess nor disobedient."

Verse 5.

The argument is from the greater [*a maiore*]. For it is easier to rule a family of a few people than the church of a whole city, region, or province. Bernard (on Song of Songs, serm. 30): "I am astonished at the audacity of many who, we see, harvest only thorns and thistles from their vineyards, and yet they are unafraid to inflict themselves upon the Lord's vineyards."

Ambrose (*De dignit. sacerd.*): "The man who cannot maintain the house of his heart, how will he apply diligence to the house of many?"

Verse 6.

Μὴ νεόφυτον. "Not recently implanted." One who recently has come to the true religion from false religion. Gregory says it beautifully (*Pastoral.*, part 3, admon. 26): "If the weight of heavy beams is laid upon new construction that has not yet been solidified, then one constructs not a dwelling but a collapse. And if women deliver the children they have conceived before they come to term, they fill not homes but graves."

Those recently baptized were called "neophytes" because they were considered Christians or believers because of Baptism.

The question arises: *Why does the apostle keep the neophyte from the episcopacy?* I respond. (1) Because he has not yet been soundly instructed in the mysteries of the faith. (2) Because his steadfastness has not yet been demonstrated. (3) He lacks authority. (4) There is the risk of envy if a new Christian is chosen while the veterans are passed over. The apostle adds another reason in the words that immediately follow.

Ambrose, who had been ordained as a neophyte, excuses this thus (Letter 82 *ad eccles. Vercellensem*): "How I resisted my ordination! When I was finally forced, I tried at least to have it delayed. But the prescription did not prevail against the [people's] insistence. Nonetheless the Western bishops approved my ordination by deciding for it while the Eastern bishops approved it by example." (He is talking about Nectarius.)[2] "Still, a neophyte is not allowed to be ordained, lest he be puffed up by pride. If there was no delay to

2 Nectarius (d. 397) succeeded Gregory of Nazianzus as bishop of Constantinople, though he was unbaptized until just prior to his ordination. See F. L. Cross and Elizabeth A. Livingstone, eds., *The Oxford Dictionary of the Christian Church* (Oxford: Oxford University Press, 2005), p. 1142.

the ordination, it was because of forcefulness. If the humility appropriate to the priesthood is not lacking, then where there is no case the crime is not imputed."

τυφωθεὶς. "Puffed up." The Vulgate has *in superbiam elatus* ["carried away into pride"].

ἵνα μὴ εἰς κρίμα ἐμπέσῃ τοῦ διαβόλου. "Lest he fall into the judgment" (or condemnation) "of the devil." That is to say, lest because of pride he be punished by God in the same way as the devil, namely, with eternal destruction (2 Pet. 2:4; Jude 6). Others take διαβόλου as a common noun ["slander"], the sense being: "Lest through pride he give his accusers material for their slander and in this way empty his office of authority."

The first explanation is better, for it would be unusual to take "judgment" as "false accusation" or "insult."

Verse 7.

By τῶν ἔξωθεν he means "those who are outside the church" (cf. 1 Cor. 5:12). By "having a good testimony toward them" he means "having a good reputation and a good name among them."

ἵνα μὴ εἰς ὀνειδισμὸν ἐμπέσῃ καὶ παγίδα τοῦ διαβόλου. ["Lest he fall into reproach and the snare of the devil."]

The Vulgate translates ὀνειδισμὸν as *opprobrium* ["disgrace"], but it is more correctly translated as *exprobrationem* ["reproach"].

Some take the noun διαβόλου as a proper noun for the evil spirit while others take it as a common noun denoting a false accuser. The former explain it thus: "Lest the devil, through his means—that is, wicked men—use reproaches as nets to trap and stop him from accomplishing anything in his ministry." Or: "Lest he fall into the reproach and snare of the devil, for he lies in wait for all ministers of the church and seeks their destruction."

The latter explain it in this way: "Lest some false accuser be able to bring a true charge against him."

("Lest the faithful, who should have been honoring him as their bishop, start to reproach him for the sins of his former life; and lest he, in despair because of this when he sees that the shame of his former life has been uncovered, return to his vomit and renounce his Christianity through apostasy, with great offense to the church," Estius, commentary on this passage, [quoting] from Thomas's commentary.)

The question arises: *Why does the apostle move on to deacons without mentioning presbyters?* I respond. This is because in apostolic times there was no difference between the episcopacy and the presbytery. Estius opposes this position on the grounds that "the apostle speaks about the bishop in the singular but the presbyters in the plural so as to imply that each city should have only one bishop but that there can be many presbyters in one city." However, in Acts 20:17 and 28 multiple men are called bishops of one city, as also in Phil. 1:1. Estius cites an argument borrowed from Chrysostom in these words: [The apostle moves on without mentioning presbyters] "because there is hardly any difference between the office of bishop and that of presbyter, especially since care for the church has also been entrusted to the presbyters. Also, what the apostle says about bishops also applies to presbyters, for they are superior to them only with respect to ordination, and this is the only thing they seem to have that presbyters do not." When Estius says "ordination," he means "the power to ordain." Even if that were the case, nevertheless, as Jerome teaches (commentary on Titus 1): "This comes only from good order in the church, but it does not prove that bishops have greater power by divine right."

Verse 8.

ὡσαύτως. ["Likewise."] The Vulgate rendered this *similiter* ["in the same way"], and based on this some conclude that deacons should not be inferior to bishops with respect to their powers. But in the Greek it is not ὁμοίως ["in equal manner"] but ὡσαύτως, which means "in like manner."

μὴ διλόγους. "Not double-tongued," those who say one thing while standing and another while sitting. Others think it means "the guileful and deceptive, those whose lips move differently than do their hearts." Both vices are unbecoming of a minister of the church.

μὴ οἴνῳ προσέχοντας. ["Not addicted to wine."] Theodoret gives this reason: "Because drunkenness is especially unbecoming of those to whom the divine ministry has been entrusted and who serve at the sacred altars."

[μὴ] αἰσχροκερδεῖς. ["Not greedy for unjust gain."] In *Trinummus* Plautus calls them *turpilucricupidos* ["greedy for shameful gain"].[3] It can be related to the object, that one not profit from something sordid, and to the mode, that one not pursue gain from something upright in a shameful way.

Verse 9.

ἔχοντας τὸ μυστήριον τῆς πίστεως ἐν καθαρᾷ συνειδήσει. ["Holding the mystery of the faith in a pure conscience."] By τὸ μυστήριον τῆς πίστεως he means "the teaching of the Gospel," which does not become known from nature but is divinely revealed through Christ (Matt. 16:17; Rom. 16:25). So the sense is: those who are well-known as to the veracity of their faith and holiness of life, for those things are required for a good conscience (1 Tim. 1:19).

A defense. Estius concludes from this passage that "one can have faith without a good conscience." I respond. We concede this as to historical faith and a hollow opinion of faith, but as to a true, living, and saving faith we deny

3 A vulgar insult parallel to "vulture" from Plautus, *Trinummus* 1.100 (LCL 328 [2013], p. 130).

it, as do even the Papists themselves. Estius says that besides faith, the apostle requires love and a good conscience, but he still does not therefore concede that a good conscience can be separated from love.

Verse 10.

οὗτοι δὲ δοκιμαζέσθωσαν πρῶτον. ["But let these be examined first."] Just as he wants a bishop to be chosen who is not a neophyte but who has first been tested by much time, so also he wants deacons to be tested before they are brought into the ministry.

ἀνέγκλητοι ὄντες. ["Being blameless."] In v. 2 he called them ἀνεπίληπτοι ["beyond reproach"], and here he calls them ἀνέγκλητοι ["blameless"]. This can be explained in two ways. Either: "That they show themselves blameless in their ministry" (Erasmus). Or: "Let them first be tested and then minister, after they have been tested and found blameless" (Theophylact, Cajetan).

Verse 11.

By γυναῖκας ["their wives"] he means both the wives of bishops and of deacons, as even Estius admits, for he immediately afterward resumes his discourse on deacons.

σεμνάς. "Grave, modest, chaste." The Vulgate rendered it *pudicas* ["chaste"].

Chrysostom claims that "the apostle is talking about women who were endowed with the honor of ministry and were called 'deaconae' or 'deaconesses.'" Epiphanius describes their duties (*Haeres.* 79, the Collyridians). They were not ordained to the office through the laying on of hands (as the Cataphrygians and the Collyridians want to prove from this passage), nor did they take part in any part of the priestly office, but [rather] certain lower acts of service [*ministeria*].

The question arises: *Why did [the apostle] want to discuss the wives of bishops and deacons?* I respond. Just as a man must be kept from the episcopacy if he has a bad reputation because of his disobedient, spoiled children, so also if it is because of his wife, whether she is unchaste, disparaging, a drunkard, or not well attested as to her faith.

διαβόλους. "Not women who give false accusations." Ambrose: "Not eager for discord."

νηφαλέους. ["Sober."] Theophylact and Oecumenius have "vigilant and prudent." Theodoret has "sober," which is also how the Vulgate rendered it.

πιστὰς ἐν πᾶσιν. ["Faithful in all things,"] because to their husbands was entrusted the keeping of the money to be distributed among the poor.

Verse 12.

διάκονοι ἔστωσαν μιᾶς γυναικὸς ἄνδρες, τέκνων καλῶς προϊστάμενοι καὶ τῶν ἰδίων οἴκων. ["Let deacons be husbands of one wife, presiding well over their children and their own houses."]

By "houses" he means "families," a word which includes more than wife and children but also manservants and maidservants.

Verse 13.

οἱ γὰρ καλῶς διακονήσαντες. ["For those who deacon well."] This is an elegant wordplay. "If deacons live up to their title by serving well," etc.

βαθμὸν ἑαυτοῖς καλὸν περιποιοῦνται. "They obtain a good standing for themselves," that they may be able to be promoted to greater offices in the church. Some interpret "good standing" as being about the advance and increase of spiritual gifts. Others take it as a reference to a good standing in the kingdom of heaven (Matt. 25:21). But the first explanation best fits the text.

καὶ πολλὴν παρρησίαν. ["And great confidence."] They have a merry and peaceful conscience together with faith and trust in God (1 John 3:21; 5:14). Some explain it as being about the confidence or freedom one uses toward men, namely, in teaching, admonishing, reproving, and rebuking (cf. Acts 6:10)—that a blameless life produces such confidence. Both explanations have their place.

Estius asks here:

> Why does the apostle, in listing the things he requires of the bishop and deacons, make no mention of the administration of the sacraments, no mention of the altar and the sacrifice, no mention of the ceremonies to be used in the ordination of a bishop and deacon? I respond. (1) Because the chief duty of a bishop is the preaching of the Word of God. (2) Because it belonged to the apostle's prudence diligently to keep hidden the sacramental ceremonies and rites and especially those that are done in secret, lest they become public.

We hold the first reason in opposition to papistic bishops who have cast aside their duty to teach onto the shoulders of others. In opposition to the second reason we note that the evangelists published the institution of the Eucharist to the whole world in their writings.

Verse 14.

ἐλπίζων ἐλθεῖν πρὸς σὲ τάχιον. ["Hoping to come to you soon."] That is, to Ephesus, where Timothy was serving as bishop. The Greek commentators note that Paul was not promising [to come] but hoping, for he did not know whether the Holy Spirit, who directed his goings, was going to promise that he would return to Ephesus.

Verse 15.

The meaning is this: "I am prescribing these things to you about everyone's duties not because I am not going to return to you myself—on the contrary, I hope to return soon—but if I arrive late, or perhaps not at all, then you will still know how those who will be placed into His ministry should carry on in the house of God and how they should conduct themselves." He calls it "the church of the living God" because life flows into it from God in a unique and proper way.

Estius concludes from this passage that "the church of God is visible and can be pointed at like a house or family of some prince to which ministers are called to preside over certain duties." I respond. We do not deny that the church is visible in a certain way and respect. But it hardly follows from this that in no way or respect is it invisible. The gathering of the called is visible while the gathering of the elect is invisible.

The church is called "the house of God" because God is present and manifests Himself in it graciously, [and] because believers are the house-members of God. The apostle is alluding to the temple in Jerusalem, which Scripture often calls the "house of God." That [temple] had its own priests and Levites to whom certain offices of duty had been prescribed.

στῦλος καὶ ἑδραίωμα τῆς ἀληθείας. ["The pillar and mainstay of the truth."] A στῦλος is a pillar (cf. Gal. 2:9). An ἑδραίωμα in general means a "support" and sort of "seat," or that upon which something leans in some way. The meaning is that through the church's ministry, testimony, confession, and industry God asserts the heavenly truth in the world and guards against all the raging of heretics and all the persecutions of the enemies.

Therefore the church is called "the pillar and mainstay of the truth" not because she presides over truth, but because (1) insofar as she is and remains the church of Christ and the house of God she does not depart from the simplicity of the Word; (2) she guards, preaches, and spreads the truth by her ministry; (3) the truth of God is found nowhere else than in the church. (See our article *On the Church* [Commonplace XXV], § 116.)

From this passage Estius concludes that "the visible church which has the bishops, presbyters, and deacons cannot err. Consequently, the council, which represents the church in matters of the faith, cannot err." The response to be given to this has been laid out in its own place [*On the Church*, Commonplace XXV, ch. 9, "Whether the church can err," §§ 104–125].

Connection. Because the apostle had said, "The church is the pillar and mainstay of the truth," he now explains what this very truth is—namely, [the truth] of that teaching which is about the mystery of the Lord's incarnation. It is not the case that this is the only thing the church teaches, but that

Christianity chiefly consists in this, even as the church's teaching is also chiefly occupied in this.

Verse 16.

καὶ ὁμολογουμένως μέγα ἐστὶν τὸ τῆς εὐσεβείας μυστήριον. ["And confessedly, great is the mystery of piety."] "Confessedly"—[that is,] "by the confession of all, beyond controversy"—"it is great."

Some interpret "the mystery of piety" generally to be "the teaching of the Gospel which teaches the true piety by which we rightly acknowledge, love, and worship God." But it is more correct to understand it specifically as about the mystery of the incarnation. He does not call it a "mystery" because it is still hidden, for he continues "which has been manifested in the world." [He calls it a "mystery"] because "it had been hidden from the ages" (Eph. 3:5), because it still cannot become known to us except through the Holy Spirit's revelation, and because we more marvel at than understand the very fact that we know about this mystery.

Leo (Sermon 10 *in natal. Domini*): "The nativity of our Lord Jesus Christ surpasses all understanding." Anselm (commentary on this passage): "Great is the mystery of piety because all the faithful know that this is so great that no one is able to consider its magnitude." It is called "the mystery of piety" because the true piety and religion by which God is worshiped is chiefly founded upon faith in this mystery. Some translate it "the mystery of piety in which God has made known His piety, that is, His faithful [*pium*] and kind disposition toward mankind." But εὐσεβείας does not denote God's piety toward men but man's piety toward God. The Syriac has *da'zna hana dci'nuta'* ("the mystery of righteousness").

θεὸς ἐφανερώθη ἐν σαρκί. ["God was manifested in flesh."] This is a description of the incarnation of the Word (ἐνσαρκώσεως τοῦ Λόγου), which he meant by the word "mystery." The Photinians distort this as "God manifested Himself through Christ and the apostles who were weak according to the flesh." However, (1) since the Father did not take up flesh, He is not said to have manifested Himself in the flesh; (2) that manifestation through the preaching of the Gospel is not that "confessedly great mystery."

The word "God," taken *personally*, denotes "the Son of God." [The word] "flesh" *synecdochically* means "human nature," with a connotation of mortality, weakness, and misery (John 1:14; Heb. 5:7).

ἐδικαιώθη ἐν πνεύματι. ["He was justified through spirit."] (1) Theodoret, Primasius, Sedulius, Anselm, Thomas, Lyranus, Cajetan, Gagnaeus, Justinianus, etc., understand "Spirit" to be "the Holy Spirit," so that the sense is: "Just as the God-man Christ Jesus was conceived by the Holy Spirit, so He was made righteous and holy by the Holy Spirit from the beginning of His conception so that

He had and committed no sin whatsoever." But nowhere else is the [verb] "to be justified" [*iustificari*] attributed to Christ in the sense of "to be made righteous" [*iustum fieri*], nor would it be denoting anything unique in Christ since it is common to all righteous people that they have been justified in the Spirit. (2) It is more correctly understood as Christ's deity, because whatever is in Christ beyond His humanity is called "spirit." Therefore the Son of God is said "to have been manifested in flesh, justified through spirit," that is, through His deity, by the power of which He performed miracles and raised Himself from the dead. Therefore it was through His miracles done by the power of the Holy Spirit and especially through His resurrection that He showed Himself to be the Son of God contrary to the false accusations of His enemies (Rom. 1:4; 1 Pet. 3:18).

Through spirit He was manifested as right and true in His works and teaching, and He was acquitted from all the false accusations of the Jews. This way of justification befits God (Ps. [50]:6; Matt. 11:18[–19]; Luke 7:29).

"He was justified"—that is, "declared to be righteous"—because in and through His resurrection Christ was released from the sins of men which He had taken up into Himself as Substitute to make satisfaction for them to the Father.

ὤφθη ἀγγέλοις. ["He was seen by angels."] (1) Gregory (*Moralium*, bk. 34, ch. 7) understands "angels" to be "the prelates and preachers, because they announce the peace of the Gospel." (2) But it is more correct to understand them as the good spirits whom Scripture calls "angels" in its usual way of speaking. Therefore, when it says that Christ was seen by the angels, some people take it in the sense that He made known the fulfillment of the divine promises regarding the Messiah to the angels and demonstrated it in His own person (Eph. 3:10; 1 Pet. 1:12). (3) It may be understood more simply in the sense that Christ was made to be the God-man and was seen by those blessed spirits as a newborn, as one raised from the dead, and, finally, as one received into heaven.

The angels saw God as man with their intellectual eyes[4] not only when they viewed Him being born; hungering; teaching; performing miracles; suffering disgrace, beatings, and wounds unto death on the cross; rising again; ascending; etc.—but also when, through the clarity of events, they afterward clearly understood the fruit of His incarnation and Passion by the calling and conversion of the Gentiles (Eph. 3:10; 1 Pet. 1:12).

ἐκηρύχθη ἐν ἔθνεσιν. ["He was preached among the Gentiles."] He calls the preaching of the Gospel among the Gentiles a κήρυγμα ["proclamation"] since it is a public proclamation about Christ's exhibition.

4 The Scholastics distinguished between spiritual, intellectual sight and physical eyesight, which, as spiritual beings, the angels lack. Cf. *On Creation and Angels* [Commonplace VIII], §§ 43–47.

This belongs to the "great mystery of piety" because Christ was preached to the Gentiles whom God had formerly forsaken (Eph. 2:12), and this so that faith might be applied to the preaching.

ἐπιστεύθη ἐν κόσμῳ. ["He was believed on in the world."] Luther has *Gegläubet von der Welt* ["believed by the world"]. But in Greek it is "believed on in the world," that is, by those with faith in the world. One should take note of this because the Calvinists want to prove from this passage that "the word 'world' is sometimes used for the elect only."

ἀνελήφθη ἐν δόξῃ. ["He was taken up in glory."] That is, in His glorious ascension which is the blessed conclusion of Christ's entire journey.

Based on this passage the Greek fathers call Christ's ascension His ἀνάληψις ["assumption"].

Apparent contrariety. (I) *Christ was taken up in glory before He was believed on in the world.* I respond. (1) The apostle's concern is not chronology but to give the reason for saying "He was believed on in the world." In other words, the world has not rashly and pointlessly believed in the Christ as preached to it since He has already been taken up into heaven with such glory that He sits at the right hand of the Father. (2) The preaching of the Gospel and faith preceded Christ's ascension in the case of some, namely, the firstfruits of the Gentiles. (3) Also, the apostle is hinting that those who have believed in Christ are called to fellowship in the same glory with Christ (Eph. 2:6).

(II) *Christ ascended into heaven by His own power, and yet it says that He "was taken up."* I respond. (1) It says "He was taken up" not as if He was aided by some external assistance as were Enoch and Elijah, but He was taken up by the divinity united with Himself. (2) This reception [πρόσληψις] can also be explained by Acts 1:9: νεφέλη ὑπέλαβεν αὐτὸν ἀπὸ τῶν ὀφθαλμῶν αὐτῶν ["a cloud took Him up from their eyes"]—for the service of the cloud confirms Christ's lordship and glory.

Note the stages in the apostle's statement: (1) "God was manifested in flesh." This is the incarnation. (2) "He was justified in spirit." This is Christ's life and conduct on earth wherein He showed through various miracles that He was the Son of God. (3) "He was seen by angels." This is His resurrection. (4) "He was preached among the Gentiles." This is the preaching of the Gospel which some received through faith. (5) "He was taken back in glory." This is His ascension.

This saying of the apostles contains (1) a general description of the mystery of the incarnation; (2) a specific unfolding of the same through five propositions.

In the former he describes this mystery's nature and dignity, from which the following aphorisms are derived:

(1) The mystery of the incarnation should not be measured by the yardstick of human reason.

(2) The mystery of the incarnation is the incentive for piety.

In the former he describes the consequent usefulness of this mystery, from which the following aphorisms are derived:

(1) Human wisdom does not perceive the mysteries of God.

(2) The mysteries of God are the angels' desires.

(3) The universal preaching of the Gospel is a great witness to God's mercy.

(4) The benefits of God are presented to us for the purpose that they be applied to us through faith.

(5) Just as Christ ascended to glory in the body so let us ascend in heart.

Chapter IV

Connection. The apostle had spoken in chapter 1 against the Judaizers. In chapter 4, having already laid out the chief mystery of piety—that is, the Lord's incarnation—as the chief foundation of Christianity, he now teaches and forewarns Timothy, and in him the whole church, as to the heresies that are going to arise.

This chapter has two parts.

(1) A prophecy about the state of the last times and the apostasy of the Antichrist (vv. 1–5). (2) A specific admonition directed to Timothy:

(1) That he give the admonitions thus far expounded to the brethren and reject empty cunning to the contrary (vv. 6–7).

(2) That he train himself in the pursuit of piety (v. 7), and he [the apostle] strengthens this exhortation from its beneficial effect (vv. 8–10).

(3) That he teach the church about the fruit of piety (v. 11).

(4) That the gravity of his conduct compensate for what he lacks in age (v. 12). Here he lists some virtues that can earn him respect.

(5) That he nurture and develop his God-given gift for teaching by reading the Scriptures as well as by teaching others (vv. 13–16).

Verse 1.

Τὸ δὲ πνεῦμα ῥητῶς λέγει. ["Now, the Spirit expressly says."] By τὸ πνεῦμα with the article he means "the Holy Spirit." Through special revelations given at that time not only to the apostles but also to other prophets in the church (Acts 11:27; 20:23; 21:4; 2 Thess. 2:3) [the Holy Spirit] predicted this, and, what is more, ῥητῶς ("expressly, explicitly, plainly, without riddle").

ὅτι ἐν ὑστέροις καιροῖς ἀποστήσονταί τινες τῆς πίστεως. ["That in latter times some will apostatize from the faith."] By the term ὑστέροις καιροῖς ["latter times"] he means that whole time period between Christ's first and second coming (Luke 18:8; 2 Tim. 3:1; 2 Pet. 3:3; 1 John 2:18; Jude 18).

Based on the fact that the apostle does not say ἐν ἐσχάτοις ["in the last"] but ἐν ὑστέροις καιροῖς ["in latter times"], Estius concludes that the apostle is speaking about a time that was soon approaching back then. I respond. (1) Estius himself reminds us that "others think that the apostle makes no distinction between 'last' and 'latter,' since here he says 'in latter times' but in 2 Tim. 3:1 he says 'in the last days.'" (2) Already in apostolic times had the mystery of anti-Christian iniquity begun to "be at work" (2 Thess. 2:7).

Furthermore, he means not the apostasy of some few but of many, as a sort of universal apostasy.

By "the faith" he means here the teaching and confession of faith (1 Tim. 1:19), so the sense is: "They will abandon the Christian faith they once defended."

προσέχοντες πνεύμασιν πλάνοις. ["Heeding erring spirits."] The Vulgate rendered it *spiritibus erroris* ["spirits of error"]. Instead of πλάνοις ["erring"], it seems to have read πλάνης ["of error"], which is in the *Editio Complutensis* and other codices. So also in 1 John 4:6 "the Spirit of the truth and the spirit of error" (τὸ πνεῦμα τῆς ἀληθείας καὶ τὸ πνεῦμα τῆς πλάνης) are set in opposition to each other. Nevertheless most Greek copies read πλάνοις ("erring and error-inducing"). Ambrose (commentary) and Hilary (*De Trinit.*, bk. 19) have "deceitful," and Augustine (*Contra Faustum*, bk. 15, ch. 10) has "seducing."

Chrysostom interprets the "imposter spirits" to be "those very people, namely, the false teachers and prophets" (1 John 4:1[–6]). Others understand the imposter spirits to be the demons, since this is connected to "the teachings of demons." The former interpretation better fits the text.

Anselm (commentary on this passage) cites the example of the people of Agen,[1] "whom the demons, appearing at night in the form of horses, carried through the air wherever they wanted, providing them with an abundance of temporal goods and at the same time instructing them with false teachings."

The abbot Serenus (in Cassian, *Collat.* 7, ch. 32) witnesses that "he very openly heard a demon confessing that he published the ungodliness of sacrilegious teaching through Arius and Eunomius." To confirm this he uses this passage from Paul and also 1 Kings 22:22.

Therefore they are called "false teachers, imposter spirits, and seducers" either because the evil spirits—that is, the devils—inspire them with all kinds of deceit or because they pretend that they have their teaching from the "Spirit of God" (1 John 4:1[–2]).

καὶ διδασκαλίαις δαιμονίων. ["And to the teachings of demons."] This latter explanation belongs with the former.

1 Probably Cathars, who in Gnostic fashion considered material creation to be evil. Anselm's commentary goes on to say that the people of Agen "forbid marriage and call it evil."

Verse 2.

ἐν ὑποκρίσει ψευδολόγων. ["Lying with hypocrisy."] Augustine rendered it *mendaciloquorum* ["speakers of lies"]; Ambrose, *falsiloquorum* ["speakers of falsehood"]. The hypocrisy refers to works that have the outward appearance of being pious. They lie by means of this holiness and make their teaching agreeable to people. This is grammatically constructed with the word δαιμονίων ["of demons"]. Therefore this means that false teachers are the devil's instruments. Through them he speaks and spreads the poisons of false teaching. Against this explanation Estius objects that "it is unusual for Scripture to ascribe the term 'demons' to people." There is, however, a clear example in John 6:70 where Judas is called "a devil" because he was a man ἐνδιαβολισμένος ("who became an instrument of Satan"). So there is no need for us to state with Estius that "the latter genitives ψευδολόγων ['lying'] and κεκαυτηριασμένων ['seared'] are used by themselves as substantives, as equally positioned as they are equally dependent on the word 'teachings,' so that the sense is: 'heeding the teachings of demons, the teachings, I say, of men speaking lies in deceit.'"

κεκαυτηριασμένων τὴν ἰδίαν συνείδησιν. ["Seared in their own conscience."] A καυτήρ is a tool used to burn on marks and brands; also medics use it on the bodies of the sick to burn an infected area. A καυτήριον ["branding iron"] is so called because it has the power to burn. Καυτηριάζω is "I burn with a branding iron; I remove with a branding iron."

Therefore some translate "seared in the conscience" as "cut off by a branding iron." Beza, Piscator, and Tossanus [do so] so that the lack of conscience or fear of God is intimated, even as elsewhere such men are called ἀπηλγηκότες ("those who have grown callous so that they do not feel remorse in their conscience though they have most severely offended God by their crimes"). But it is better to translate it "whose consciences have been seared by the iron; who have consciences marked by the iron." Commentators differ as to in what sense this is attributed to the false teachers:

(1) Ambrose (commentary on this passage) notes thus: "Having a seared conscience, that is, one marred by deception. For just as the branding iron mars the hide and inflicts its mark, so also falsehood marks for destruction the conscience which by the trickery of an evil disposition knows one thing but speaks another."

(2) Theodoret (commentary on this passage): "He calls them 'those having a seared conscience,' thus indicating an utter numbness. For the place deadened by the branding iron loses its former feeling."

(3) Some explain it in terms of the recalcitrant malice of heretics, for marks burned on with the iron cannot be removed.

(4) Others want to explain it with respect to the conscience's inner fire and the flames of lusts.

(5) Others join these explanations together: "Just as we mark an evildoer with the iron so that everyone will recognize him and regard him as infamous; or just as the members of animals are burned by the iron and toughened, so to speak, so as to lack all feeling—and sometimes, yes, they are even cut off—so also is the seared conscience the same as one that is twisted or hardened, without any sense of remorse, and so it is utterly cut off." (Cf. Balduin, *De casib. consc.*, p. 30.)

(6) Some want it to be "a metaphor drawn from criminals who are often permanently marked by a glowing iron. So are those who want to be considered saints, and yet they carry a conscience permanently marked by the scars of a most impure life" (Estius).

(7) There are some who think that the apostle has in mind what the Carpocratian heretics were going to do. On them see Irenaeus (bk. 1, ch. 24) and Epiphanius, who relate that they would mark their followers on the upper part of their right ear, as if the apostle were saying, "Just as they have a seared ear, so they have a seared conscience."

Verse 3.

κωλυόντων γαμεῖν. ["Forbidding marriage,"] under the guise of holiness and unique chastity.

The apostle describes two kinds or aspects of false teaching: the law of celibacy and the distinction of foods.

ἀπέχεσθαι βρωμάτων. ["To abstain from foods."] But as to heretics who introduce a distinction of food, it would have needed to be said κελευόντων ἀπέχεσθαι βρωμάτων ["commanding to abstain from foods"] rather than κωλυόντων ἀπέχεσθαι ["forbidding abstinence"]. Costerus (*Enchir.*, ch. *de ieiun.*, p. 108): "Here it seems that it is instead referring to the heretics who forbid abstinence from foods which God created for mankind to use rather than the Catholics who command abstinence." (In the same place, however, he admits that this response is to be given to the unlearned.)

Isidore of Pelusium (*Letters*, bk. 4, Letter 112) tries to prove that instead of ἀπέχεσθαι it should read ἀντέχεσθαι ["to hold on to"], which signifies the contrary. "Take care," he says, "lest perhaps a mistake was made here revolving around one letter, one little mark: κωλυόντων γαμεῖν, ἀντέχεσθαι βρωμάτων ['forbidding one to marry, to hold on to food']." But the Greek copies consistently read ἀπέχεσθαι, nor should we mangle the text.

What, then, is to be made of the way the apostle speaks? I respond.

(1) One must bear in mind the apostle's aim, which entirely consists in his prediction that these false teachers are going to introduce a ban on marriage and certain foods.

(2) The preceding and following contexts show the same thing. For the apostle adds an argument against the distinction of foods. Therefore he is rebuking those false teachers on the grounds that they prohibit certain foods.

(3) Add to this the admission of Bellarmine, Costerus, and other Papists who admit that the apostle is censuring the prohibition of foods.

(4) One must also consider the grammatical connection (συνάφεια), how γαμεῖν and ἀπέχεσθαι βρωμάτων are closely joined together by the same participle.

(5) The proper meaning of this Greek expression is best explained by Oecumenius, a Greek himself:

> Οὐκ ἔστι σφάλμα καλλιγραφικόν, τὸ ἀπέχεσθαι βρωμάτων, ὡς ἐνίοις ἔδοξεν, οὐδὲ παρόραμα Ἀποστολικόν, ἀλλ' καὶ ὀρθῶς εἰς τὴν Ἀτθίδα συνήθειαν διαπεφρασμένον, ὥσπερ τὸ ἐκώλυσεν αὐτὸν μὴ ποιεῖν τὰ ἄτοπα, οὐ λέγει, ὡς εἰς ἀτοπίαν αὐτὸν προὔτρεπεν καὶ τὸ ἀπέτρεπεν αὐτὸν μὴ προσκρούειν φίλοις, οὐχὶ φίλοις προσκρούειν, ἀλλὰ τοὐναντίον, καὶ πάλιν, ἐκώλυεν μὴ κλέπτειν, οὐχ ὅτι ἐπέτρεπε τὴν κλοπήν καὶ ἐκώλυεν ἀπέχεσθαι ἀρρητοποιίας, ἀντὶ τοῦ ἀπῆγεν ἀπὸ τῆς τοιαύτης πράξεως. οὕτως καὶ ἐκώλυον ἀπέχεσθαι βρωμάτων ἀντὶ τοῦ ἐκώλυον ἀπὸ τῆς βρώσεως.
>
> It is not, as some think, a mistake or departure from elegant speech when he says "to abstain from foods." Nor is this language representative of apostolic carelessness, but an example of good Attic usage. It is like when one says ἐκώλυσεν αὐτὸν μὴ ποιεῖν τὰ ἄτοπα ("he forbade him that he not act stupidly"); this does not mean that he encouraged him to be stupid. And when one says ἀπέτρεπεν αὐτὸν μὴ προσκρούειν φίλοις ("he deterred him that he not conflict with his friends"), this does not imply that he encouraged him to oppose his friends, but rather the contrary. And again, when one says ἐκώλυεν μὴ κλέπτειν ("he forbade him not to steal"), this does not mean that he encouraged him to steal. Moreover, when one says ἐκώλυεν ἀπέχεσθαι ἀρρητοποιίας ("he gave a prohibition to abstain from evil"), it means that he discouraged such action. So also ἐκώλυον ἀπέχεσθαι βρωμάτων ("they gave a prohibition to abstain from foods") means "they were prohibiting foods."

Budaeus (*Comm. ling. Graecae*, f. 935) agrees with Oecumenius's explanation: "The Attic Greeks add a negation to verbs that are of themselves negative (ἀποφατικὰ καὶ ἀπαγορευτικὰ), such as to ἀπαγορεύω, κωλύω, ἀρνέομαι, and ἀπέχω ['I dissuade,' 'I forbid', 'I deny,' and 'I abstain from']." From this comes the rule that "according to Attic usage, the verb κωλύω with a particle or verb of negation has a greater force of commanding and bidding."

(6) Some respond that a verb of related meaning such as κελευότων ["commanding"] must be supplied. Even Epiphanius says this when he cites this passage against the Cataphrygians. This is similar to when Homer says

σῖτον καὶ οἶνον, ἔδοντες ["men devouring bread and wine"].[2] There is a similar ellipsis in 1 Cor. 14:34: ἀλλ' ὑποτάσσεσθαι (δεῖ), that is, (they ought) "to be in submission."

(7) Others want to explain this ellipsis based on Hebrew idiom. For them the verb *tswh* means "to command what should be done" and "to forbid that from which one should abstain."

(8) The Syriac translator seems to have read ἀπεχομένων ["abstaining from"], and that as if it were in the Hiphil: "making people abstain" (*maprqiyn*). Of all these Oecumenius has the simplest explanation. (Cf. Chamierus, tom. 3, bk. 19, ch. 5, § 34.)

When we set this passage in opposition to the Papists who bring into the church the law of celibacy and abstinence from certain foods under the opinion of necessity, worship, and merit, they object that "the apostle is speaking about the Tatians, Encratites, and Manichaeans," etc. (Benedict Justinianus, commentary on this passage, p. 479).

Estius (commentary on this passage): "The apostle is talking about those who would condemn marriage of any kind as evil and illicit and those who would reject certain kinds of food as impure in themselves. For when he says 'forbidding marriage, to abstain from foods,' he also adds 'because every creation of God is good.'" Based on this he concludes the apostle's words here were directed against the Encratites, Marcionites, Manichaeans, etc., and even those who, according to Ignatius (Letter *ad Philadelph.*), detested certain foods and marriage even in apostolic times.

I respond. (1) The apostle is not talking about a kind of apostasy that would happen right after the apostolic age in the time of the early church but one that would happen later, namely, under the Antichrist.

(2) The apostle is making a prediction about those who would have the power to command abstinence from foods and to forbid marriage. This does not seem to describe the heretics—who could indeed teach this but could not command it or enforce it—as well as it describes the Roman pope. Hence Theodoret comments on this passage: "He was right to claim that 'they forbid marriage.' Of course, he is attacking neither celibacy nor continence, but rather he accuses those who pass a law and compel [people] to follow it."

(3) The apostle is not talking about those who were to condemn marriage and foods but those who through hypocrisy and the appearance of a unique [degree] of perfection would prohibit marriage and certain foods. For it is one thing to condemn as the Marcionites, Tatians, and Manichaeans did, but it is another thing to forbid, as the Papists do. Nor indeed is Paul talking about those who would condemn marriage and certain foods with open blasphemy

2 *Odyssey* 16.110 (LCL 105 [1953], p. 124).

against God, the Author of marriage and the Creator of foods (as the ancient heretics did), but [he speaks of those] who, in hypocrisy and under the guise of some kind of superb holiness, would forbid certain people from marriage and command abstinence from certain foods.

(4) The apostle is talking about those who do this with a "seared conscience." This is especially descriptive of the Papists, for they know that this distinction [of foods] is not a command of God.

(5) Even if he were talking about those ancient heretics, this would still not exempt those in later times who would prohibit foods as a pretense for some kind of holiness and worship.

Estius himself writes: "It is more than likely that here the apostle predicted the Ebionites, Saturnius, the Encratites, the Marcionites, the Manichaeans, etc. And yet his teaching still stands for the condemnation of all those who teach similar things after them."

ἃ ὁ θεὸς ἔκτισεν εἰς μετάληψιν μετὰ εὐχαριστίας τοῖς πιστοῖς. ["Which God created for partaking with thanksgiving by the faithful."] For it is because of the faithful as beloved children that God creates and preserves all things, and they alone rightly receive the gifts of God.

The emphasis is on the phrase εἰς μετάληψιν ["for partaking"], which describes a legitimate use and excludes gluttony and overindulgence. Theophylact: "Partaking involves moderation; overindulgence and extravagance, immoderation."

πιστοῖς καὶ ἐπεγνωκόσιν τὴν ἀλήθειαν. ["By the faithful and those who know the truth."] The latter part explains the first, for "the faithful" are those who know the truth revealed by God.

Verse 4.

ὅτι πᾶν κτίσμα θεοῦ καλόν. ["That every creation of God is good."] He is transitioning from his premise to his main proposition and refutes the false teachers by a clear proof.

The Greek commentators, whom Erasmus follows in his translation, take this part with the preceding like so: "Who know the truth, namely, that every creation of God is good."

καὶ οὐδὲν ἀπόβλητον. "And nothing is to be rejected." Nothing is to be spurned as if it were unclean and unlawful.

μετὰ εὐχαριστίας λαμβανόμενον. ["When it is received with thanksgiving."] He adds this: (1) Because though the partaker's thanklessness does not defile the food, his very partaking is defiled through it and rendered unclean. (2) Because thanksgiving is a sort of declaration that the food one receives is given by God and thus not to be rejected.

Verse 5.

ἁγιάζεται γάρ. ["For it is sanctified,"] so that it can be received in good conscience as holy and pure.

This is an anticipation of an objection. Some believer could say:

> It is true, no creation of God is evil or unclean of itself. Nevertheless, through the first transgression where man subjected himself to the devil, even those things which belong to man, and especially things having to do with food and drink, have so come under the devil's power that he can hurt man through them bodily as well as spiritually. So what, then, is the remedy against this evil?

The apostle responds: "There is no danger for the faithful and those who partake with thanksgiving because what they receive is sanctified through the Word of God and prayer, that is, it is taken away from the devil's power."

διὰ λόγου. ["Through the Word."] Through faith which believes God's testimony that all foods were especially made for the sake of believers and that the right of dominion over the earth and animals has been restored to believers through Christ; likewise, that the distinction of foods sanctioned in the Old Testament has been removed in the New Testament, and thus "all things are pure for the pure" (Titus 1:15).

Estius: "He means 'the Word of God as believed,' that is, the faith by which [*fides qua*] one believes in Christ and resists the devil."

καὶ ἐντεύξεως. ["And prayer."] Through [prayer] (1) we ask God to bestow on us His divine blessing and to sanctify "the gifts which we receive from His bountiful goodness."[3] (2) We give thanks for the [gifts] received.

Chemnitz (*Exam. Conc. Trid.*) compares this passage with 1 Cor. 7:14: "Just as marital cohabitation is clean and lawful for the believing person, and he can enjoy it with a good conscience, so food is sanctified—through the Word of God in His very act of creation."[4]

Estius (commentary on this passage): "On this Scripture is founded the very ancient church practice of applying exorcisms and blessings to water, salt, breads, fruits, and various things. Through these [exorcisms and blessings] the power of the demons is repressed and these things become salutary for those who use them." I respond. The apostle teaches that it is not through exorcisms nor through the sign of the cross but through the Word and prayer that food is sanctified.

3 SC, "Daily Prayers" (*Concordia*, p. 345).

4 See Martin Chemnitz, *Examination of the Council of Trent*, trans. Fred Kramer, Chemnitz's Works 4 (St. Louis: Concordia, 1971), p. 288.

Verse 6.

Ταῦτα ὑποτιθέμενος. "Presenting these things, bringing these things to mind." "If you impress these things upon the faithful, if you pass on these things I have said about the great mystery of piety, about avoiding the teachings of demons, etc., you will show yourself to be a faithful minister of Christ."

ἐντρεφόμενος τοῖς λόγοις τῆς πίστεως. "Nurtured on the words of faith." That is, reared in the true religion.

Against this explanation Estius raises the objection that "Timothy, being a bishop, was not still being nurtured by the words of faith and good teaching but had already long since been nurtured by them (2 Tim. 3:15)." I respond. (1) The present tense is often used for the past. (2) Chrysostom and Theophylact think this verb is commending Timothy for his perseverance in learning and meditating upon the sound teaching of the faith. They say, "Just as the body needs nourishment every day, so we must always be nourished by the words of faith."

ᾗ παρηκολούθηκας. "To which you have always adhered; which you have ever followed." Luther: *bey welchen du immerdar gewesen* ("from whose side, so to speak, you have never departed").

Verse 7.

τοὺς δὲ βεβήλους καὶ γραώδεις μύθους παραιτοῦ. ["But decry profane and old-ladies' tales."] He calls the talking of the false teachers that true holiness consists in external ceremonies and in the distinction of foods γραώδεις μύθους ["old-ladies' tales"]. To these he opposes εὐσέβειαν ["piety, godliness"], which consists of inner faith, love, and fear toward God.

Chrysostom says that "εὐσέβειαν includes a pure faith, an upright life, since God is worshiped by these things." Therefore he trains himself unto piety who diligently devotes himself to actions that please and serve God; such are the actions of all the virtues done with reference to God.

Verse 8.

Connection. From the antithesis of bodily training [the apostle] shows how beneficial training unto piety is.

ἡ γὰρ σωματικὴ γυμνασία πρὸς ὀλίγον ἐστὶν ὠφέλιμος. ["For bodily training is somewhat beneficial."] He opposes bodily training to spiritual training unto piety. Through this [bodily training]:

(1) Some understand training the body in obeying ceremonies.

(2) Theophylact explains "bodily training" as "an activity of the body that, though it has great effort, will still be of little, temporary benefit to the body."

(3) Akin to this is the explanation of those who take it as a reference to bodily exercising for strength, as athletes do (1 Cor. 9:25), or to stay healthy, such as walking and horseback riding.

(4) Some think that the apostle has in mind abstaining from foods as he discussed in v. 3. But the apostle did not say of such dietary laws that they were "somewhat useful," but utterly useless, even harmful and ungodly.

(5) Some understand it to be about the bodily toil by which the necessities of this life are obtained, such as the mechanical arts.

(6) The simplest way to take it is about the training by which the body is treated harshly with respect to sustenance through fasts, vigils, etc. Such training has little benefit with respect to the spiritual training unto piety so that we may all the more apply concerted effort to sacred meditations and prayers, for of itself it does not commend anyone to God since it gives neither true holiness nor purifies the heart from sins. To be sure, Theophylact rails against this interpretation: "Some say that 'bodily training' is fasting, but this is different since it" (the training through fasting) "is spiritual. For though the body is weakened through fasting, the spirit becomes more wakeful." But in fact that explanation—that "bodily training" means fasting—comes from Ambrose and other fathers whom Anselm, Theophylact, Aquinas, and Cajetan follow.

Against this explanation Estius raises the objection that "it is true that fasting and abstinence from foods is of little value unless piety is added. But it is not therefore simply true that these are of little value since the external works of piety are not to be separated from piety itself whether you understand that to be piety toward God or toward your neighbor." I respond. Hypocrites separate this "bodily training" from piety, and it is about them that the apostle is speaking here.

Again, Estius (following Chrysostom) offers proof that this passage cannot be understood about fasting: "(1) Because fasting is not a bodily exercise but a spiritual one since it does not nourish but weaken the flesh. Nor is it training just with respect to the body but a cessation of a certain work. (2) Because Christ promises a heavenly reward for fasting (Matt. 6[:18])."

I respond to (1): The words σωματικὴ γυμνασία ["bodily training"] taken generally stand for everything by which the body is treated harshly and forced into order. Such exercises are common to the pious and to the hypocrites.

[I respond] to (2): A reward is promised to fasting not through itself but with respect to its attendant prayer, repentance, and other good works.

ἡ δὲ εὐσέβεια, etc. ["But piety."] Just as "the present life" means "the rewards of this life" and not the present life itself—since no one obtains it because of his piety but from the absolute grace of God—so also "the life to come" does not mean "eternal life itself" but "the rewards of eternal life or in eternal life," which are called "nonessential rewards."[5]

---

5 On the distinction between the "essential reward" and "nonessential rewards," see below, pp. 186–87.

πρὸς πάντα. ["For all things"] (1) that we are to desire; (2) for both kinds of goods: those that are of this life and those looked for in the life to come. Some copies read the plural ἐπαγγελίας ["promises"] with the meaning that there are many such promises in Holy Scripture.

Estius (commentary on this passage): "This passage means that piety merits eternal life, not by its very nature but by the generosity of the Promiser." I respond. (1) Just as "the present life" does not mean "the present life itself" but "rewards of the present life," so "the life to come" does not mean "the life to come itself" but "the nonessential rewards of the life to come." (2) Where the generosity of the Promiser is predominant, there merit, properly speaking, has no place.

Verse 9.

πιστὸς ὁ λόγος. ["The saying is trustworthy."] He means what he said in the previous verse about piety and its rewards.

Verse 10.

Connection. From the trials and persecutions that Christians were suffering the apostle now proves the "saying" that he said "was trustworthy," that is, "certain and undoubted." He says, "Because of this we labor"—that is, endure all troubles of the body—"and suffer insults, because we have our hope fixed in the living God." That is to say, "The reason we do not succumb to so many adversities is because we not only receive this present life from God, but we also look for the life to come from Him."

εἰς τοῦτο γὰρ καὶ κοπιῶμεν. ["For to this we both labor,"] "that we may become partakers of the promises made to the pious and those who believe."

καὶ ὀνειδιζόμεθα. ["And are reproached."] "We endure all manner of false accusations and disgrace which afflict us in this world."

ὅτι ἠλπίκαμεν ἐπὶ θεῷ ζῶντι. ["Because we have set our hope on the living God."] The apostle includes both the past and the present: "We have hoped and do now hope in God."

There is an emphasis on the word ζῶντι ["living"]. God is living—indeed, is life itself (1) οὐσιωδῶς ["substantially"], (2) ἐνεργητικῶς ["actively"], and (3) ἀντιθετικῶς ["antithetically"] with respect to false gods.

ὅς ἐστιν σωτὴρ πάντων ἀνθρώπων, μάλιστα πιστῶν. ["Who is the Savior of all, especially of believers."] Piscator, Tossanus, and other Calvinists do not understand σωτὴρ ["Savior"] to mean "the Giver of eternal, spiritual salvation," but "the Author of rescue from the dangers of this life." They say that

> Paul is not discussing the salvation of souls accomplished through Christ but the universal providence of God by which He preserves all people in this life and especially believers. God is the Savior, that is, Preserver of all

people (Ps. 36:7; 107:2; Acts 17:28), but He is especially the Preserver of believers, for He not only keeps them in this bodily life but also in the spiritual life, and He reserves the blessedness of eternal life for them in heaven (Ps. 36:8–10).

Estius yields to the Calvinists, saying (commentary on this passage): "This passage is wrongly cited by some to strengthen their teaching about grace sufficient for salvation, which they say is offered to all people. In vain does Ambrose Catharinus try to import this meaning here."

But it is more correct to say that the apostle is directly and immediately discussing the spiritual salvation from sins and God's beneficent will to give people eternal salvation, but that in an indirect way he understands the preservation of God's providence, since the latter is included in the former. Accordingly, the latter must be stated so as not to deny the former. This is proved:

(1) From the apostle's purpose. The apostle's purpose is that he wants to admonish Timothy—and, under his person, all people—toward the exercise of piety (v. 7). He uses a twofold argument. The first (v. 8) is drawn from its contrary, namely, the usefulness of bodily exercise. The second is drawn from its effect or the outstanding usefulness of piety, because piety is useful for all things. This he proves from the fact that it holds promise for the present and future life. He asserts the certainty of the promise (v. 9), from which it is clear that the apostle is directly and chiefly not discussing a bodily benefit but a spiritual one.

(2) From the true foundation of consolations. Various kinds of calamities could have deterred Timothy from the exercise of piety since the pious are subject to them in this life. Therefore Paul gives him a true and firm consolation, which is that they should hope in the living God who is the Savior of all people. But if the word "Savior" did not mean "spiritual Savior" or "Giver of eternal salvation" but merely "a bodily Savior" (one who preserves people in their body), then the power of this consolation would be gone. Indeed, the examples of the martyrs show that God does not always deliver the pious from bodily hardships in this life.

(3) From the specific use of the word σωτὴρ ["Savior"]. When the word "Savior" is used about God or Christ in the New Testament, then it never means "Preserver" in bodily and external things to the exclusion of spiritual salvation, but it always denotes that He is the spiritual Rescuer and Savior (Luke 1:47; 2:11; John 4:42; Acts 5:31; etc.). Compare 1 John 2:2, where the apostle progresses ἀναβατικῶς ["inductively"]; even here Paul is progressing καταβατικῶς ["deductively"], and again ἀναλυτικῶς ("from the general to the specific"). God is the Savior of all because of the universal acquisition of salvation accomplished through Christ and with respect to the universal mercy of God who earnestly

desires the salvation of all. Moreover, He is especially the Savior of believers because of its acquisition and also its application.

The fathers do not agree in their explanation, as some relate the first part to temporal salvation while others relate it to eternal salvation.

Ambrose (commentary on this passage):

> He is the salvation[6] of all because, as concerns the present life, all live from Him and through Him; but as concerns the promised salvation, [He is the salvation of] believers. For after this life is finished by death, He has promised to give another life to those who know Him. That life will flourish in immortality, and for this reason he says "especially of those who believe."

Jerome: "He is the Savior of all now; of believers, in the future."

Theophylact explains this passage by means of 1 Tim. 2:4: "God wants all people to be saved."

Prosper (*De vocat. gent.*, bk. 2, ch. 10): "By saying 'He is the Savior of all people,' he is confirming that the goodness of God is universal upon all people. But in adding 'especially of believers,' he is showing that there is a part of humanity that is carried upon His particular benefits into the highest, eternal salvation by the merit of faith, which is inspired by God."

Lyranus: " 'Of all' as to sufficiency on His part, but especially of believers. It says 'especially' because He is their Savior as to sufficiency and efficacy."

Chrysostom recalls that "even in this life God is the Savior of believers in a unique way, because He helps them as they struggle so that they may come to eternal salvation; because He makes temporal salvation salutary for them, that is, beneficial and profitable for eternal salvation; and, finally, because all things, both adversity and prosperity, work together for them for good."

Verse 11.

Παράγγελλε ταῦτα καὶ δίδασκε. ["Command and teach these things."] The former belongs to moral precepts; the latter, to the mysteries of the faith.

ταῦτα. ["These things,"] that is, "everything I have said about the great mystery of piety, avoiding heresies, keeping to the sound teaching, and what I said about piety being useful for all things."

"Command and teach," that is, "when commanding, teach; deliver [these things] to the faithful with authority as a bishop who has the power to teach and command" (Estius).

Verse 12.

Μηδείς σου τῆς νεότητος καταφρονείτω. ["Let no one look down on your youth."] The Greeks explain it: "Do not give anyone a reason to look down on your youth." This can be taken in two ways: (1) "Do not allow yourself, though

6 *Salus* can mean both "salvation" and "well-being, health, safety."

you are young, to be despised by those under your charge, but use the authority of your office" (cf. Titus [2]:15). (2) "So conduct yourself with proper dignity—uprightly, soberly, and prudently—that no one will think less of you because of your age. Act in such a way that no one will have just cause to despise your youth." This meaning is deduced from the antithesis.

"Youth" [*iuventus*] extends into one's thirties. No one should think that Timothy was an adolescent of twenty years or so when these words were written to him. In Acts 7:58 Paul is called a νεανίας ["young man"], though at the time he was about thirty-five.

Connection. Lest Timothy be despised for his youth, the apostle admonishes him to present himself to the faithful as an example and pattern to which they may direct their lives and order their doings.

A τύπος is a clear form to which something else answers as its ἀντίτυπον ["antitype, copy"].

ἐν λόγῳ. ["In word."] "That you sincerely set forth the teaching of the heavenly Word." Or: "That you speak with dignity and prudence for the edification of others." The first explanation is confirmed by 2 Cor. 6:7, where it adds ἐν λόγῳ τῆς ἀληθείας ["in the Word of the truth"].

ἐν ἀναστροφῇ. ["In conduct."] "So that you may edify others by your holy way of living."

ἐν ἀγάπῃ. ["In love."] "That from all your doings love toward the neighbor shines forth."

ἐν πνεύματι. ["In Spirit."] "In zeal of spirit, in pious devotion, in holiness." Chrysostom and the translator of the Vulgate do not read this. Theophylact and Oecumenius interpret this "as a spiritual order or gift, as if the apostle is reminding Timothy not to become elated because of such [a gift]." But it is better to understand this as the Holy Spirit (2 Cor. 6:6), the sense being that Timothy should make known by his actions that he has the fervor of the Holy Spirit and zeal for God.

ἐν πίστει. ["In faith."] "That you preach faith freely." Or: "That you show your faith by good works" (James 2:17).

ἐν ἁγνείᾳ. ["In chastity."] "That you show chastity in your words and actions."

A defense. At this point Estius seeks to find proof for the celibacy of priests, "since to be content with one wife is the lowest kind of chastity." I respond. (1) Ἁγνείᾳ also signifies purity or being unstained from human lusts. (2) Conjugal chastity is often more honorable than virginal chastity. (3) They admit that celibacy is not of divine right.

Verse 13.

The apostle had mentioned his hope to come to Timothy ([1 Tim.] 3:14). Meanwhile, while [his coming] is delayed, he tells Timothy what he should be doing: πρόσεχε τῇ ἀναγνώσει ["Devote attention to the reading"], namely, of Holy Scripture. Therefore, first of all, he commends to him the assiduous reading of Holy Scripture so that he may learn from it what to teach others. Second, he admonishes him to devote attention to exhortation and to teaching, that is, to others. For by exhortation he will continuously urge his hearers toward constancy in faith and holiness of living; but by teaching he will teach the ignorant what they should believe and do.

Theophylact understands παρακλήσει ["exhortation"] to be "consolation," thinking that "here is commanded the pastor's obligation to sorrowful and downcast spirits." But it is better to take this as about exhortation, for it includes consolation (Rom. 12:7–8).

Verse 14.

μὴ ἀμέλει τοῦ ἐν σοὶ χαρίσματος. "Do not neglect the gift [*gratiam*] that is in you."

Some understand χαρίσματος ["gift"] to be "the order itself" or "the rank of bishop which consists of the power to exercise everything that has to do with the office of bishop."

(1) Jerome (commentary on this passage): "The bishop used to have prophecy with ordination." Therefore, according to Jerome, Timothy had some kind of miraculous gift simultaneously communicated [to him] when he was admitted [to the episcopacy] through the laying on of hands.

(2) The ministers of Greifswald (*De vocat. ministrorum*) explain it thus: "Paul calls the very ministry of teaching the Gospel 'a gift' along with the gifts of the Holy Spirit. At the same time, however, he teaches that the rite of ordination should be done in the presence of the church with prophecy, that is, with the reading and explanation of the Word of God about the ministry of the Gospel and also with prayer and the laying on of hands by the presbyters, who are partakers and witnesses of his examination."

(3) Bellarmine (*De sacram. ord.*, ch. 2) explains it thus: "'Do not neglect the gift that was given to you when you were ordained a bishop by me according to the revelation given to me about you.' For God had revealed to Paul and commanded him that he ordain Timothy, which is also mentioned in [1 Tim.] 1[:18]."

(4) It is simplest to say that χαρίσματος comprises both the very ministry of the Gospel to which Timothy had been called and also the gifts of the Holy Spirit needed to carry it out, gifts he had received at the same time, such as the gift of teaching, exhorting, interpreting the Scriptures, and refuting contradictors.

Estius (commentary on this passage): "Since the apostle speaks about the grace given to Timothy through the ceremony of ordination by which he was made a bishop, it becomes clear from this that ordination is a sacrament of the new law by which a grace is conferred that is not only free but also makes [its recipient] acceptable [*gratificans*]."[7] I respond. (1) Ordination lacks an external element. (2) The promise of grace is proper to the Gospel.

ὃ ἐδόθη σοι διὰ τῆς προφητείας. ["Which was given to you through prophecy."] Timothy was first called and appointed to the church's ministry through a special revelation of the Holy Spirit given to the prophets who were in the Christian church at the time. Afterward he was confirmed and invested, so to speak, through the laying on of hands on him (1 Tim. 1:18).

The apostle recalls this prophecy to commend Timothy as well as to excuse himself, for without such testimony he would not have dared to lay an office of such great dignity upon Timothy, who was still young.

Apparent contrariety. *1 Tim. 1:18 speaks in the plural: "according to the previous prophecies about you." But here it is singular.* I respond. There were several prophecies with respect to the "previous prophecies," but there was only one prophecy with respect to the content predicted and revealed.

μετὰ ἐπιθέσεως τῶν χειρῶν τοῦ πρεσβυτερίου. ["With the laying on of hands of the college of presbyters."] Some interpret this as about the *office*, the sense being that Timothy received the laying on of hands so that he became a presbyter. But πρεσβυτερίου ["presbytery"] is not "the office of presbyter" but "the college of presbyters." In Luke 22:66 the Vulgate renders πρεσβυτερίου as *seniors plebis* ["elders of the people"]. It renders πᾶν τὸ πρεσβυτέριον (Acts 22:5) as *omnes maiores natu* ["all those elder by birth"]. In that sense it is an unusual way of speaking: "the laying on of hands of the presbytery."

According to Scripture's usage, the word "presbyters" also means "bishops," for the apostle says that he himself was one of them (2 Tim. 1:6).

Apparent contrariety. *"With the laying on of hands of the presbytery." But in 2 Tim. 1:6 the apostle mentions only his own laying on of hands.* I respond. It is likely that only the apostle laid on hands, but that this laying on of hands still happened in the congregation of presbyters and was done in their name. Or, what is more likely, Paul laid hands on Timothy together with the presbytery at the ordination. Estius says, "Although the ceremony of the laying on of hands was done by many, only Paul did those things that were essential for the sacrament." But now, if the laying on of hands is not essential for ordination, then what external element will they say is divinely commanded to be employed in ordination?

---

7 See *On the Ecclesiastical Ministry* [Commonplace XXVI/2], § 165.

Verse 15.

ταῦτα μελέτα. "Attend to these things." "Do these with all zeal; take pains for this care." Luther has *solches warte* ["attend to this"]. Oecumenius applies the demonstrative pronoun to what he had said: "Be a type for the faithful" [v. 12]. Chrysostom and others claim that the apostle had in mind the hearer: "Devote attention to the reading, to exhortation, to teaching."

ἵνα σου ἡ προκοπὴ φανερὰ ᾖ ἐν πᾶσιν. ["So that your progress may be manifest in all."] This can refer to both things and people: "So that your progress may be manifest in all things and among all people." Luther followed the former; the Vulgate, the latter: *ut omnes tuum profectum intelligant* ["so that all may perceive your progress"].

Chrysostom and Theophylact explain this "not only in his manner of life but also in his speech when teaching."

Verse 16.

ἔπεχε σεαυτῷ καὶ τῇ διδασκαλίᾳ. "Pay attention to yourself" (that you live rightly) "and to the teaching" (that you rightly instruct others).

ἐπίμενε αὐτοῖς. ["Persist in them."] Some relate this to everything that precedes in general: "I have admonished you to devote attention to the reading, to exhortation, and to teaching. In addition to this I now admonish you to persist in these." But it is more correct to take this with respect to what precedes immediately: "Persist in these two things I mentioned, that you pay attention to yourself and to the teaching."

σώσεις σεαυτὸν. ["You will save yourself."] Tossanus (commentary on this passage): "Not by your own merit, but because of the gratuitous promise of God you will save yourself (Phil. 2:12). You will flee the curse which God has threatened to all negligent ministers, and, on the other hand, you will receive the crown promised to faithful workers and stout athletes (Ezek. 33:19; 2 Tim. 4:7)." However, the second part [of this statement] sheds light on the first.

"You will save those who hear you" as a salutary instrument through whose teaching and ministry God works efficaciously in hearts (Acts 26:18; Rom. 11:14; 1 Cor. 9:12; James 5:20). This explanation of the second part [of this statement] should also be applied to the first part.

Estius (commentary on this passage):

> Note that the apostle had said earlier that God is the Savior of all people, especially of believers, but that now he attributes to a man the fact that he both saves himself and others. Clearly [this is] so that we would understand the ability and operative power of free choice within man. Hence Scripture also says that man sanctifies, justifies, purifies, and cleanses himself and his soul. Moreover, he saves himself with good works by meriting life, and he saves others by leading them to salvation with examples and teaching.

I respond. (1) Timothy and other ministers of the church save themselves and others and are called θεοῦ συνεργοί ["co-workers of God"] (1 Cor. 3:9) not by their natural powers but by the new powers given by the Holy Spirit. (2) Neither do they act meritoriously but instrumentally in this work of salvation by preaching the Gospel of Christ, "which is the power of God unto salvation for all who believe" (Rom. 1:16).

Estius (commentary on this passage): "Catholics are right to call the mother of God their 'life and hope,' for they can also call her a 'savior' since she obtains salvation for so many people by her intercession before God." I respond. (1) They not only trust in Mary's intercession but also in her merits. (2) The reason why Timothy is said "to save" does not coincide with Mary.

Chapter V

There are two parts [to this chapter].

The first part contains certain specific rules for how Timothy should conduct himself in his office (1) toward men and women of advanced age (vv. 1–2); (2) toward widows (vv. 3–16); (3) toward presbyters working in Word and teaching (vv. 17–19).

The second part contains some general rules that should be carefully observed in carrying out the office of the church (vv. 20–25).

[This chapter] can also be divided into three parts:

(1) How Timothy should conduct himself in private rebukes (vv. 1–2).

(2) How he should conduct the care of widows (vv. 3–16).

(3) How he should behave toward presbyters (vv. 17–25).

Verse 1.

Connection. The apostle now moves from general precepts in which a bishop should be instructed to specific ones.

Πρεσβυτέρῳ μὴ ἐπιπλήξῃς. "Do not rebuke an older man," namely, due to the respect and honor owed to old age.

Here the noun πρεσβυτέρῳ is one of age, not office and rank, as is clear from what follows.

The Greek ἐπιπλήξῃς properly means "to inflict a blow," but later it is used figuratively for "to rebuke bitterly and harshly."

Apparent contrariety. "Do not rebuke an older man." But Christ (Matt. 23:13), Paul (Acts 23:3), and Daniel (ch. 11) harshly rebuked older men.

I respond. Gregory (bk. 7, Letter 1): "This apostolic rule should be kept when an older man's sin does not draw the hearts of younger men to their ruin by his example. But when an older man provides younger men with a destructive example, then he must be hit with a severe rebuke."

παρακάλει ὡς πατέρα. ["Admonish him as a father."] Some translate this "exhort," but the context shows that it is not about exhortation but about correction. So it is more correct to translate it: "By entreaty admonish and correct him as father would his son."[1]

νεωτέρους, ὡς ἀδελφούς. ["Younger men as brothers."] Understand "admonish them" or "correct them." The comparative **νεωτέρους** ["younger men"] is used as a substantive, as also with the word **πρεσβυτέρῳ** ["older man"].

Verse 2.

πρεσβυτέρας. "Older women."

ἐν πάσῃ ἁγνείᾳ. ["In all chastity,"] lest spiritual love (as expressed by the term **ἀδελφάς** ["sisters"]) become tainted with carnal desire. For the devil especially lies in wait for the chastity of the young, and he easily takes advantage of a friendly conversation to misuse it for harm.

Thomas, Lyranus, and the *Glossa ordinaria* relate these two verses to the previous chapter 4.

Verse 3.

He gives instructions to Timothy as to what the selection should be for honoring widows, that is, for caring for them at the public expense of the church. **Χήρας τίμα** ["honor widows"] in such a way that you make them known, since certain ones are to be charged with the ministry of the sick and sojourners and are to be supported by the church's goods. This support is signified by the word "honor" because it also served as a testament to the virtue of those who were being thus supported. Compare this to Acts 6:1, where the opposite of this honor is "disregarded."

τὰς ὄντως χήρας. ["The ones who are truly widows."] They are utterly deserted; they do not have help from their parents, children, and relatives; and they lead a life according to the pattern given in vv. 5, 9–10.

He is alluding to the derivation of the word **χήρα** ["widow"], for it is derived from **χηρεύω** ("to be deprived of, to lack, to be without").

Chrysostom asks: "Why does the apostle make no mention of honoring virgins?" He answers: "Maybe there were no virgins then, that is, ones who had resolved to grow old in virginity." But the simpler answer is that virgins were not supported by the church's resources as were needy, desolate widows.

Connection. Through contrariety he makes known who truly is a widow, namely, not merely one deprived of her husband but also one who is without the help of her children.

---

1 Gerhard's paraphrase reads "father" in the nominative, though in the Greek it is in the accusative.

Verse 4.

μανθανέτωσαν πρῶτον. ["Let them learn first."] That is, before her own [children] burden the church with her necessary support.

Some take this with respect to the widows. But since it is in the plural, Theophylact and Oecumenius are more correct to take it with reference to their children and grandchildren, as the following words also prove: καὶ ἀμοιβὰς ἀποδιδόναι τοῖς προγόνοις ["and to return payment to their parents"] (cf. v. 16). The verb εὐσεβεῖν ["to show devotion"] itself confirms this explanation.[2]

The little word πρῶτον ["first"] points out the order of giving support. "Let them learn in the first place to employ devout care for the support of those of their own house, and parents are especially such. Then, if they can, let them also be generous toward others" (cf. v. 8).

εὐσεβεῖν τὸν ἴδιον οἶκον. ["To show devotion to their own house."] The Vulgate has *domum suam regere* ["to rule their own house"]. Luther has *jhre eigne Häuser Göttlich regiren* ["to rule their own houses in a godly manner"], "to exercise devotion among the members of one's house," that is, to serve one's mothers and grandparents and give support for their livelihood. Augustine (*Confess.*, bk. 9, ch. 9; and *Quaest.* 43 on Deuteronomy) translates εὐσεβεῖν as *pie tractare* ["treat dutifully"]. Jerome (Letter *ad Ageruchiam*) translates it *colere* ["cherish"]. It can also be translated *pie curare* ["to care for dutifully"].

ἀμοιβὰς ἀποδιδόναι. "To return payment," that is, in giving support. The Greeks call it ἀντιπελαργεῖν ["to cherish in return"], from the nature of the πελαργός ("stork").

τοῦτο γάρ ἐστι καλὸν καὶ ἀπόδεκτον ἐνώπιον τοῦ θεοῦ. ["For this is good and pleasing in the sight of God."] Some copies do not have the added καλὸν ["good"], and so it is thought that it was transferred here from [1 Tim.] 2:3. The Syriac translation, Theophylact, and Oecumenius omit it.

This should be well inculcated into children, that this work of devotion toward parents is exceedingly dear and pleasing to God.

Verse 5.

Connection. He teaches that widows who are truly widows should be honored. Now he subsequently explains who the true widows are. She is truly a widow who should be employed in the service of the poor, the sick, and the sojourners and should be supported at the church's expense.

μεμονωμένη. ["Left alone."] "Who has no children or relatives to support her." The Vulgate has *desolata* ["forsaken"]. She is not only destitute of a

2 Εὐσεβεῖν usually means to show devotion (piety) to God or to one's parents.

husband but also of children and grandchildren, as well as of all human support by which she could be helped.

ἤλπικεν ἐπὶ τόν θεόν. ["She has set her hope on God."] The preterit has the force of the present, as in [1 Tim.] 4:10.

προσμένει ταῖς δεήσεσιν. ["She persists in prayers,"] [following] the example of Anna the prophetess (Luke 2:37). "She persists, continues, perseveres in prayers." The Greek word signifies more constancy than "perseverance." Based on this passage, Jerome (Letter *ad Ageruchiam*) describes widows thus: "They are devoid of all help from their own relations; they cannot work with their own hands; poverty debilitates them; and age weakens them. For them God is their hope, and all their work is prayer." [The apostle] left it to Timothy to conclude that only women such as this were to be received into the number of the church's widows.

Connection. The apostle now interposes an antithesis so that Timothy will know which widows he should reject from the support of the church as unworthy.

Verse 6.

ἡ δὲ σπαταλῶσα. ["But she who lives for indulgence."] The Vulgate rendered this as causal: *nam quae in deliciis est* ["for she who is in pleasure"]. But in Greek the particle is adversative ["but"]. [The word] σπαταλῶσα has the meaning of "itching with desire for pleasure." Therefore she who is σπαταλῶσα is "wanton and shameless" (cf. James 5:5). Augustine (*Q.* 43 on Deuteronomy): "She who lives in pleasure." Cyprian (*Ad Quirinum*, bk. 3, ch. 74): "She who is spoiled with indulgence."

ζῶσα τέθνηκεν. ["She is dead though living."] Drusius (*Adag. Hebr.*, decur. 13, prov. 3, taken from commentary on the book of *Avoth*, ch. 3): *resha'im behayehem niqere'im methim* ("the ungodly are called 'dead in their life'"). Therefore the apostle is right to say of the wanton and ungodly widow that "she is dead though living." She is alive in her bodily life but is devoid of spiritual life, because she is dead to every good work and subject to everlasting death (Rev. 3:1; Matt. 8:22).

Estius (commentary on this passage): "The apostle means that the widow devoted to pleasure is a sort of monster, because she is dead while living. For though she is alive and well in the body and lives so delightfully according to the flesh, nevertheless she is dead in spirit, seeing as she lacks God's grace."

Verse 7.

καὶ ταῦτα παράγγελλε. "Command these things too," that is, besides those discussed above ([1 Tim.] 4:11).

ἵνα ἀνεπίληπτοι ὦσιν. ["So that they may be irreproachable."] Some think that the particle ἵνα signifies the *material*, but others think it signifies the *end purpose*. The latter is more fitting. "The things that I just mentioned—namely, that they hope in God, be resolute in prayers, flee pleasure—command them to widows, so that no one will dare reproach them."

Verse 8.

εἰ δέ τις τῶν ἰδίων καὶ μάλιστα τῶν οἰκείων οὐ προνοεῖ. "If anyone has no concern for his own [relatives] and especially those of his own household." "If anyone does not provide for his own relatives," etc. This refers back to v. 4.

The relative τις ["anyone"] is common for both genders. Therefore some think it should be rendered in the feminine gender ("if any woman"), since the apostle is continuing his discourse on widows. That is how the Greek commentators and Erasmus take it. But it is more correct for it to be rendered in the masculine, for it refers to the children and grandchildren of widows (v. 4).

He calls people who are related in any way "relatives" [*suos*] while those who are related closely by blood he calls "of one's own household." These would be parents, siblings, children, and grandchildren, because they are often joined together in the same residence.

τὴν πίστιν ἤρνηται. ["He has denied the faith."] He acts contrary to the nature and character of true faith and by doing so testifies that he does not have true faith, since it is "effectual through love" (Gal. 5:6). There is a similar form of speech in 2 Tim. 3:5 and Titus 1:16.

One is particularly considered to be denying the faith in deed through those sins which cause others to blaspheme the God of Christians or which turn others away from faith and religion in Him. In the early church such was the case if children abandoned the care of their needy parents, if servants refused to obey their masters, [or] if Christians refused to pay taxes to rulers.

ἔστιν ἀπίστου χείρων. ["He is worse than an unbeliever."] (1) With respect to culpability, because [even] the unbeliever or pagan recognizes from the light of nature that parents should be shown support. (2) With respect to punishment, because that kind of ingratitude [ἀχαριστία] will be punished more severely. For surely he whom God has called through the light of grace to the knowledge of the truth sins more grievously by violating that natural obligation, and accordingly he makes himself liable to a more severe judgment.

However, this should be understood with this limitation: "He is worse than an unbeliever" in this respect, for it is not necessarily the case that he is worse absolutely.[3]

---

3 See above, p. 31 n. 1.

Estius (commentary on this passage) notes: "It should be noted that the apostle did not say 'he has lost his faith,' but 'he denied it.' Again, neither did he say 'he is an unbeliever,' but 'he is worse than an unbeliever." So one should not deduce from the apostle's words that faith is lost by any mortal sin. This was asserted by Luther and condemned by the fathers of the Council of Trent." I respond. To deny the faith by one's deeds is to lose true, saving faith. "Through faith Christ dwells in the believer's heart" (Eph. 3:17). But now, where mortal sins rule, there Christ does not dwell through grace. (2) One who is worse than an unbeliever no longer has true, saving faith but has lost it. (3) Whoever does not care for his relatives lacks love. But where there is no true love, neither is there faith, because true "faith is effectual through love" (Gal. 5:6).

Verse 9.

Χήρα καταλεγέσθω. ["Let a widow be enrolled"] for service to the poor and sick, for which service they were supported at the church's expense (Acts 6:1; Rom. 16:1). Epiphanius seems to be discussing these widows (*Haeres.* 79, p. 883):

> Although in the church there is an order of ministering women called "deaconesses," it does not exist so that they may preside or be allowed to usurp anything. It exists to respect womankind when it comes time for Baptism, or for the inspection of an affliction or pain, or for whenever a woman's body would [need to] be uncovered, so that it would not be seen by the presiding men but [only] by an assisting woman whom the priest orders temporarily to exercise care for a woman in need—in a time when her body is uncovered. So it is that order for good discipline and for the church's good arrangement is greatly and wisely protected by the extent of this rule.

καταλεγέσθω, etc. ["Let her be enrolled."] This can be taken in two ways: either as "Let her be chosen for admission into the company of widows" or as "Let her be put in charge of others." Cajetan follows the latter meaning because such a great age is required. But the Greek word demands the first meaning, for it does not properly signify "let her be chosen" but "let her be enrolled," as Erasmus renders it. That is, she was added to the list and enrolled in their company. This meaning fits with the aim and context, for the apostle is continuing his description of the widow who is being received into the generous support from the offerings of the faithful. Neither does the apostle contrast this widow whom he commands to be enrolled with widows who, on the other hand, should obey her, but with the younger ones whom he wants disqualified [from enrollment].

μὴ ἔλαττον ἐτῶν ἑξήκοντα. ["Not less than sixty years of age."] (1) "So that there will be less of a danger that they may start to grow indulgent and scandalize the church by defiling themselves in lusts" (Chrysostom). (2) Lest they want to marry and leave the service of the church. (3) Before that age women are still able enough to gain a living for themselves by some kind of work (Jerome, Letter *ad Salvinam*; Thomas, commentary on this passage).

Lest the church be burdened or gain a bad reputation, he wants diligent consideration to be given when electing such widows. He prescribes conditions: for example, that younger widows and those suspected of lacking self-control not be accepted. Likewise, [that they not accept] those who can be supported by near relatives or those who have the means to support themselves. But [they are to enroll] those who are old, chaste, poor and alone, and who have demonstrated that they are worthy of this benefit by showing good works toward the church and their own children.

γεγονυῖα ἑνὸς ἀνδρὸς γυνή. ["Having been the wife of one husband."] One who has not left her husband or had an affair. Or one who remained in widowhood after her husband's death and gave evidence of her chastity.

Estius (commentary on this passage) notes: "It is absurd for Paul to demand of a woman who is going to be supported by the church's alms that in her whole life she have had but one husband, but then for him to allow a bishop, who is supposed to be in charge of the church, to be married twice." I respond. (1) If we accept the explanation above, then the force of this argument is removed. (2) Marriage could not have existed simultaneously with the public enrollment of widows who were to be supported by the church's alms, but the office of bishop and marriage can exist simultaneously in one subject. (3) If an argument for the requirements of a bishop is to be deduced from the requirements of these widows, then it will follow that no one should be chosen for the episcopacy before the age of sixty.

Verse 10.

ἐν ἔργοις καλοῖς μαρτυρουμένη. ["Well attested in good works."] "For whom many will give their testimony that she has diligently applied herself in good works."

εἰ ἐτεκνοτρόφησεν. ["If she has reared children,"] that is, "well." "If she raised her children in a godly way, in the fear of the Lord." Some explain it thus: "If she has reared children and in that way made it clear that she is not spoiled with indulgence, lazy, and addicted to pleasure."

εἰ ἐξενοδόχησεν. "If she has exercised hospitality." This virtue was most necessary in the beginnings of the church because public inns were full of idolatrous filth as a result of the extremely corrupt morals of the pagans. Chrysostom (on this passage): "Even the pauper still has a house in which to receive a traveler."

εἰ ἁγίων πόδας ἔνιψεν. ["If she has washed the feet of saints."] In this passage "saints" means "traveling and wandering Christians." The sense is: "If she has shown ready service and ministry to travelers and wanderers." Indeed, the general is understood from the specific, because in those hot regions this kind of duty was frequent and common (Gen. 18:4; 19:2; Luke 7:44).

Some specifically understand this about ministers of the church in whom holiness should be more apparent.

εἰ θλιβομένοις ἐπήρκεσεν. "If she helped the afflicted" with money, intercession, consolation, and [in] other ways [that] she could.

εἰ παντὶ ἔργῳ ἀγαθῷ ἐπηκολούθησεν. "If she pursued good works of every kind with great zeal." Jerome (on Zechariah 8): "If she pursued every good work." Erasmus: "If she was constant in every good work." Even if she could not perform many good works because of poverty or by reason of her sex, she is still such a one who showed willingness and participation for every good work.

Verse 11.

After he has taught which widows should be chosen, he now teaches which are to be rejected.

χήρας νεωτέρας παραιτοῦ. "Turn [younger widows] away," not absolutely but in a certain respect, namely, that you not set them over the ministries to the poor or enroll them in the number of the widows being supported by the church. Cyprian (*Ad Quirin.*, bk. 3, ch. 74): "Pass over younger widows." The comparative is being used substantively, for the apostle is not demanding that fifty-year-old women marry (cf. v. 2).

ὅταν γὰρ καταστρηνιάσωσιν τοῦ χριστοῦ. ["For when they behave wantonly toward Christ."] The uncompounded verb στρηνιάω is used of the "great whore" in Rev. 18:7 and of those "fornicating with her" (Rev. 18:9).

As for its compound καταστρηνιάω, (1) the commentators Chrysostom and Erasmus translate it in this passage as "to fornicate." Jerome (Letter *ad Gerontiam*) expresses it in the same way. But neither does the force of the verb mean that nor would the apostle ever speak like this: "After they have fornicated, I want them to marry." This would censure marriage more than the fornication itself.

(2) Oecumenius gives this paraphrase: "When they become lazy, debauched, that is, when they become flippant, when they treat Christ with disdain." In the same way Theophylact interprets it through ἀκκισθῶσι καὶ θρύψωνται ("they become flippant and debauched"). That first verb is derived from the manners of a most flippant woman, called an ἀκκώ.

(3) Sophilus (in Athenaeus, bk. 3) uses it for "to indulge in pleasure."

(4) Joachim Camerarius: "Στρηνιάω signifies the swelling of intoxication and luxury as well as the titillation of filthy lust."

(5) Chemnitz: "Στρηνιάω is to rage with unfettered wild arrogance and flippancy."[4]

Some explain it like this: "When they have an abundance of temporal goods through Christ, that is, in view of the profession by which they dedicated themselves to Christ" (Thomas and Cajetan).

Others, for the most part, translate the Greek verb as "when they have tasted the riches of Christ, the latter start to scorn them and want to marry" (Stapulensis and Hentenius). But the original text does not allow these explanations. Erasmus (*Annot.*): "Καταστρηνιάω means 'to be wanton and rage against someone for pleasure,' like beasts which, when they have grazed too much, rage against their masters and, having burst their reins, move about as they please. Therefore the sense is: 'When they have started to act wantonly against Christ.' The preposition κατὰ, which forms the compound of the Greek verb, signifies opposition when joined with the genitive (Ps. 2:2)."

Some think that this verb is derived from στερεῖν ["to deprive"] or from a metaphor taken from beasts of burden which, when they become unruly for food, tear off their reins and move about as they please. Others think it comes from στρηνόν ("harsh"); hence Hesychius interprets στρηνὲς βοᾶν as τὸ σκληρὸν βοᾶν ("to shout harshly or fiercely"). For to the Greeks στρηνές ["harsh sounds"] sound σαφὲς, ἰσχυρὸν, τραχὺ, στυγνὸν, ἀνατεταγμένον ("clear, strong, bitter, unpleasant, lingering").

Therefore καταστρηνιάσωσιν τοῦ χριστοῦ is by words, gestures, and works to show wantonness and ferocity against Christ, that is, against faith shown to Christ and the church.

Verse 12.

ἔχουσαι κρίμα. ["Having the judgment."] They are reproachable, they incur reproach and the permanent mark of shame. They have deserved to be sternly censured by the church's elders and leaders. The Vulgate rendered it *damnationem* ["condemnation"] as if the uncompounded κρίμα stands for κατάκριμα. But the Greek and the Syriac have "judgment."

ἠθέτησαν. "They have rejected, cast off." The Vulgate rendered it *irritam fecerunt* ("nullified"), for whoever rejects the faith He gave and abandons it nullifies it.

By τὴν πρώτην πίστιν ["the first faith"], (1) he does not mean monastic vows and their denial through πρώτης πίστεως ἀθέτησις ["a breach of former faith"]. For in the apostle's day monastic vows were not yet in use, nor does "first faith" mean "a vow" anywhere in Scripture.

4 Chemnitz, *Examination of the Council of Trent*, Chemnitz's Works 3:102.

Estius cites many fathers to support this explanation. But they are talking about a promise, not a solemn vow. Estius himself is forced to admit that "the vow of these widows was not solemn in the way the nuns' vow is today."

(2) Therefore Luther (*De capt. Babyl.*, Lat. Jen., tom. 2, f. 514) takes it as about "faith in Christ or the religion which those mercy-working women denied the more freely to marry and return to Judaism or paganism."[5] Chemnitz (*Exam. Conc. Trident.*, part 3, p. 59; *Loci*, part 2, p. 510),[6] Calvin (commentary on this passage), and Whitaker (*De script.*, p. 541) explain it in the same way.

Such faith is simply "first" for the Christian, since from it one is named a "Christian." Moreover, this usage of "faith" is very common in the apostolic Epistles.

To this explanation Estius raises an objection: "If the apostle was talking about Christian faith, it would have been completely pointless to mention 'they desire to marry.' For whether they want to marry or not, they have condemnation since they depart from the faith of the Gospel." I respond. Those younger, wanton widows were denying the Christian faith so that they could marry more freely and not be accused of levity.

(3) Others, however, explain it in terms of "the promise by which they devoted themselves to the ministry of the poor and the sick in the church" (Beza, *Tract. de polygam.*, p. 206; Hunnius, *Tract. de lege et evang.*, p. 82; Tossanus, commentary on this passage).

·The apostle calls their promise "first faith" not because no faith preceded it as its cause, but because in the Hebrew way of speaking it was "first," that is, "former" or "previously given" (cf. Rev. 2:4–5; Acts 1:1). "Faith" is used for faithfulness in keeping promises in Rom. 3:3 and 2 Tim. 4:7. (Cf. Chamierus, *Panopl.*, tom. 3, bk. 20, ch. 16.)

Some explain it as being about one's profession of faith given at Baptism. This explanation can be put back under the second.

"They abandon their first faith," namely, through a new marriage which forces them to desert the ministry of the church.

·*Connection.* He lists other things that make younger widows unfit to be taken into the college of widows who are supported by the church's funds.

Verse 13.

ἀργαὶ. "As idlers" they wander about, seeing as they have been supported by the funds and support of the church. Idling and having nothing to do at home nor a husband whom they fear, they learn—that is, grow accustomed

5 See *Judgment on Monastic Vows* (1521), AE 44:397.

6 Cf. Chemnitz, *Examination of the Council of Trent*, Chemnitz's Works 3:104.

to—wandering about through homes, which is foreign to a woman's honor and dangerous to her chastity.

οὐ μόνον δὲ ἀργαί, ἀλλὰ καὶ φλύαροι. "But not only idlers but also gossips" and inappropriate chatterboxes. The conjunction **δὲ** (which the Vulgate translator omitted) adds emphasis.

περίεργοι. ["Meddlesome."] "Women who pry into the affairs of others who have nothing to do with them." This meddling is a fruit of their idling.

λαλοῦσαι τὰ μὴ δέοντα. ["Saying things they should not,"] because they divulge secrets they have heard, because they are harming the reputation of others, or because they are saying words now and then that are hardly virtuous and chaste.

Verse 14.

Βούλομαι οὖν νεωτέρας γαμεῖν. ["Therefore I want the younger ones to marry."] That is, "if they cannot remain continent," for the apostle thus explains himself in 1 Cor. 7:9.

[The question arises:] *How does this fit with what he says in 1 Cor. 7:7: "I want all people to be as I am"?* Estius responds not absurdly: "In this passage the apostle says that he wants what seems best for those younger widows absolutely, all circumstances considered. But in 1 Cor. 7:7 he merely expresses his desire, though he sees that it cannot be fulfilled. So he adds: 'But everyone has his own gift from God.' "

Again, Estius says: "In this passage, **βούλομαι** does not command but urges and counsels a lesser good." I respond. Actually, widows who lack the gift of continence should marry, lest they fall into the sin of fornication. From this Cajetan (on this passage) notes: "Would that we today would learn from such practical knowledge whether the solemn vows of sacred orders or of religious orders are good for young people of either sex."

μηδεμίαν ἀφορμὴν διδόναι τῷ ἀντικειμένῳ. ["To give no opportunity to the adversary."] Some take this as a proper noun for the devil, whose instruments are false accusers. Some take it as being about adversaries or enemies of the church in such a way that the singular stands for the plural. But the latter explanation is more fitting, for the devil always curses and makes false accusations even without any occasion given.

λοιδορίας χάριν. ["For slander."] "For accusing the church of God and falsely accusing the morals of Christians." Therefore he is indicating the reason for the preceding: he wants younger widows to marry and be housemothers, so that, having been brought back under the bond of matrimony and engaged in the obligations of marriage, they may not have the freedom to wander about and commit other evils that would give the adversaries of Christianity an opportunity for cursing.

Verse 15.

ἐξετράπησαν ὀπίσω τοῦ Σατανᾶ. ["They have turned away after Satan."] Through fornication and lusts they have turned away from Christ and His holy commands after Satan, the author of fornication. Some take this as being about apostasy from the faith that they had been following so that they could more freely fornicate. Others interpret it that they married contrary to their vow. But Estius himself rightly recognizes that it is more correct to take it in the sense that "they fornicated, and because of this," he says, "they gave the adversary greater opportunity to curse."

Verse 16.

εἴ τις ἔχει χήρας. ["If anyone has widows,"] that is, "who are related to them." The Vulgate has only the masculine: *si quis fidelis* ["if any believing man"]; but the Greek has both the masculine and the feminine: εἴ τις πιστὸς ἢ πιστὴ ἔχει χήρας ["if any believing man or believing woman has widows"].

Estius:

> This is a universal statement, not one that applies only to children and grandchildren who are obligated toward widows by a closer bond, about whom he spoke in v. 4. But it also encompasses the widows' relations and kin—yes, even their lords and ladies who employed their help and service. He is admonishing all these to support from their own means such widows who are bound to them by any close connection if they cannot endure normal work because of age or infirmity.

Connection. He moves from the honor of widows to the honor owed presbyters.

Verse 17.

"Those who preside well," that is, over church discipline. He means presbyters ["elders"] not by age but by order.

διπλῆς τιμῆς ἀξιούσθωσαν. ["Let them be counted worthy of double honor."] Some understand "double honor" to mean "greater compensation" based on a comparison with the verse that follows.

Hieronymus Weller (*De off. eccles.*) explains "double honor" as being about "sustenance and obedience, that not only reverence be shown to them on account of their office, but also there be provision for the sustenance they need."

Ambrosiaster explains "double honor" as "earthly and heavenly." Some [interpret it] as "the honor of reverence and support"; others, "a double honor of sustenance" which they think should be given to presbyters doubly, that is, as compared to the widows. Others [take it to be] "a generous and liberal support and assistance of necessities." The word "honor" signifies "the support of one's life" inasmuch as it is given as a witness to one's virtue or excellence. For the

Hebrews "double" means "abundant, much," etc. This last explanation is confirmed by the following verse.

οἱ κοπιῶντες. ["Those laboring."] For, as it should be, teaching sacred doctrine is no small[7] labor.

Connection. He now confirms his command from Scripture.

Verse 18.

"For Scriptures says." See Deut. 25:4 (cf. 1 Cor. 9:9), where the meaning of the law is set forth. This means that preachers of the Word should be given a living not sparingly but generously, as if "from a full heap."[8]

ἄξιος ὁ ἐργάτης τοῦ μισθοῦ αὐτοῦ. ["The laborer is worthy of his wages."] This statement is found in Matt. 10:10 and Luke 10:7. Therefore Paul, by his assent, thus asserts the canonical authority of the evangelists.

Estius objects to this explanation that "it is unlikely that Paul would have cited anything from the Gospel of Luke, his disciple, especially since it does not seem to have been written at the time." However, neither reason has any weight. For why would Paul not use his authority to confirm the Gospel of Luke as canonical and divine? Besides, many people agree that 1 Timothy was written after Luke's Gospel.

Some claim that this is a reference to a passage in Moses, Lev. 19:13: "The pay of your hired hand shall not remain with us until morning." But here the wording is not similar, though the content applies to some extent.

Some say that no testimony of Scripture is being cited, and they claim that the preceding "for Scripture says" should merely be related to the testimony of what immediately follows: "You shall not muzzle an ox while it threshes." To this Scripture, [they say,] the apostle adds another statement from human affairs and common sense, for reason dictates to everyone that a worker is owed his wages.

Apparent contrariety. The Gospel should be proclaimed for free—therefore not for wages. I respond. This comparison only has in view the support owed to the worker, the sense being: "Just as the worker is worthy of wages so that he can live, so also the minister of the Gospel is worthy of an honorarium or the means to support himself." Hence Christ uses the word "food" in place of "wages" (Matt. 10:10).

Connection. Just as he has to this point given a command about honorably supporting presbyters, so now he gives commands about how they are to be judged if perhaps they have transgressed. Here, as above, a bishop is included.

---

7 Reading *parvi* instead of *pravi*.

8 Juvenal, *Satires* 6.364 (LCL 91 [2004], p. 270).

Verse 19.

κατὰ πρεσβυτέρου. ["Against a presbyter."] Erasmus (*Annot.*, on this passage) says, "It is unclear whether this passage is talking about a bishop or an elder." Cyprian (*Ad Quirinum*, testim. 76), Chrysostom, Theophylact, and Oecumenius (commentary on this passage) take it as being about an elder by age. But Ambrose and Theodoret (commentary on this passage) more correctly interpret it as being about a presbyter by rank and office.

The context demands this explanation, for the apostle has been speaking about presbyters by rank and office since v. 17.

Cyprian (on this passage), Ambrosiaster, Primasius, and Oecumenius (commentary on this passage) do not read the added exception: ἐκτὸς εἰ μὴ ἐπὶ δύο ἢ τριῶν μαρτύρων ["except on the basis of two or three witnesses"]. But they still understand it as saying that an accusation should not be admitted easily or rashly. Jerome, however (Letter *ad Marcellam*, p. 102), prefers the common reading that has the exception included.

Ambrose gives this reason for the apostle's edict: "Because the honor of this order is lofty" (for such men are vicars of Christ), "and therefore an accusation should not be easily admitted about such a person." The meaning is that, because of the dignity of the office, a presbyter should not rashly be suspected of evil. Add to this the fact that the office of presbyters is subject to various acts of hatred and false accusations; they can easily become weighed down by false accusations. The first reason comes from the rank of presbyters; the latter, from the disposition of their hearers.

Apparent contrariety. *The law is common to all: "That no one be condemned by only one giving testimony against him" (Deut. 17:6; 19:15). So why is something particular established concerning presbyters?* I respond. It is one thing "to admit an accusation" and another "to condemn." Thomas (commentary on this passage): "The apostle commands that an accusation against a presbyter should not even be admitted by a judge unless it is established by suitable and sufficient witnesses."

Verse 20.

Τοὺς ἁμαρτάνοντας ἐνώπιον πάντων ἔλεγχε. ["Those who keep on sinning rebuke in the presence of all."] Some understand this specifically about presbyters, for the apostle had spoken about them in the preceding verse: "Just as an accusation should not easily be admitted against presbyters, so also, if they are convicted by a lawful judgment, they should not be spared but should be sternly rebuked in the public gathering of the church as an example for others." But it is more correct to take this generally about all who sin publicly, who are notorious of themselves or who are convicted by public judgment—not of just any sin but of more grave, scandalous sins. The added reason shows that this qualification is implied.

ἐνώπιον πάντων. ["In the presence of all."] "Rebuke before the whole gathering of the church" (cf. Matt. 18:17; 2 Cor. 2:6). For this qualification does not belong to the participle ἁμαρτάνοντας ["sinning"] but to the verb ἔλεγχε ["rebuke."]

ἵνα καὶ οἱ λοιποὶ φόβον ἔχωσιν. ["So that the rest also may have fear."] Those who take this apostolic command only about sinning presbyters interpret οἱ λοιποὶ ["the rest"] to be "those who are not in the number of the presbyters." But it is more correct to understand them as those who are not guilty of the same crime. He wants them to be restrained by this public rebuke and have fear put upon them as a restraint for sin so that they may fear receiving a similar rebuke—that is, one that is public and connected with public shame—and so that they may be deterred from committing similar sins.

Verse 21.

Διαμαρτύρομαι ἐνώπιον τοῦ θεοῦ καὶ κυρίου Ἰησοῦ χριστοῦ καὶ τῶν ἐκλεκτῶν ἀγγέλων. ["I implore you before God and the Lord Jesus Christ and the angels."] The Vulgate rendered the verb διαμαρτύρομαι as *testor* ["I bear witness"], but it is more correct to render it *obtestor* ["I implore by"]. For these are not properly the words of one making an oath, but of one imploring. The apostle is declaring that by the weightiest of witnesses he is commanding to Timothy those things which he said about the carrying out of judgment (1 Tim. 6:13; 2 Tim. 4:1). He lists God first, in whose stead stand judges and who is present in their judgment (2 Chron. 19:6). He lists Christ second, for He is the "Mediator between God and men" (1 Tim. 2:5), and He is lower than the Father with respect to His human nature. In the third place he cites the presence of the angels as being diligent observers of our actions and as those who will come with Christ at the judgment.

Some understand "the angels" to be "the teachers of the church, for they are also called 'angels' (Mal. 2:7; Rev. 1:20)," through which the apostle implores Timothy, because teachers of the church should revere and esteem one another. But it is more correct to understand them as being those blessed spirits who serve before the throne of God and Christ and who execute the divine commands. The apostle adds them to Christ in the church as spectators and future witnesses against negligence or faithlessness, just as he wants good order to be observed in the church "on account of the angels" (1 Cor. 11:10).

From the fact that he calls them "elect angels" the Calvinists deduce that "the object of election" (which they claim is absolute[9]) "is not only men but also angels." Calvin (commentary on this passage): "He calls them 'elect

9 See above, p. 31 n. 1.

angels' not only to distinguish them from the reprobate but also for the sake of excellency, that their testimony should be more respected." (Cf. Ravensperg, *Decad.* 3. *globor. sacror.*, q. 6). But I respond. (1) The object of election, properly so called and which occurred in view of faith in Christ, is not the angels but men. (2) Hence Paraeus admits that "the word 'election' is not used here as it is used elsewise in the article on the election of men." (See Bellarmine, *De grat. et lib.*, bk. 2, ch. 17, p. 369.) (3) The angels are called "loved [*dilecti*] and choice," for in Greek ἐκλεκτῶν often means the same thing as "select and excellent," even as "blossoming young men" (*bahure hemed*, Ezek. 23:6) are named from the root *bahar* ("he chose"; cf. Ps. [78:63]; 148:12; Ezek. 9:6). The Son of God, who in Isa. 42:1 is called *bahir* ("elect"), is then in Matt. 12:18 called by the equivalent term ἀγαπητός ("beloved"). The substantives *mibekar* ["choicest"] and *mibekhor* ["choice"] denote something that is choice and outstanding, because in a free and right election one does not usually choose the worst but the best (Gen. 23:6; Jer. 48:15; 2 Kings 3:19; 19:23). From all this it is clear that the word ἐκλεκτῶν does not denote election, properly speaking, but the excellence of the angels, and in this sense it is attributed even to other creatures (Exod. 14:7; Jer. 22:7).

Ambrosius Catharinus wants "elect angels" to be understood as "not all the blessed angels but the seven primary ones" whom he thinks are signified by "'the seven spirits of God' (Rev. 1:4) and 'the seven angels' (Tobit 12:15), who are called 'elect' because they excel the other angels (Ps. 78:31)." But to understand them as the blessed angels in general is more correct; they are called "elect" to distinguish them from the evil, reprobate angels, namely, the demons.

ἵνα ταῦτα φυλάξῃς. ["That you guard these things."] Some relate the pronoun ταῦτα ["these things"] to everything he has commanded Timothy thus far, but the Greeks relate it only to what just precedes it, as is clear from the fact that he adds "without prejudice."

χωρὶς προκρίματος. ["Without prejudice."] "Without preferring one over another through partiality." Luther: *ohne eigen gutdünckel* ["without one's own opinion"]. Ambrosiaster connects it with the following, so as to make the apostle's command: "Do nothing without pre-judgment; that is, do not confer ecclesiastical rank on anyone without first having examined and judged his life and morals." Cajetan interprets it in the same way. But the Greeks and Latins more fittingly join it with the preceding part, [the sense being] that he not give judgment based on a hastily conceived opinion and without sufficient investigation. Luther: *Dass du solches haltest ohne eigen gutdünckel* ["that you should hold this without your own opinion"].

μηδὲν ποιῶν κατὰ πρόσκλισιν. "[Doing nothing] according to inclination" or "partiality." Some copies read κατὰ πρόσκλησιν ("according to legal summons"). Theophylact and Oecumenius mention both readings, but the former is genuine. "Do nothing through the inclination of your heart" by which you are inclined toward this or that, preoccupied by some bias, "but rather show yourself fair to all."

Judges must chiefly guard against two vices: hastiness to judge as well as bias. The apostle is excluding both vices.

Verse 22.

χεῖρας ταχέως μηδενὶ ἐπιτίθει. ["Do not lay hands on anyone hastily,"] lest anyone come to the ministry of the church by a quick ordination, but first diligently examine everything. To be sure, by "the laying on of hands" here he means ordination, in which this ceremony was customarily employed. Some take this as a reference to the absolution of penitents, but the former explanation fits better.

Pope Leo (Letter 87 *ad episcopos Africanos*, ch. 1): "What is it 'to lay on hands hastily' if not to bestow the order of priest on those who have not been tested, before the time of maturity, before the time of examination, before the merit of labor, before the practical knowledge of discipline?"

μηδὲ κοινώνει ἁμαρτίαις ἀλλοτρίαις. ["Nor participate in the sins of others."] Ambrosiaster: "Nor defile yourself by the sins of others." But the Greek κοινώνει does not mean "defile" but "participate in." This can be taken as the reason for the preceding command. In other words: "If you hastily ordain someone who is not worthy, you will participate in the sins of another when he teaches or lives badly." This can also be taken as a second part of the apostle's command, that Timothy not consent with the other presbyters if they are electing someone for the ministry of the church who is not worthy. Some offer this explanation: "Nor ordain anyone before you are sure about his worth. But if he performs his office badly after ordination, rebuke him before all, lest you make his sins your own by looking the other way."

σεαυτὸν ἁγνὸν τήρει. ["Keep yourself pure."] Some take this as being about purity of the mind in judging, others as about bodily chastity and purity, so as to rebuke those sinning with greater authority. The Greeks explain ἁγνὸν as "temperate and chaste." Therefore the apostle is admonishing Timothy to preserve his chastity—that is, his virtue—diligently and zealously. [He did this] both because [Timothy] was a bishop (and a crime of unchasteness seriously defames that office) and because he was young and chastity tends to be easily endangered at that age. This can also be understood generally as: "Keep yourself pure from sins so that you will be irreproachable, nor [will you] cause others to stumble."

Augustine (*Contra epist. Parmen.*, bk. 2, ch. 21): "The apostle is teaching from what follows how to understand what he said before. For whoever keeps himself pure does not participate in the sins of another. For if he participates, he consents. If he consents, he is defiled. If he is defiled, he is not keeping himself pure."

Estius concludes from this that "celibacy is an apostolic institution." But he cannot prove this unless he first[10] proves that chastity is not in marriage.

Verse 23.

Μηκέτι ὑδροπότει. ["No longer drink water."] These words do not seem to cohere with what precedes or follows them. It is noteworthy, however, that v. 24 coheres with v. 22, where the apostle commands Timothy not to lay hands on anyone hastily. In other words, though the sins of some are conspicuous and make it easy to exclude them from ecclesiastical offices, the sins of others are hidden and come to light as time goes on. Therefore assent for ordination is not to be given rashly and hastily. Verse 25 fits in with this in a similar way, the sense being: "Those whose piety and worth are evident can be quickly ordained into the ministry. But as for the rest, who are not so well-known, though they are pious, their ordination can still be delayed a little until their worth becomes more evident." Verse 23, then, which contains private advice, is inserted, so to speak, parenthetically, as often happens in letters to family and friends where a precise order of subjects is not always kept. Gregory (*Moral.*, bk. 5, ch. 29): "Divine Scripture has this habit where, when discussing something, it inserts a statement on another topic and then suddenly returns to the previous discussion." He illustrates this rule with this passage from the apostle.

Μηκέτι ὑδροπότει. "No longer drink water." Timothy was drinking water, not wine, and his stomach was upset and suffering frequent illnesses. So the apostle advises him to change his habits so as to be mindful of his health. "Although I am reminding you about purity, I do not want you to sin on the other side and harm yourself by drinking water." Ambrosiaster (commentary on this passage): "God wants people to serve Him wisely, not in such a way that they grow weak from excess and then need the help of doctors."

The question arises (1) *Why did the apostle want to give Timothy this command, which is more fitting for a doctor to give?* I respond. Its aim is not merely bodily health, but it goes beyond that to strength of the mind and to the service of God.

The question arises (2) *Why did the apostle not heal Timothy's illness?* Chrysostom responds: "Because it was advantageous for Timothy to suffer this illness even as it was for Paul to feel a 'thorn in the flesh,' for the Lord's power is perfected in weakness [2 Cor. 12:7, 9]. Just as the death of his hostess's son was not revealed to Elijah [1 Kings 17:17–24], so the apostles did not have the power simply to heal all the diseases of all people." Some respond that

10 Reading *prius* instead of *pius*.

Timothy's weakness was able to be healed by using wine, and therefore it was not required to have recourse to a miracle.

οἴνῳ ὀλίγῳ χρῶ. ["Use a little wine."] He does not want Timothy to be πάροινον ["addicted to wine"] ([1 Tim.] 3:3) but to use wine sparingly and in moderation. Moreover, in Timothy he teaches all bishops and presbyters to exercise moderation.

By this instruction the apostle is commending rules for health and the study of medicine.

Verse 24.

Τινῶν ἀνθρώπων αἱ ἁμαρτίαι πρόδηλοί εἰσιν. ["Some men's sins are conspicuous."] Here he gives the reason for v. 22, as we said a little earlier.

Some translate πρόδηλοί as "manifested beforehand," but the order of time is signified by the following participle: "leading on into judgment." The compound Greek word is used for the uncompounded, so that it signifies nothing other than "conspicuous" with some intensity.

προάγουσαι εἰς κρίσιν. ["Leading on into judgment,"] so that they can easily be repudiated as unserviceable for the church's ministry since they are punishable for their sins.

Some explain this passage in terms of the judgment of God which He will carry out in the age to come. Others explain it in terms of human judgment, such as that by which a bishop judges those placed under him.

Furthermore, it may be explained about the *judgment of God* in two ways. (1) "Some men's sins are conspicuous to men. Accordingly, they can be known and judged in this life before they come into the judgment of God. The sins of some others, however, are hidden to men, and so they cannot be judged in this life but must be referred to the future, final judgment." Thus Basil (*De vera virgin.*) and Augustine (*De serm. Dom. in monte*, bk. 2).

(2) "Many sins of wicked men precede their death and the judgment—or condemnation—that happens in death. But some men's many sins also follow after their death, namely, those which are committed afterward by others through their wicked teaching and the examples of their wicked life. The same holds true in reverse for good men." Basil (ibid.) gives this meaning, and based on him Theophylact and Oecumenius also relate it. But according to these explanations it is not clear enough how the words of Paul fit with what precedes them.

Therefore it is more correct to take Paul's words in terms of human judgment (which is also what he was discussing earlier), yet in such a way that it is taken as a general reference to human judgment under which is included the judgment of a bishop. Jerome (Letter 10 *ad Furiam de viduitate servanda*, ch. 3): "As to what the apostle says, he means this: Some men sin so freely and openly that, when you see them, you know right away that they are sinners. But others shrewdly hide their vices, and we only come to recognize them from further interaction."

But this explanation still produces two senses, for this judgment is either one of examination and inquiry or of decree, as when someone is elected or rejected. In the former way the sense is: "When I said not to lay hands on anyone quickly, I was not talking about men who are openly wicked, but secretly [wicked]. It is already obvious that those who are openly wicked should be rejected even before they receive the judgment of an examination because their sins are so conspicuous that they preclude this judgment. Hence in the case of such men there is no need for judicial order. However, those who are secretly wicked should not be rejected or condemned before their life is examined, namely, because their sins, with respect to their manifestation, follow this examination's judgment. Because of this, therefore, I warn you not to lay hands on anyone quickly." The following confirms this sense.

Verse 25.

ὡσαύτως καὶ τὰ καλὰ ἔργα. ["Likewise also the good words are conspicuous."] The sense is this: "Those whose piety and worth are evident[11] can be quickly ordained into the ministry. But as for the rest, who are not so well-known, though they are pious, their ordination can still be delayed a little until their worth becomes more evident." Just as the preceding part had a fourfold sense, so also this part has a fourfold sense. The first two pertain to divine judgment; the latter two, to human judgment. But the third sense more fits the text: "Just as when I advised you not to ordain anyone quickly I did not say that on account of those who are openly wicked, so neither [did I say it] on account of those who are openly and famously known to be good and suitable, but on account of those whose virtue is hidden." For some men's good works are also so evident that they preclude the judgment of an examination. There is no need to deliberate receiving them [into the ministry]. But some men's good works are not so evident and require investigation. But if that happens they will not easily be kept hidden, but at least after the judgment of such an inquiry they will be evident and show the men worthy to have hands laid on them.

In the latter way the sense is: "If you ordain open sinners, you will participate in the sins of others. If, however, you ordain those who are exposed or discovered to be wicked after ordination, then such a thing will not weigh heavily on your conscience so long as you diligently examined them beforehand, because you could not have known things that are hidden or yet to happen. For some men's sins are known openly before their election or rejection, but other men's [sins] lie hidden, and they do not reveal themselves before they have been ordained and advanced into office."

11 Reading *perspecta* instead of *perfecta*.

Chapter VI

Connection. After his admonishment regarding honoring and judging presbyters, he adds an instruction about servants.

There are four parts [to this chapter].

(1) A reminder about the office of servants (vv. 1–2).

(2) An exhortation about avoiding false teachers (vv. 3–5).

(3) An exhortation against greed, which combats αὐταρκείας ["contentment"] (vv. 6–10).

(4) An exhortation to various Christian virtues, especially to fortitude in fighting out the good fight of faith and to the duty required in teaching the rich (vv. 11–21). Finally, the entire Epistle closes with the apostolic greeting.

Verse 1.

Ὅσοι εἰσὶν ὑπὸ ζυγὸν δοῦλοι. "As many as are [slaves] under the yoke," that is, "of servitude." This is a metaphor.

The question arises: *Why did the apostle want to add this admonition?* I respond. Christianity was gaining a bad reputation from the fact that Christian slaves were not so readily obeying their masters, and their masters were becoming estranged from Christianity. Some think that in that region there were some who taught that after slaves were converted to Christ they were freed from the yoke of human servitude. This teaching of the apostle stands in opposition to this pernicious teaching.

πάσης τιμῆς ἀξίους ἡγείσθωσαν. ["Let them regard them as worthy of all honor,"] so that they give them not only respect but also obedience, for the greater part of honor is obedience and the desire to be useful to one's masters.

ἵνα μὴ τὸ ὄνομα τοῦ θεοῦ καὶ ἡ διδασκαλία βλασφημῆται. ["That the name of God and the teaching not be blasphemed."] Some apply τοῦ θεοῦ ["of God"] to both τὸ ὄνομα ["the name"] and ἡ διδασκαλία ["the teaching"]. But it is more correct to say that the word "teaching" is used absolutely for "the teaching of the Gospel" ([1 Tim.] 5:17). The sense, then, is: "So that unbelievers will not speak poorly of Christian teaching if slaves present themselves as disobedient and stubborn, as if it dissolves the order of the state."

Verse 2.

οἱ δὲ πιστοὺς ἔχοντες δεσπότας. ["Those who have believing masters."] Those who happen to have Christian masters. He had spoken about slaves of unbelieving masters, now he goes on to speak about slaves of faithful—that is, Christian—masters.

ὅτι ἀδελφοί εἰσιν. ["Because they are brothers,"] that is, in Christ. To be sure, masters and slaves are equal in Christ's kingdom and with respect to their common participation in spiritual goods. At the same time, however, the Gospel does not abolish the civil realm [*politias*] nor erase the distinction of stations in civil life.

ἀγαπητοὶ. ["Beloved,"] that is, (1) by God, who has called them to acknowledge Him; (2) by the members of the church, who are joined together by the bond of faith and love.

Note that there the apostle piles up three names by which Christians were calling one another: ἀδελφοί, πιστοί, ἀγαπητοὶ ["brothers, faithful, beloved"].

οἱ τῆς εὐεργεσίας ἀντιλαμβανόμενοι. ["Those who lay claim to the benefit."] He means the inheritance of eternal life which Christ merited for all who believe and serve Him.

Some take this with reference to the masters, the sense being: "They are partakers of the benefit of Christ just as are their slaves." The Syriac also relates it to the masters, but in a different sense: "who are content with their service," that is, they consider their service pleasing and acceptable and count it as an act of kindness.

Those who take this as being about the slaves explain it like this: "Who are partakers of the kindness of their masters, and now more freely than before. For now that their masters have become Christians, they increase their kindness toward their slaves, love them as brothers, and compensate them more kindly for the obedience they have shown." Most Greek commentators take it this way, so that the apostle's words contain a hyperbaton.[1]

Ταῦτα δίδασκε ["teach these things"], that they may know them, καὶ παρακάλει ["and urge them"], that they may do them.

Verse 3.

εἴ τις ἑτεροδιδασκαλεῖ. "If anyone teaches otherwise." Or: "If any teaches other things." Cf. [1 Tim.] 1:3.

---

1 See above, p. 10 n. 2.

Some apply this only to what immediately precedes so as to rebuke those who were teaching that Christian slaves are freed from human service. In this way they were confusing spiritual, inner freedom with bodily, external freedom. But it is more correct to take it generally, as referring to those teachings on account of which he commands [1 Tim. 1:3] certain persons to be commanded not to teach differently.

Some understand τοῖς ὑγιαίνουσιν λόγοις τοῦ κυρίου ["the sound words of the Lord"] to be "the words Christ taught." But it is more correct to understand it generally as the teaching about Christ, His person, office, and benefits. This is the foundation and sum of the apostolic teaching.

τῇ κατ' εὐσέβειαν διδασκαλίᾳ. ["The teaching that accords with piety."] This is a most lovely definition of Christian teaching, that it promotes piety. By εὐσέβειαν ["piety"] he means the true and sincere worship of God.

Verse 4.

τετύφωται. "He is puffed up, frenzied, raving mad." Luther has *er ist verdüstert* ["he is in darkness"]. This word is believed to come from a typhoon, which the ancients thought robbed men of their mind and reason, causing them to go insane once seized by such a wind. [He is puffed up] either because he places his own understanding before the apostolic teaching or because he flatters himself as if he were gifted with great knowledge. The following antithesis confirms this explanation.

Ignorance is always bold and proud.

μηδὲν ἐπιστάμενος. ["Knowing nothing."] Because he does not rightly acknowledge Christ, "who became to us wisdom from God" [1 Cor. 1:30], nor does he remain constant in His teaching. Either because he knows none of the things that he boasts he knows before others or because he lacks saving knowledge of Christ, without which all other knowledge is useless for salvation.

νοσῶν περὶ ζητήσεις. ["Obsessed about disputes."] He labors in intellect and reason. He is ruined in mind and understanding. Luther has *er ist seuchtig in fragen* ["he is addicted to questions"]. This stands elegantly opposed to what was said before (v. 3): προσέρχεται ὑγιαίνουσιν λόγοις ["consent to the sound words"].

Erasmus rendered it "being of unsound mind" to make clearer the antithesis the apostle is making between the soundness of Christ's teaching and the unsoundness of the teaching of those spoken against in this passage.

Estius (commentary on this passage):

> According to the Greek commentaries, they linger over questions who seek the truth with a feeble and unsound mind. Such are those who apart from faith seek and strive to learn about things for which we are required to have faith before anything else. Indeed, those who use their reason to pry

> into and investigate things that they should believe make poor judgments about them, like feverish people and like lunatics who choose one thing for another. "Faith is the eye," says Theophylact. Therefore, just as he who lacks eyes does not find that for which he is looking, so it is with the one who lacks faith.

It is more likely that the apostle is speaking in general about frivolous, useless, meddlesome, and superfluous questions that contribute nothing toward the fruit of salvation.

The word λογομαχίας ["word fights"] means arguments about useless questions. Therefore it denotes two vices: pointless questioning and combativeness in disputing.

Some understand βλασφημίαι ["blasphemies"] to mean "perverse teachings about God and the things of God," and ὑπόνοιαι πονηραί ["evil suspicions"] to mean "false and unworthy beliefs about God." But it is more correct for "blasphemies" to be understood as the insults and abuse which such contentious disputants hurl at one another. The "evil suspicions" are those which they stir up against one another out of formal hostility.

Verse 5.

διαπαρατριβαὶ. "Useless contentions." "Meddlesome disputes." For διατριβαὶ are conversations and friendly talks. Luther has *Schulgezenck[e]* ["scholastic disputes"]. Erasmus adds "superfluous" while others add "wicked." Oecumenius thinks that it is a metaphor drawn "from sheep infecting other healthy sheep because they are near them and rubbing up against them." The Syriac also translates it "rubbing against." But this meaning is a departure from the accepted meaning of the Greek word.

ἀπεστερημένων τῆς ἀληθείας. ["Deprived of the truth."] Not because the truth they once held has been taken from them, but because with them there is no truth nor is it found.

νομιζόντων πορισμὸν εἶναι τὴν εὐσέβειαν. ["Thinking that piety is a means of gain."] Under the guise of confessing the Christian faith, they seek their own honor and advantage (Titus 1:11; 2 Pet. 2:3). They consider piety a means of gain, and whatever they seem to do, say, or teach piously and scrupulously goes back to their own personal advantage.

ἀφίστασο ἀπὸ τῶν τοιούτων. ["Stand apart from such as these."] The Vulgate omits this phrase, but the Greek copies consistently read it, and all the Greek commentators expound upon it. Ambrosiaster reads "depart from them," that is, "after one or two warnings." This he adds in Titus 3:10.

Connection. This is a rhetorical correction in which one turns around what he has already rejected, but with the meaning changed. In other words, [the apostle is saying]: "If one considers it rightly, piety itself is a great source of gain—not earthly but heavenly; not bodily, but spiritual.

Verse 6.

Ἔστι δὲ πορισμὸς μέγας ἡ εὐσέβεια μετὰ αὐταρκείας. ["But piety is great gain with contentment."] This is a remarkable **συζυγία** ["coupling"] of two very outstanding virtues: **εὐσέβεια** ["piety"] toward God and **αὐταρκείας** ["contentment"] toward one's self. If you add **ἀγάπη** ["love"] toward the neighbor, then you will have the best triplet.

Now "piety is great gain" because through it we receive eternal, heavenly goods. "Contentment" here pertains to the judgment of the mind and the disposition of one's spirit when one says that he has enough and desires nothing more since he is content with his lot. Others, however, think that "contentment" does not signify the spirit content with its lot but the spirit that is content with the things needed for life so that it does not seek more than what is necessary.

Verse 7.

οὐδὲν γὰρ εἰσηνέγκαμεν εἰς τὸν κόσμον. ["For we brought nothing into the world."] This comes from Job 1:21: "Naked I came forth from my mother's womb, and naked I shall return." Eccl. 5:15: "Just as a man has gone forth naked from his mother's womb, so shall he return so that he departs as he had come and will take nothing with him in his hand when he departs."

Verse 8.

ἔχοντες διατροφὰς καὶ σκεπάσματα. ["Having foods and coverings"] with which we are nourished and clothed. Jerome (*Contra Jovin.*, bk. 2): "Having nourishment and clothing." The Syriac has: "Because of this, nourishment and clothing is enough for us." Baptista Mantuanus (*Ecl.* 5): "I ask for clothing; I seek food at a small hearth."

Σκεπάσματα ["coverings"] is broader than just clothing but also includes one's dwelling.

ἀρκεσθησόμεθα. "We will be content." But in the Hebrew way of speaking, the future stands for the imperative.

Apparent contrariety. *"Having food and clothing we are content." But wealth is a gift of God, and parents should save riches for their children (2 Cor. 12:14).* I respond. With these words the apostle is not forbidding an abundance of wealth ([1 Tim. 6:]17), but he commends "contentment" in the absence of an abundance.

Verse 9.

οἱ δὲ βουλόμενοι πλουτεῖν. ["But those who desire to be rich."] "Those who exert all their effort and all their thoughts to heaping up riches." "Those who act to become rich."

Note that the apostle does not say "those who are rich," but "those who want to become rich," lest anyone think that here the possession of riches is condemned.

They fall into many occasions for sin and become ensnared by them as by snares and nets. Some think that this means only that they fall into many dangers of this life. However, from what follows it is clear that it means the temptations by which they are incited to sin. Therefore the sense is that they are overcome by temptation and are engulfed as by a snare.

καὶ παγίδα. "Into a snare," that is, of the devil, who hastens them into various sins and, as a consequence, into eternal destruction through that insatiable lust for riches. The Vulgate added *Diaboli* ["of the devil"]. Although this should be understood here, it is still not in the Greek or Syriac text.

καὶ ἐπιθυμίας πολλὰς ἀνοήτους. "Into many senseless and absurd desires." This is how the Syriac rendered it also. The Vulgate rendered it *inutilia* ["useless"], and hence Erasmus conjectures that the Latin translator read one letter more than is in the Greek: ἀνονήτους ["useless"]. Even to this day this reading is found in some Greek copies, namely, in the *Exemplar regium*. But the first reading, which Chrysostom and the other Greek fathers follow, is to be preferred.

αἵτινες βυθίζουσιν τοὺς ἀνθρώπους εἰς ὄλεθρον. ["Who plunge people into ruin."] This is an elegant metaphor. **Βυθίζουσιν** properly means "to sink into the depths."

εἰς ὄλεθρον καὶ ἀπώλειαν. ["Into ruin and destruction."] The apostle uses this doublet to be emphatic or to signify a twofold destruction: temporal and eternal.

Connection. The apostle proves what he has now said: that those who want to become rich fall into many evils because they seek riches from greed, which is a root and seedbed of all evils.

Verse 10.

ῥίζα γὰρ πάντων τῶν κακῶν ἐστιν ἡ φιλαργυρία. ["For the lust for money is a root of all evils."] Just as various branches stem from the root, so many sins stem from greed. Furthermore, he means not only evils of fault but also evils of punishment; not only evils of future punishment but also of the present age.[2]

---

2 Evil of fault (*malum culpae*) is constituted by deliberate fault or guilt. Evil of punishment (*malum poenae*) is that punishment that God renders for sin according to His justice. This is not "evil" in the English sense of the word, but rather "bad" to the one who experiences it.

Augustine (*De Genes. ad lit.*, bk. 11, ch. 15; *De lib. arbitr.*, bk. 3, ch. 17; on Psalm 118, conc. 11) thinks that the specific stands for the general—that is, greed stands for lust—whereby one seeks after more than what is enough, not only in money and external riches but also in anything, such as honor, power, knowledge, and pleasure. But in the Greek text it is not πλεονεξία ["the desire for more"] but φιλαργυρία, which denotes "the lust for money," which is also what the apostle's speech is about here.

ἧς τινες ὀρεγόμενοι. ["Some by striving for it."] The disposition is used in place of its object, greed in place of the things one covets.

ἀπεπλανήθησαν ἀπὸ τῆς πίστεως. ["Have been led astray from the faith,"] because true faith requires us to put all our trust in God. Some claim that the apostle means that greed is so much a root of all evils that it even leads to unbelief.

ἑαυτοὺς περιέπειραν ὀδύναις πολλαῖς. ["Pierced themselves through with many sorrows."] The verb περιέπειραν properly means "piercing," as when one falls on a sword. So the sense is: "They have pierced themselves through with many sorrows." For they are worried and anxious about increasing and keeping riches, and beyond that they are also tormented by the pricks of their conscience over riches unjustly gained.

Verse 11.

ὦ ἄνθρωπε τοῦ θεοῦ. ["O man of God."] A "man of God" is a minister of God in proclaiming the Word (1 Sam. 2:27; 2 Tim. 3:17).

ταῦτα φεῦγε. ["Flee these things," namely,] greed and the things that stem from that root. The verb φεῦγε is emphatic: "Be far removed from things such as this."

δίωκε δὲ δικαιοσύνην. ["And pursue righteousness."] He is exhorting him to the virtues contrary to greed and the sins that come from it. The verb δίωκε ["pursue"] stands in opposition to the verb φεῦγε ["flee"], the sense being that one must flee the vices and pursue the virtues with equal zeal and single-mindedness.

Verse 12.

ἀγωνίζου τὸν καλὸν ἀγῶνα τῆς πίστεως. ["Contend the good contest of the faith."] "Remain steadfast in the true faith and by it bravely resist all wicked desires and temptations." (Cf. 1 Cor. 9:25; 1 Tim. 1:18; 2 Tim. 4:7).

This metaphor does not come from warfare but from a running contest in a stadium (1 Cor. 9:24; Phil. 3:14; 2 Tim. 2:5). Moreover, the race of the ecclesiastical ministry is called a "contest" because of the hardships the contender suffers from adversaries both internal and external who strive to obstruct his course and cheat him out of the prize.

He calls it "the contest of the faith" (1) because one undertakes it to spread and defend faith in Christ, and (2) because whoever begins this contest only wins it through faith.

ἐπιλαβοῦ τῆς αἰωνίου ζωῆς. "Take hold of eternal life," like a contest's prize or reward. He is sticking with the metaphor, for "contend the good contest of the faith" preceded. "With all your strength strive so that you can obtain the prize of eternal life set before you and reach the goal." (Cf. Phil. 3:12; 2 Tim. 2:5.)

Estius (commentary on this passage): "Contrary to the sectarians, this passage teaches that eternal life has been set as a prize before those who contend well and vigorously. Theophylact expressly comments as much. 'Look,' he says, 'eternal life is both a wage and a reward.'" I respond. There is a wage of merit and wage of grace. Here it means a wage of grace, which is called τὴν ἀνταπόδοσιν τῆς κληρονομίας ["the reward of the inheritance"] (Col. 3:24). With respect to consequence, a great inheritance is the wages of filial obedience, but not the wages of merit.

εἰς ἣν ἐκλήθης. ["To which you were called"] by a calling that is not only external but also internal, to which you were called and invited by the contest superintendent, Christ.

ὡμολόγησας τὴν καλὴν ὁμολογίαν. ["You confessed the good confession,"] either in receiving Baptism or, what is more fitting, at your solemn inauguration into the ecclesiastical ministry.

This "confession" is explained variously. (1) Some explain it thus: "You have many witnesses of your outstanding confession, for they saw you faithfully engaged in confessing the Gospel."

(2) Others think that at some point Timothy was in danger by persecution and confessed faith in Christ before many people.

(3) Others take it as a reference to a confession of faith which Timothy made at Baptism, that he had confessed the creed. This kind of confession regularly happened in a solemn rite with many people present. This is how the Greeks explain it; and of the Latins, Ambrosiaster, Primasius, and Haymo.

(4) Still others explain it as being about a confession Timothy made when he was ordained a bishop by Paul along with the laying on of hands of the presbytery. This was not a confession of faith but the profession and promise to rightly and faithfully fulfill the ministry of the Gospel (Lombard, Thomas, and Cajetan).

Connection. Not content with an exhortation, he continues by calling God to witness.

Verse 13.

τοῦ ζωοποιοῦντος τὰ πάντα. ["Who gives life to all things."] He gives and preserves life for all living things (Acts 17:25), and He can punish disobedient transgressors of His Commandments with eternal death. But the apostle especially has the resurrection in mind, for he means to say, "You should bear all adversities and all dangers with a cheerful and brave spirit—yes, you should not even fear death, for you are a servant of that Lord who can call the dead back to life."

καὶ χριστοῦ Ἰησοῦ τοῦ μαρτυρήσαντος ἐπὶ Ποντίου Πιλάτου τὴν καλὴν ὁμολογίαν. ["And of Christ Jesus, who testified the good confession under Pontius Pilate."] He mentions Christ, not only that He sees all our doings and is our coming Judge, but he also sets Him before Timothy as an example of confession to be imitated. Some think that [the apostle] has in mind Matt. 27:11, but it is more correct to say that the apostle is thinking of John 18:37. Christ's example of steadfastness of confession to the end of life should be followed by all those who are truly pious, but especially by ministers of the church.

"Who testified the good confession." This is the same as "to confess the good confession," because confession itself is a kind of testimony.

Some render ἐπὶ as "before," but it is more correctly translated "under" (Acts 11:28). Some think that here the word "testimony" or "testimony sealed with blood" [*martyrium*] means not a testimony that happens by just any work but by one that is perfect and complete unto death, the sense being: "The truth Christ had often confessed He sealed with His martyrdom when He suffered death on the cross for that truth."

Verse 14.

τηρῆσαί σε τὴν ἐντολὴν. ["That you keep the commandment."] Some take this generally as being about all the commands given to Timothy by the apostle. Some take it specifically as being about the commands laid out in vv. 11–12. Others take it as being about the commandment of love.

ἄσπιλον, ἀνεπίληπτον. ["Unblemished, irreproachable."] Both of these can be applied to the commandment as well as to Timothy's person. Ambrosiaster does the former while the Greek commentators do the latter. Some take the first word with reference to the commandment and the second with respect to Timothy. The Vulgate translator seems to apply the latter to the commandment and the first to Timothy's person.

μέχρι τῆς ἐπιφανείας. "Until the appearing," that is, until the second coming of Christ when He shall come openly and with great power, etc. He does not say "that you keep the commandment until death" (Rev. 2:10), but "until the coming of Christ," "in order to stir him up more by the mention of His tremendous glory" (Theophylact).

Apparent contrariety. The apostle knew that Christ was not going to come while the recipients of his writing were still living (2 Thess. 2:2). So why does he command Timothy to keep the commandment until Christ's coming? I respond. The meaning is that he should keep [the commandment] until the end of his life because that is when the day of the Lord's coming will come to each person, since that is when he will depart such as he will be judged on that day (Augustine, Letter 80 *ad Hesychium*).

Verse 15.

ἥν (ἐπιφανείαν) δείξει. ["Which (appearing) He will manifest."] Luther referred this to Christ: [*welche*] *wird zeigen* ["which He will show"]. It does not make much difference for the meaning, because "to show the appearing of Christ" is nothing else than "to show the appearing Christ."

καιροῖς ἰδίοις. "In His own time," that is, "preordained by God for this and known [only] to Him."

μακάριος. ["Blessed."] God alone is blessed because He lacks no good thing. He is *El Shaday*, αὐταρκέστατος ["self-sufficient"].

He calls Him "blessed" so that we would not doubt that He, who is essentially blessed, is going to share with us His promised blessedness.

μόνος δυνάστης. ["The only Potentate,"] because He is essentially and independently powerful—indeed, almighty—yes, even Almightiness itself.

They are called δυνάστης ("potentates") because they have the most power. Such especially are kings and princes.

ὁ βασιλεὺς τῶν βασιλευόντων, καὶ κύριος τῶν κυριευόντων. ["The King of kings and Lord of lords."] (1) Because He lords over all kings and lords as their superior. (2) Because all kings and lords have their power from Him, but He receives lordship from no one else.

Verse 16.

ὁ μόνος ἔχων ἀθανασίαν. ["Who alone has immortality."] After blessedness and power, he adds other properties of the divine Majesty. In the first place he lists immortality, by which He is distinguished from all earthly kings—indeed, from every created thing.

Apparent contrariety. The angels and souls of men are also immortal. I respond. (1) Jerome (*Contra Pelag.*, bk. 2) and Damascenus (*De orth. fid.*, bk. 2, chs. 3 and 12): "The angels and souls of men have immortality not by their own nature but by the grace of God. Only God has immortality in and of Himself. The angels and souls of men have it from God."

(2) Augustine (*Contra Maximin.*, bk. 3, ch. 12) takes the word "immortality" as standing for "immutability." [Again,] (*De cognit. verae vitae*, ch. 31): "Only God has immortality because He admits no mutability."

Chrysostom (commentary on this passage) thinks that this was said "in comparison to earthly kings, for it is preceded by 'the only Potentate, the King of kings and the Lord of lords.'"

φῶς οἰκῶν ἀπρόσιτον. ["Inhabiting unapproachable light."] These words describe God's standing and ours. God's standing is described as glorious, for it denotes:

(1) The invisibility of God, for it is called "unapproachable light" with respect to us. Elsewhere this difficulty of approaching and seeing it is described as dwelling in darkness and cloud. "For every body of light that one cannot gaze at for its excessive brightness is rightly called darkness and unapproachable" (Anselm, commentary on this passage, *Oper.*, part 1, p. 366). Hence it immediately follows: "Whom no one has seen nor can see."

(2) The incomprehensibility of God. Dionysius Carthusianus (commentary on this passage): "It is called 'unapproachable light' because it cannot be comprehended by any created intellect. Hence it also says that He makes the darkness as His hiding place. Nevertheless man can approach [the light] on the way through faith and grace, and in the fatherland through the bright vision."

(3) The purity of God's essence. For that light is and remains completely pure, and access to it is not open to any other thing.

Our standing is described as miserable. By "light" he means the majesty and glory of God, to which no one can come, that is, of himself and by his own powers, unless the Lord brings him to it. The light in which God dwells is inaccessible to us while situated outside of Christ, and the way to the throne of the divine Majesty is shut to us.

Ambrose (*De Abraham*, bk. 2, ch. 8) recalls that "some have taken this passage as being about a created light that consists of some quintessence or fifth substance." But the apostle is speaking about uncreated light which is God Himself (1 John 1:5). It says that "He dwells in light" even as He is [light] and dwells in and remains in Himself [light]. For one is especially said to dwell where he always is and from where he never departs.

ᾧ τιμὴ καὶ κράτος αἰώνιον. "To whom be honor and eternal power," so that all may acknowledge Him as the almighty King and Lord. The Vulgate has *imperium sempiternum* ["eternal dominion"]. Luther has *dem sey ewiges Reich* ["to whom be eternal rule"].

Κράτος means more literally "the power to rule" than the act [of ruling].

This can be understood as *optative* ("to whom be honor") or as *indicative* ("to whom is honor"). Likewise, "power"[3] can be taken either way.

The fact that "eternal power" is ascribed to God stands contrary to earthly kings who rule only for a time and merely have limited power.

3 Reading *robur* instead of *amor*.

Connection. Lest anyone think that riches in general are condemned because of what he said before against greed and the desire for riches, he now gives commands to the rich which show the holy use of riches.

Verse 17.

πλουσίοις ἐν τῷ νῦν αἰῶνι. ["To those rich in the present age."] Contrary to this stand the rich who are not "rich toward God" (Luke 12:21). Moreover, in this and the following two verses he commands them to beware of two things about riches: (1) pride and (2) false confidence. From their opposite three things are commended to them, namely, (1) true trust in God, (2) spiritual richness, (3) free generosity.

μὴ ὑψηλοφρονεῖν. "Not to be prideful." Not to have a lofty spirit, for wealth is often the mother of pride and arrogance. The Vulgate unsuitably translates it *non sublime sapere*[4] ["not to have high tastes"].

μηδὲ ἠλπικέναι ἐπὶ πλούτου ἀδηλότητι. ["And not to set their hope on the uncertainty of riches."] Estius (commentary on this passage): "It is the nature of earthly riches to be uncertain because they are subject to many misfortunes: theft, fraud, pillaging, fire. By these they are carried away and perish even against the will of their owners." Augustine (*De civ. Dei*, bk. 5, ch. 18): "Earthly riches do not make us or our children blessed. They must either be lost while we are alive, or, when we are dead, they will be taken by those we do not know or by those we do not want [to have them]. It is God, rather, who makes us blessed, who is the true wealth of minds."

ἐπὶ πλούτου ἀδηλότητι. "On the uncertainty of riches," that is, "on uncertain riches." To hope in wealth is the reason why the rich are proud. For those who have much are confident that they can do much, and because of this their thinking becomes elated.

ἐν θεῷ τῷ ζῶντι. ["In the living God."] This epithet is added either to distinguish Him from false gods or to indicate the certainty of the hope that is placed in God.

τῷ παρέχοντι πλουσίως. ["Who richly provides."] He is talking about the generosity of God toward all people, which the greedy ruin for the poor (Acts 14:17).

Verse 18.

ἀγαθοεργεῖν. ["To do good."] This can be taken generally about good works and specifically about kindness and generosity.

---

4 Reading *sapere* instead of *serpere. Sublime sapere* could mean "to be high-minded, proud," but usually the verb *sapere* ("to be wise, to have good taste and discernment") is positive, e.g., *homo sapiens.*

He is exhorting the rich not to hoard their riches greedily or to use them for pride, vanity, and pleasures, but for good works.

πλουτεῖν ἐν ἔργοις καλοῖς. ["To be rich in good works."] He is referring to v. 17: "Command those who are rich in the present age." That is to say: "If those who are rich in this age also want to be rich in the age to come, then they must become rich in good works in this present age."

The verb πλουτεῖν means "to become rich" and "to be rich." Both meanings fit with this passage. His speech is growing lofty: it should not be enough for the rich to do good in just any way, but as they abound in riches so also they should abound in good works (Estius).

Estius (commentary on this passage): "This passage shows how false it is that the heretics teach that all the works of the righteous are sins, since even the rich can do what is good—yes, even abound in good works." I respond. We can and should abound in good works. Nonetheless it still remains true that the works of the righteous are sins—that is, tainted by sin—since they are imperfect and unclean.

εὐμεταδότους εἶναι, κοινωνικούς. ["To be generous and sharing."] That they generously and richly share their goods (2 Cor. 9:7). Luther: *Das sie gerne geben, behülfflich seien* ["that they give gladly, be helpful"]. Still, some render κοινωνικούς as "communicable," that is, gentle and affable, those who present themselves as polite and kind, not at all haughty. But the Greek word properly means the communication by which one communicates what he has by giving it to others who have not (Rom. 12:13; Heb. 13:16; 2 Cor. 8:4; Gal. 6:6; etc.).

Verse 19.

ἀποθησαυρίζοντας ἑαυτοῖς θεμέλιον καλὸν εἰς τὸ μέλλον. "That they store up for themselves a good foundation for the future."

The θεμέλιον ["foundation"] is faith in Christ, from which flow out works of mercy done from love which God most bountifully promises to reward, but not by merit but by grace.

A defense. Estius (commentary on this passage): "Just as faith is the foundation of all our good works and all our righteousness, so good works are the foundation of salvation which we await in the future." To this he applies the saying of Thomas Aquinas (commentary on this passage): "All preparation for future glory is through merits which we acquire through grace."

I respond. (1) Faith is not only the foundation of righteousness but also the instrumental cause[5] through which we apprehend the righteousness of Christ

5 Also called a "secondary cause" or "organic cause." In producing an effect, the instrumental cause makes a specific contribution, but it operates only in virtue of motion or power given it from the principal cause.

so that it is imputed to us. (2) Faith is the foundation of actual righteousness,[6] but because that actual righteousness is imperfect and impure we cannot rely on it before the judgment of God, nor can we obtain eternal life because of it as if it were merit. (3) Good works are the fruit of faith, but still Christ alone, apprehended by truth faith, is the foundation of our salvation (Acts 4:12; 1 Cor. 3:11; etc.). (4) Just as our works are not the foundation of our election but Christ is, so also Christ alone is the foundation of our justification and glorification (2 Tim. 1:9; Titus 3:5).

ἵνα ἐπιλάβωνται τῆς αἰωνιόυ ζωῆς. ["That they may take hold of eternal life."] He is explaining εἰς τὸ μέλλον ["for the future"], which he just said. The Vulgate rendered it *veram vitam* ["true life"], "because when compared to eternal life, this temporal life should be called 'death' rather than 'life' " (Gregory, Hom. 37 *in evangel.*).

Based on this passage, Estius concludes that "eternal life is apprehended through good works and not through faith alone." But the apostle has made it abundantly clear elsewhere that faith is the means of apprehending Christ and that eternal life is in Christ.

Connection. As he is about to draw his Epistle to a close, he once again reminds Timothy faithfully to guard the deposit of true teaching that he has received.

Verse 20.

τὴν παραθήκην φύλαξον. ["Guard the deposit."] He means the purity of teaching, which is the most precious deposit. Vincent of Lérins (*Adversus profanas heresium novitates*, ch. 24):

> What is the deposit? It is what is entrusted to you, not what has been discovered by you. It is what you have received, not what you have thought up. It is not a matter of talent but of the teaching, not of private usurpation but of public tradition. It is a thing delivered to you, not invented by you. In this you should not be the author but the guardian, not the institutor but the follower, not leading but following. "Guard," he says, "the deposit. Preserve inviolate and unscathed the talent of the catholic faith. What has been entrusted to you—may it stay with you and be handed down from you. You have received gold. Return gold. Do not add for me some things instead of others."

Therefore the apostle calls sound teaching a "deposit" because it has been entrusted to his faith so that he may administer it in the church just as a money deposit is usually given and entrusted to a friend.

Some explain the deposit as the talent or grace of the Holy Spirit which Timothy had received through ordination. But based on the order of the text

6 That is, righteousness in one's actions.

and parallel passages (2 Tim. 1:13–14; 2:2; 3:14), it is clear that he is talking about the deposit of the teaching.

A defense. Estius (commentary on this passage) concludes that "traditions, written or unwritten, that are in the deposit of the church belong to Christian teaching, for Paul not only deposited the Scriptures with Timothy but also delivered orally the sound teaching."

I respond. (1) When Paul wrote this, the New Testament canon had not yet been finished. (2) The unwritten traditions Paul had deposited with Timothy did not contain other teachings at odds with the written word or different from the teachings extant today in written Scripture. (3) We do not simply reject all traditions but those which fight against the written Word or those which are forced into the articles of faith as simply necessary. (4) It is not enough to say that these or those traditions were handed down by the apostles to their successors outside of and beyond Scripture, but one must prove it. Therefore we greatly approve of what Estius goes on to note: "We learn from this passage that bishops (whom the apostle instructs in Timothy) have been appointed guardians and trustees of the teaching. Accordingly, they are not permitted to change anything in it nor to diminish it nor to add to it. For this, too, is outside the nature of a deposit, to add anything to it. Hence Basil said that bishops are guardians of the deposit, not inventors of any teaching (*Histor. tripart.*, bk. 7, ch. 36)."

ἐκτρεπόμενος τὰς βεβήλους καινοφωνίας. ["Avoiding] profane novelties of speech." Thus read the Latin commentators. Some copies read κενοφωνίας ("profane empty talk," 2 Tim. 2:16), which is how most copies read, as well as Theophylact and Oecumenius.

However, as between the words (καινοφωνίας and κενοφωνίας) so also between the things signified there is a great resemblance. New things are quite often empty, hence Acts 17:21 connects the zeal for novelty and vanity. There is the well-known line: "Whoever produces new words also produces new teachings."[7]

However, from the attached epithet βεβήλους ["profane"] it is clear that it should be read καινοφωνίας, because all κενοφωνίας are in error. Hilary (*Contra Constantium*): "The apostle commands word novelties to be avoided, but profane ones. Why do you exclude pious ones?" (He is talking about the word "consubstantial.") Athanasius (*Disp. contra Arium*): "Do you take offense at the novelty of the word, or do you flee from the truth of the matter this word has obtained? Indeed, an ancient reality is receiving a new word; no new real truth is entering in by a new word."

7 *Qui gignit nova verba, simul nova dogmata gignit.*

Estius (commentary on this passage) thinks that "profane word novelties" include "specific faith," "imputed righteousness," and "bound choice." But we reprint for him what he soon adds: "They are not 'profane word novelties' when, for the sake of teaching and explaining, things believed from the beginning are adapted to new words, such as 'incarnation,' 'Trinity,' 'not made' [*ingenitus*], etc." Therefore, if the teachings about imputed righteousness and bound choice are shown from Scripture, then the novelty of the name should not offend anyone. In fact, let Estius show us from Scripture both the name and the reality of "transubstantiation," "the work worked" [*opus operatum*].

καὶ ἀντιθέσεις τῆς ψευδωνύμου γνώσεως. "The oppositions of the false name 'knowledge,'" that is, "falsely named 'knowledge.'" He means objections that are contrary to the teaching of the faith bearing the specific title "knowledge," but falsely so. For it cannot be true knowledge if it is contrary to the truth. The Greek commentators say that the Gnostic heretics are meant. Irenaeus (bk. 1, ch. 20) writes that "it was from the Simonians that the false name 'knowledge' took its beginnings."

Haymo and Cajetan suspect that "the apostle means the questions of the Jews that they promoted against the Christians on the basis of the falsely named 'knowledge' they call 'Cabala.'"

But the apostle is speaking generally, about whatever oppositions that are contrary to the teaching of the faith.

ἐπαγγελλόμενοι. ["Professing."] The Vulgate has *promittentes* ["promising"], but *profitentes* ["professing"] is better.

Verse 21.

περὶ τὴν πίστιν ἠστόχησαν. ["They swerved from the faith."] They do not arrive at the knowledge of the true teaching about faith, but fall into all manner of errors. "They have wandered from the wholeness and purity of the faith as their aim" (cf. [1 Tim.] 1:6).

Ἡ χάρις μετὰ σοῦ. ["Grace be with you."] "In his usual way at the end of an Epistle, he prays for the grace of God as the source of all good things" (Estius).

Commentary on St. Paul's Second Epistle to Timothy

Introduction

§ 1. The principal efficient cause[1] or primary author is the Holy Spirit, by whose impulse and inspiration Paul also wrote this Epistle to Timothy (2 Tim. 1:1).

§ 2. *The material or argument.* This Epistle is mostly about admonishing Timothy of his office and encouraging him in the face of threatening afflictions and persecutions by Paul's own example. He adds in many things about false teachers (both present and future) of unholy teachings and tells him to avoid them.

This Epistle can be arranged into three integral parts. (1) He urges Timothy to be supremely zealous for purity of doctrine and not to allow himself to be dissuaded from his confession by any dangers. (2) He forewarns him about seductive spirits, who already were appearing in the church at that time. (3) He explains his own situation to him and asks him to come to him.

§ 3. *Form or arrangement.* The Epistle contains (I) the preface, (II) the treatment, (III) the conclusion.

(I) The preface is finished within the first five verses of chapter 1.

(II) The treatment contains: (1) an exhortation to (a) patience and endurance under the cross (1:6–18); (b) constancy in teaching and faith (2:1–13).

(2) A digression on reproving vices: (a) those particular to teachers of the church, including fighting over words (λογομαχία), idle talking (κενοφωνία), youthful desires, foolish questions (2:14–26); (b) those common to teachers and hearers, a list of which is given in 3:1–9.

(3) A return to the aforesaid exhortation to being patient under the cross, which he repeats from 3:10–17 and concludes in 4:1–8.

(III) The apostle's conclusion contains various private concerns from 4:9–22.

---

1 See above, p. 3 n. 1.

§ 4. Paul's purpose for writing this Epistle is identical to the purpose and aim of 1 Timothy, namely, the instruction, encouragement, and comforting of Timothy and, under the person of Timothy, all faithful teachers of the church.

Furthermore, since by a revelation of the Spirit Paul knew that his death was near, he wanted to make arrangements while he was still alive for future affairs: a cloak, parchments, and Timothy's arrival.

§ 5. *Place of writing.* It is clear from this Epistle that it was written in Rome under imprisonment, for he recalls his chains and bonds in [2 Tim.] 1:8 and 2:9. "This was Paul's second imprisonment. Almost a full decade has passed between this and his first imprisonment" (Cosmas Magalianus, preface, sect. 1).

§ 6. *Time of writing.* Nearly all commentators both ancient and modern agree that among Paul's Epistles this one was written last, with martyrdom nearly upon him. This can be gleaned rather clearly from [2 Tim.] 4:6–8: "For I am already being poured out, and the time of my departure is upon me. I have fought the good fight, finished the race, kept the faith. As to what remains, there is laid up for me the crown of righteousness." (Cf. Eusebius, *Hist. eccles.*, bk. 2, ch. 22; Chrysostom, *Homil.* on 2 Timothy; and Jerome, *De scriptor. eccles.*)

Estius (preface to his commentary on 2 Timothy) disagrees with this opinion. (He followed Baronius, who said the same: "Paul wrote this Epistle shortly after he arrived in Rome, and thus long before he died." So also Salmeron, commentary on 2 Timothy, disp. 1.) Estius claims that "this Epistle was written first or second among those sent from Rome, many years before Paul's death, that is, in the third or fourth year of Nero's reign, while his martyrdom occurred in the thirteenth year of Nero's reign." He gives the following argument:

(1) Since Paul had recently arrived in Rome, he wanted to inform his dearest disciple Timothy about his affairs, namely, as to the success of his first defense before Nero. This he does at the end of the Epistle ([2 Tim.] 4:16).

(2) This Epistle contains some things which clearly argue for his recent arrival in Rome. [2 Tim.] 4:13: "When you come, bring with you the cloak I left in Troas." Verse 20: "Erastus stayed in Corinth, but I left Trophimus sick in Miletus."

(3) In this Epistle Paul does not think that the end of his life is upon him yet. To the contrary, rather, he indicates that he is still being kept to fulfill the office of preaching among the Gentiles. For he writes thus ([2 Tim.] 4:17): "The Lord was with me and strengthened me so that through me the preaching might be fulfilled and all Gentiles hear."

Swayed by these arguments, Baronius and Estius claim that this

Epistle was sent either with the one written to the Ephesians or not much later—that is, before three others were written: Philippians, Colossians, and Philemon. You see, in this Epistle, Timothy is summoned to Rome. In those [three], Timothy's name is listed as one now present and participating in

> writing. Likewise, in this Epistle, Mark is told to be taken to Rome, and he is also one of those sending greetings in Colossians and Philemon, which were written in Rome.

They base their conjecture that it was written shortly after the Epistle to the Ephesians from the fact that "those were sent through Tychicus, but in this one it says, 'Tychicus I sent to Ephesus' [2 Tim. 4:12], as if it just happened."

But anyone can see that these arguments (which are merely probable) do not contain such weight as to be able to dissuade us from the clear wording of [2 Tim.] 4:6 and the universal consensus of commentators, nor should they.

Benedictus Pererius (commentary on Romans, disp. 2, n. 55) agrees with us. Cosmas Magalianus (preface to 2 Timothy, annot. 3) expressly refutes Baronius. He says:

> Baronius wants the apostle's words—"For I am already being poured out" [2 Tim. 4:6]—to mean only that maybe God had revealed to him that he was about to be crowned with martyrdom under Nero's reign and that the time for this could have seemed to be very much upon him since it did not extend beyond the life span of one emperor. Nevertheless I scarcely think [Paul's words] allow for this meaning. For can the time of his death be said to be "upon him" if it was going to be delayed for nearly ten or more years, as [Baronius] does not deny?

And later on:

> Chrysostom, Theophylact, and nearly all of the most accurate commentators assign this Epistle to the end of [Paul's] life and think that no other was written after this one. Moreover, the idea that a death which is still a long way off can be called "imminent" is inept. For it is one thing to speak of a delaying of time as compared to the brevity of life (Heb. 10:37), but to speak of our actions is another. For who has ever called a death that would happen in ten years "an imminent death"? Who has ever said, "I have finished the race," unless he was at the finish line?

§ 7. *The use and worth.* This Epistle is full of salutary precepts necessary for a shepherd of souls duly to fulfill his office, which primarily is to handle the Word of truth rightly and purely [2 Tim. 2:15] and not to depart at all from the teaching he has been given and has received. Chrysostom calls this "the testament of Paul on his deathbed."

Chapter I

The parts of this chapter.

(1) The inscription and greeting (vv. 1–2).

(2) Thanksgiving for and commendation of Timothy (vv. 3–5).

(3) An exhortation directed to Timothy that he be steadfast in faith and preaching the Gospel, that he persevere, and that he not let himself be discouraged from this because of Paul's chains or the apostasy of others (vv. 6–15).

(4) Praise for Onesiphorus (vv. 16–18).

Verse 1.

Παῦλος, ἀπόστολος Ἰησοῦ χριστοῦ διὰ θελήματος θεοῦ. ["Paul, an apostle of Jesus Christ through God's will."] He attributes his apostleship not to his own merits but to the will and free choosing of God.

κατ' ἐπαγγελίαν ζωῆς τῆς ἐν χριστῷ Ἰησοῦ. ["For the promise of life that is in Christ Jesus."] He describes the material and purpose of his apostleship. "God chose and appointed me for apostleship to proclaim the promise of God by which He promises eternal life to believers in Christ Jesus."

Κατὰ has the same force here as εἰς or πρὸς (cf. Titus 1:1).

Life in the Gospel is said to have been promised in Christ because: (1) Christ acquired it for us by His most precious merit. (2) Christ is the foundation, source, and origin of that life.

The Vulgate is ambiguous. *Secundum promissionem vitae, quae est in Christo Iesu.* ["According to the promise of life which is in Christ Jesus."] Here one cannot tell whether the relative *quae* ["which"] belongs to *promissionem* ["promise"] or to *vitae* ["of life"]. But from the Greek text it is clear that it belongs to the nearer, that is, to ζωῆς ["of life"].

Verse 2.

Τιμοθέῳ ἀγαπητῷ τέκνῳ. ["To Timothy, my beloved son."] See commentary on 1 Tim. 1:2, where the reasons are given why he calls him "a son."

χάρις, ἔλεος, εἰρήνη. ["Grace, mercy, peace."] This greeting is given verbatim in 1 Tim. 1:2.

Verse 3.

Χάριν ἔχω τῷ θεῷ. ["I thank God,"] namely, "because God gave you sincere faith and other wonderful gifts."

ᾧ λατρεύω ἀπὸ προγόνων. ["Whom I worship from my ancestors."] The Vulgate rendered it *cui servio* ["whom I serve"] as if it was ᾧ δουλέυω. Now, because in the dispute over the invocation of the saints it is a matter of religion for the Papists to distinguish between λατρεία ["worship"] and δουλεία ["service"], Estius recommends "the Greek be read *quem colo* ['whom I worship'], since the verb λατρεύω is used in the Scriptures for divine worship." But what, then, is to be done with the Vulgate translation, which the Council of Trent declared authoritative? Therefore we rightly press against the Papists the fact that the Vulgate translator did not so strictly observe their distinction between λατρεία and δουλεία, worship and service.[1]

ἐν καθαρᾷ συνειδήσει. ["With a pure conscience."] *But how could Paul have been worshiping God with a pure conscience already from his ancestors when purity of conscience cannot exist apart from true faith in Christ?* I respond.

(1) Some people restrict these words to the present or at least to the time since he became a Christian, so that he means all true Israelites who call upon and worship the true God by faith in the promised Messiah. He claims to be following in their footsteps.

(2) But according to the explanation of the Greek fathers (which the parallel passages Acts 23:1; 24:16; 26:4; and Phil. 3:6 support), this also includes his time spent living in Judaism. He claims to have been worshiping God from his youth with a pure conscience in the ancient religion received by his forefathers.

(3) You see, though at one point he persecuted the church of God, he claims that he still never did or taught anything but what his conscience demanded, though prior to his conversion to Christ it was in error.

(4) Therefore he is answering the false charges of the Jews, who were accusing him of having abandoned the ancient religion and of having withdrawn from the ordinances of the fathers. He responds to this accusation in such a way as to assert that he never deserted the ancient religion, but that he has been worshiping God "from his ancestors," that is, by the religion received by the fathers and continued all the way down to him.

(5) At the same time, however, he maintains that he, who has shown faithfulness in preaching the Gospel, should be considered worthy now, after his conversion to Christ, because he has been better instructed by divine

---

1 See *On the Law* [Commonplace XV], § 89.

revelation, called to the apostleship, and even his former manner of life had integrity and sincerity.

ὡς ἀδιάλειπτον ἔχω τὴν περὶ σοῦ μνείαν. "As also without stopping"—that is, assiduously—"I keep remembrance of you."

But how is this connected to the preceding?

(1) Ambrose connects them thus: "I thank my God, for whenever I pour out prayers to Him, I also remember you and pray for you. It is the gift of God that I am doing this, and therefore it is right that I give thanks about it."

(2) But others explain it thus: "I thank God for you, my dearest son, faithful co-worker in the Gospel, pointing out to you that in my prayers to God I keep assiduous remembrance of you, praying that He would bring to completion what He began in you." This second sense fits with other openings of Paul's Epistles.

νυκτὸς καὶ ἡμέρας. ["Night and day."] Some apply this to the following words which express his desire to see Timothy. But it is more correct to take them with the preceding, that is, Paul's prayers. The meaning is that he very often, even by night and by day, pours out prayers to God for Timothy. Parallel passages are Rom. 1:9–10; 1 Thess. 1:2; 3:10; 1 Tim. 5:5.

Verse 4.

ἐπιποθῶν σε ἰδεῖν. ["Longing to see you."] This does not give the theme of his prayers but states absolutely that he longs to have Timothy present.

μεμνημένος σου τῶν δακρύων. ["Remembering your tears."] (1) Some understand this as being about tears Timothy shed out of earnest contrition for sins and love for God.

(2) Others take it as being about tears Timothy shed out of sympathy for the calamities that befell the apostle.

(3) But it is more correct to take them as being about the tears he and the other bishops of Ephesus shed when Paul left (Acts 20:37). By these tears he had testified to his own devotion and love for his teacher.

ἵνα χαρᾶς πληρωθῶ. ["That I may be filled with joy."] This should be taken with the words at the beginning of the verse: "Longing to see you so that your presence may bring me comfort and joy in these chains of mine."

Verse 5.

ὑπόμνησιν λαμβάνων τῆς ἐν σοὶ ἀνυποκρίτου πίστεως. ["Keeping remembrance of the sincere faith that is in you."] "When I recall to mind your sincere faith that lacks any hypocrisy, I cannot but fervently hope and long for you to come." Therefore this is another thing on Timothy's part that moves the apostle to long for the presence of his student.

He calls "sincere" that faith which is true, living, and saving, by which Timothy has believed in Christ from the heart without hypocrisy. *But did the apostle know this for sure since he was unable to know the heart?* I respond. Either he is making his judgment based on love, because Timothy had made his faith known by good works, or by revelation from the Holy Spirit he knew that Timothy's faith was unfeigned.

ἥτις ἐνῴκησεν πρῶτον ἐν τῇ μάμμῃ σου Λωΐδι. ["Which first dwelt in your grandmother Lois."] "Which first dwelt," that is, "she had it steadfast and firmly seated." "It was rooted and implanted, so to speak, in the heart of your grandmother." The Vulgate adds the copulative *et* ["also"] which is not in the Greek.

By grandmother he means maternal grandmother, for Timothy was born to a Gentile father (Acts 16:1). Hence the Syriac rendered it *bema' de'mak* ("in your mother's mother").

καὶ τῇ μητρί σου Εὐνίκῃ. ["And in your mother, Eunice."] She was a Jew by birth but had married a Gentile and later was converted to Christ. Hence she is called "faithful" (Acts 16:1).

Apparent contrariety. *Christians are made, not born. So how can one say that sincere faith was propagated to Timothy from his grandmother and mother?* I respond. This did not happen through the generation of the flesh but through faithful teaching and instruction.

πέπεισμαι δὲ ὅτι καὶ ἐν σοί. ["And I am convinced that also in you,"] understand, "dwells sincere faith." The Vulgate rendered the verb πέπεισμαι *certus sum* ["I am certain"]; others have it *persuasum habeo* or *persuasus sum* ["I am convinced"].

The Papists want to show from this passage that "certainty of grace cannot be proven from Rom. 8:38 since here he is talking only about moral certainty but not the immovable certainty of faith, as also in Rom. 15:14."

I respond. (1) The verb πέπεισμαι can be understood in two ways. First, *abstractly*, and then it often signifies some sort of probable opinion. Second, *concretely* or materially. In this way it has a different meaning for different subjects. "Words for things that are spoken of in various ways (ἐκ τῶν πολλαχῶς λεγομένων) come to have different meanings for different subjects."[2] When the word πέπεισμαι is used about others, then it signifies [certainty] that is not conclusive (ἀποδεικτικήν) but probable (τοπικήν),[3] not the certainty of faith and infallible truth but the conviction of love, that is, a probable opinion. You see,

2 For this axiom, see Aristotle, *Metaphysics* 1 (LCL 271 [1933], p. 271).

3 Johann Micraelius, *Lexicon philosophicum . . . Editio Secunda ab ipso Authore correcta & aucta, cum novis novorum terminorum & vocabulorum indicibus.* ([Electronic edition.] Stetini: Mamphrasius, 1661; PURL: http://diglib.hab.de/drucke/201-29-quod/start.htm), col. 1137: "Logicians distinguish between an argument or syllogism that is necessary or apodictic (one which cannot be denied); a syllogism that is probable (which they call topical and dialectic); and, finally, one that is sophistic or false."

we cannot make a determination about our neighbor *a priori* but *a posteriori*, that is, from his doings or actions. But when it is used about ourselves, then it signifies a certain, unmovable conviction, which is the certainty of faith and truth, for it relies on the unmoving, unchanging foundation: the promise of God and the witness of the Holy Spirit.

(2) The Papists themselves are forced to admit this because Paul uses this verb about himself in this very chapter (v. 12): πέπεισμαι ὅτι δυνατός ἐστιν ["I am convinced that He is able"]. But now, they teach that it was through a special revelation from God that Paul had certainty about God's grace and his own salvation (Pistorius, *Hodeg.*, p. 201; Duraeus, *Contra Witaker.*, f. 259). Therefore, when Paul uses the verb πέπεισμαι about himself, he is using it in another sense than when he uses it in this passage about Timothy.

(3) For this reason Guilielmus Estius comments on this passage thus:

> The word πέπεισμαι is general for signifying the conviction by which something may be considered certain, be it moral certainty, as they say, or the certainty that comes from divine authority, that is, the certainty of faith. For the apostle was certain by faith that God was able to preserve his deposit. But it was not in this way that he knew about how unfeigned faith dwelt in Timothy. This he had learned from long-standing experience, and thus he came to this certainty in a human way.

Verse 6.

Δι' ἣν αἰτίαν. ["Because of this reason."] That is, "Because God has given you true faith, which is the root of good works, do not let it be idle."

Some relate this to the more remote: "Because I keep assiduous remembrance of you in my prayers, from that sincere disposition of love I want to admonish you of your office through a letter also."

ἀναμιμνήσκω σε. ["I remind you."] The apostle is arriving at his main purpose for writing, which was to admonish Timothy of his office.

ἀναζωπυρεῖν τὸ χάρισμα τοῦ θεοῦ. ["To rekindle the gift of God."] The Vulgate rendered it *ut resuscites* ["that you revive"]. Ambrose expresses it through [the verb] *recreare* ["renew"]. The Greek verb literally signifies "to stir up a flame that has been hidden and diminished or covered in ash; not to allow it to be extinguished, but if it needs wood or is dying from lack of oil to kindle it and renew it." Therefore some people claim that the metaphor was derived from a spark preserved in ashes which may be kindled by gently blowing on it so that it gives rise to a flame. However, it is more appropriate to have in view the type of the Old Testament priests, by whose daily, assiduous ministry the fire that had come down from heaven was kindled.[4] In a similar way, Timothy is being commanded to stir up and preserve the gifts of the Holy Spirit which he

4 See *On the Ceremonial and Forensic Laws* [Commonplace XVI], § 15.

has received, to strive by faithful and pious zeal to have the gift of God to shine and burn forth (cf. 1 Thess. 5:19; 1 Tim. 4:15).

τὸ χάρισμα. ["The gift."] The Vulgate rendered this through [the word] *gratiam* ["gift" or "grace"]. But τὸ χάρισμα properly signifies "a gift given by grace." It should be renewed in a pious man by prayer, meditation, reading, and a zeal for sacred things, as well as by frequent use and exercise of the gifts of God.

ὅ ἐστιν ἐν σοὶ διὰ τῆς ἐπιθέσεως τῶν χειρῶν μου. ["Which is in you through the laying on of my hands."] Through "the laying on of hands" he means ordination, which happens with the laying on of hands.

Apparent contrariety. *It says here that Paul laid hands on Timothy, but in 1 Tim. 4:14 it says the presbytery did.* This was explained in [the commentary] on that passage.

From this passage Estius tries to prove that ordination is a sacrament, properly speaking. "Through the application of episcopal ordination on the ordinands," he says, "grace is given to them that they may fulfill their ministry well and in holiness. Accordingly, it should be counted among the sacraments of the new law."

I respond. (1) For a sacrament, not only is the promise of grace required but also an external sacramental sign commanded by God, one which is also proper to the sacrament. But there is no such external sign in ordination since no divine command has been given about the laying on of hands. Estius himself admits here that the laying on of hands is "a sort of common term that applies to many things." (2) Not just any grace is required of a sacrament, properly speaking, but that which is proper to the Gospel, namely, the grace of the forgiveness of sins. Such grace is not given in ordination.

Estius retorts that it may be concluded from this apostolic passage that "in ordination are given not only gifts which are called 'graces given by grace' but also those gifts which make one acceptable to God, for such are virtue, love, and sobriety, under which the other gifts required of a bishop must also be included." I respond. (1) Bellarmine admits that (*De sacr. ordin.*, ch. 2) "ordination was not instituted for the bestowal of justifying grace but rather for another purpose." From this we draw the following conclusion: Every sacrament, properly so called, has been instituted to the end that it may apply and seal the promise of grace. Ordination was not instituted to the end that it may apply and seal the promise of grace. Therefore it is not a sacrament, properly speaking. (2) Even if gifts that make one acceptable to God were sometimes also given in ordination, they still would not be given through any sacramental sign instituted by God but through the prayers customarily used in ordination.

Verse 7.

οὐ γὰρ ἔδωκεν ἡμῖν ὁ θεὸς πνεῦμα δειλίας. ["For God has not given us a Spirit of fear."] Some people want to take the pronoun ἡμῖν in reference not only to bishops and ministers of the church but also generally to all the truly pious. They compare this passage with the apostle's statement in Rom. 8:14. However, it is more correct to say that this should mainly and mostly be related to bishops. The context proves this, for the apostle is showing the nature of the gift [*gratia*] Timothy had received in his ordination and which all ministers of the church receive.

Therefore the sense is: "God has not given us a Spirit of δειλίας ('fear'), which very often hinders those to whom God has given outstanding gifts from using them for the church's benefit, but rather they allow them to be extinguished and die out within themselves." Here "fear" means human or worldly fear and also that perverted modesty by which one is afraid to perform the things belonging to his office, such as (in the ministry of the church) preaching the Gospel, reproving delinquents, etc.

Δειλίας signifies timidity, weakness of courage [*animi*], avoiding the dangers one must face in his vocation. To this is opposed ἀνδρία ["manliness, bravery"]. In this passage the apostle set δυνάμεως ["power, strength"] in opposition to it, for it follows in the antithesis.

ἀλλὰ δυνάμεως καὶ ἀγάπης καὶ σωφρονισμοῦ. ["But of strength and love and self-control."] "God gave us a Spirit of δυνάμεως ('strength, courage, vigor'), ἀγάπης (that is, God's love which drives us to serve the church), and σωφρονισμοῦ (by which is meant the self-control that keeps us from allowing our faulty affections, especially fear and dread, to carry us the wrong way)." The Vulgate rendered it *sobrietas* ["moderation"], but the Greek σωφρονισμοῦ properly signifies the self-control by which one bears in moderation whatever happens, good or bad. The Syriac translates it *martyanuta'* ("tranquility").

By "Spirit" is meant "gift" in the common way Scripture speaks, for it often happens that the name of the gift is appropriated to the Holy Spirit, who is the giver of gifts in the church.

Verse 8.

μὴ οὖν ἐπαισχυνθῇς τὸ μαρτύριον τοῦ κυρίου ἡμῶν. ["Do not, therefore, be ashamed of the testimony about our Lord."] This is derived from the preceding, as the particle οὖν ["therefore"] shows. "Because God has given you a Spirit not of fear but of strength, for this reason do not be ashamed of your confession and ministry by which you preach Christ."

By τὸ μαρτύριον some understand "Christ's confession," but it is more correct to take it as about the preaching of the Gospel, which is the testimony about Christ Jesus (cf. John 15:27; Acts 1:8).

μηδὲ ἐμὲ τὸν δέσμιον αὐτοῦ. ["Nor of me, His prisoner."] "Do not be ashamed either of me or of my chains, for I am a captive of Christ, that is, because of the preaching of the Gospel about Christ. It is because of the name of Christ that these chains have been placed upon me, not because of anything disgraceful."

ἀλλὰ συγκακοπάθησον τῷ εὐαγγελίῳ. ["But rather, suffer along with the Gospel."] Some explain it: "Empathize with me as I suffer because of the Gospel as if you yourself were bearing it" (cf. Phil 1:7; 4:14). But the more accurate explanation is this: "Suffer along with the Gospel. Participate in the afflictions of the Gospel. Just as the Gospel suffers antagonism from false teachers, so suffer persecution from the world yourself on account of preaching the Gospel." In this way the Gospel is personified in that it is said to labor and suffer persecution when those who preach it suffer for its sake. One could also explain it thus: "Do not be ashamed of my chains, and—what is more—patiently bear your share of adversities for the sake of the Gospel. If it should happen that you also must suffer some for preaching the Gospel, take my example, and bear it with patience."

κατὰ δύναμιν θεοῦ. ["By the strength of God."] This can be taken in two ways. (1) "According to the strength" that God gives man. (2) "By the strength" with which God is at work in man. The first sense fits with the preceding words "God has given us the Spirit of δυνάμεως"; the latter sense fits with the words that follow. The apostle's aim is to direct Timothy away from trusting in his own powers and, contrariwise, to exhort him to trust in God alone and in the power of His strength.

Verse 9.

τοῦ σώσαντος ἡμᾶς. ["Who saved us."] Here "to save" does not mean bodily, temporal salvation but one that is spiritual and eternal. The apostle says this as a sort of digression, so that by recalling and magnifying the salvation given through Christ he might encourage Timothy all the more vehemently to preach the Gospel unhindered.

καὶ καλέσαντος κλήσει ἁγίᾳ. ["And who called us with a holy calling."] The Vulgate made an addition: *vocatione sua sancta* ["with His holy calling"]. But the pronoun "His" is not in the Greek, nor is it in the Syriac paraphrase. In fact, it is missing in some ancient Latin copies.

He labels the calling "holy." (1) Because it proceeds from Him who is Holiness itself and from whom nothing comes but what is holy [cf. Lev. 19:2]. (2) Because it happens "through the holy men of God" (2 Pet. 1:21) as they preach the holy Gospel. (3) Because by it we are called "to holiness that we may be holy and blameless" (Eph. 1:4). "God did not call us for impurity but for sanctification" (1 Thess. 4:7).

οὐ κατὰ τὰ ἔργα ἡμῶν. ["Not in response to our works."] From this passage, Estius, contrary to other Papists, rightly concludes that "the grace of God is not given according to our merits, and our predestination does not come from merits but from the pure good-pleasure of God's grace." The apostolic text clearly asserts this.

At the same time, however, Estius is incorrect when he claims:

> By these words the apostle does not exclude the merits of works from our justification and salvation. The apostle does not deny that eternal life comes from works since he teaches in several places that God will render to each according to his works (Rom. 2:6; 2 Cor. 5:10; and elsewhere). Also, at the end of the previous Epistle he taught that eternal life is apprehended from good works (1 Tim. 6:19). Rather, [the apostle says] that the entirety of salvation, whose beginning comes from faith, does not come from the merit of works. The reason for this is clear, since good works themselves, by which we are brought in some way to eternal life, are also included in that salvation which comes entirely from God.

I respond. (1) If the grace of God is not given because of our merits, then eternal life is not given because of our merits either. The reasoning behind the logical connection is this: eternal life is likewise a free χάρισμα, a gift of God given by grace to believers in Christ (Rom. 6:23). (2) If predestination is not because of merits but from the sheer good-pleasure of God's grace, then salvation, too, is not because of merits but from the sheer good-pleasure of God's grace. The reasoning behind the logical connection is this: The reasons why God saves us in time are the same as why He determined to save us from eternity. Contrariwise, the reasons by which He did not determine to save us from eternity are also not those for which He saves us in time. You see, His decree and His execution of the decree correspond to each other in the most precise way. (3) Our merits are not only excluded from the beginning of our salvation but also from its middle and end, as is shown by the perpetual opposition between God's grace and our merits, faith and works, believing and working within the act of justification and salvation (Rom. 3:28; 4:5; Gal. 2:16; Eph. 2:8–9; Titus 3:5; and this verse [2 Tim. 1:9]). (4) "According to works" is one thing, and "because of works" is another. The phrase κατὰ τὰ ἔργα ["according to the works"] (Rom. 2:6) is explained as πρὸς ἃ ἔπραξεν ["for what He has done"] (2 Cor. 5:10) and ὡς τὸ ἔργον αὐτοῦ ἔσται ["as His work is"] (Rev. 22:12). (5) Moreover, here κατὰ τὰ ἔργα ["according to the works"] is used for ἐξ ἔργων ["due to works"] (Titus 3:5). Thus, when God is said to render to everyone according to works (Matt. 16:27; Rom. 2:6), κατὰ does not signify ἀξία ("merit," "worthiness") but only the witness that works give. (6) In 1 Tim. 6:19 Paul does not attribute the apprehension of eternal life to good works since they lack that power to apprehend. He merely describes the resulting reward for which the faithful rich who do good works from faith are to hope. All of Scripture ascribes the apprehension of eternal life to faith, for it grasps Christ and, in Christ, eternal life (John 3:16; 1 John 5:10). (7) Not only does the apostle say that salvation as a whole does not come from the merit of works, but he also says that no part of salvation comes from the merit of works. Therefore Estius is begging the question when he says that we are brought to eternal salvation by good works, if he means this in terms of the merit of works (as he surely must according to his hypotheses). That is the very issue at question and what we—nay, the apostle—rejects. Estius, then, overcome by the power of the truth and restrained by its clarity, comments on the following words κατ' ἰδίαν πρόθεσιν ["according to His own purpose"] thus: "The apostle wants to exclude any looking at our merit from our salvation" (take note!) "and calling; he wants us to consider only the purpose and grace of God."

ἀλλὰ κατ' ἰδίαν πρόθεσιν. ["But according to His own purpose."] The Vulgate has *secundum suum propositum* ["according to His purpose"], but in Greek it is "according to His own [*proprium*] purpose," which is more emphatic.

By πρόθεσιν the apostle means that purpose by which God decreed from eternity to save those who believe in Christ (Rom. 8:28).

Estius carelessly writes here that "the apostle understands 'purpose' as the previous and eternal will or decree which elsewhere he calls 'predestination.'" However, the πρόθεσις ["purpose"] according to which election or predestination happened (Eph. 1:11) is not the predestination itself. So also the πρόγνωσις ["foreknowledge"] according to which election happened (Rom. 8:29; 1 Pet. 1:2) is not the predestination itself.

καὶ χάριν τὴν δοθεῖσαν ἡμῖν ἐν χριστῷ Ἰησοῦ πρὸ χρόνων αἰωνίων. ["And grace which He gave us in Christ Jesus before time began."] It is clear that χάριν means "the freely given mercy of God" and not "an infused habit of grace," since the latter could not be given us before time began. This is so obvious that it earns even Estius's vote, for he comments on this passage thus:

> He does not mean a created grace that is in us, for this is a product of predestination; rather, he means an uncreated grace, that is, the freely given kindness of God which he next says was made known by the coming of Christ and which in Titus 3:5 he calls "mercy." Therefore, this word "grace" intentionally adds an aspect of it being freely given. In other words, the apostle is saying "according to His own purpose" by which He freely and apart from any merit of ours determined to save us.

These are Estius's words from which we may assemble an immovable argument against such Papists: The grace by which God determined from eternity to save us is the same by which He saves us in Christ and because of Christ in time. (The reason for the logical connection has already been explained above.)[5] But now, it was not because of a created grace or an infused habit of grace that He determined in eternity to save us but because of uncreated grace, that is, His freely given mercy. Therefore.

τὴν δοθεῖσαν ἡμῖν. ["Which He gave us."] Piscator explains it [as that] "which God decreed to give us through efficacy, that is, a calling in time." But the Papists could easily adapt this to suit their own interpretation wherein some of them also explain "grace" here to mean the infused habit of grace. Hence Estius adds a little later on: "Grace—or mercy—with respect to its effects was given us through Christ; that is, in view of Christ's merits it was prepared from eternity." But now, the apostle is not saying that God decreed to give us grace in time through His calling or that God decided to prepare it for us, but he expressly asserts that His grace was given to us in Christ before time began.

Tossanus explains the grace given us in Christ before time began thus: "In that eternal decree Christ was appointed our Mediator, and the faithful were elected in Him." Given this assumption, which accords with this apostolic passage and also with Eph. 1:4, 6, an absolute decree of election collapses. For those who were elected in view of faith in Christ were not elected by an absolute decree.

πρὸ χρόνων αἰωνίων. ["Before time began."] The apostle is referring to the passage of the times and ages from the beginning of the world. Since whatever precedes this passage of the times and ages is eternal, the apostle is denoting "eternity" through the phrase πρὸ χρόνων αἰωνίων.

Verse 10.

φανερωθεῖσαν δὲ νῦν διὰ τῆς ἐπιφανείας τοῦ σωτῆρος ἡμῶν χριστοῦ Ἰησοῦ. ["But which now has been manifested through the appearing of our Savior, Christ Jesus."] By "the appearing" he means Christ's first coming, and so "in flesh" is implied. 1 Tim. 3:16: ὁ θεὸς ἐφανερώθη ἐν σαρκί ["God appeared in flesh"].

From the word ἐπιφανείας ["appearing"] one may conclude that the Son of God was already in the world before His incarnation (John 1:10), but by taking up visible flesh His presence has been manifested.

Apparent contrariety. *How can one say that this grace has finally been manifested through Christ's coming since it was not entirely unknown to the faithful even in the Old Testament?* The answer comes both from the broadness of the object and also the clarity of the manifestation. Yes, this grace was known to the faithful in the Old Testament, but more obscurely. Also, it was not made known to the whole world through the universal preaching, but only to the faithful few.

5 See above, pp. 122–23.

καταργήσαντος μὲν τὸν θάνατον. ["Who abolished death."] The Vulgate has *qui mortem quidem destruxit* ["who indeed destroyed death"]. The Greek means "to abolish, to render null and void." Luther has *zu nicht gemacht*. Now, this abolition of death happened: (1) Through the full satisfaction Christ offered for sins. Since "the sting of death is sin" (1 Cor. 15:56), if this sting is abolished, death will be abolished. (2) Through Christ's death, which was "the death of death" (Hosea 13:14). Hence the church sings of Christ: "By His dying He has destroyed death."[6] (3) Through His winning glorious victory from the devil, death's parent. Heb. 2:14: "So that through death He might destroy the one who had the strong power (τὸ κράτος) of death, that is, the devil."

The question arises: *Is the apostle talking about temporal or eternal, the first or second, death?* I respond. He is talking about both, because through Christ believers are set free from both in the blessed resurrection to eternal life.

φωτίσαντος δὲ ζωὴν. ["And who also brought life forth into light."] Φωτίζειν means "to illuminate" and "to bring forth into light." The Vulgate translator takes it in the first sense, but the additional word "life" shows that it should be taken in the latter sense and rendered: "who brought life forth into light."

καὶ ἀφθαρσίαν. ["And immortality."] He could have given us life without immortality, but He wanted the life to be immortal and eternal so that His kindness to us would be full and complete.

By "life" is meant spiritual life in this age through which we come to life again out of the death of sins (Eph. 2:5). Through immortality and incorruptibility there is heavenly life in the age to come. Life and incorruptibility—that is, incorruptible and eternal life—stand in opposition to both deaths, temporal and eternal.

διὰ τοῦ εὐαγγελίου. ["Through the Gospel."] Because the Gospel promises eternal life to all who believe in Christ.

Verse 11.

εἰς ὃ ἐτέθην ἐγὼ κῆρυξ. ["For which I was appointed a preacher."] The Vulgate has *in quo positus sum ego praedicator* ["in which I was appointed a preacher"]. But in Greek it is "for which" or "unto which I was appointed," that is, by Christ.

The apostle describes his office with three words. (1) He calls himself a κῆρυξ, a public herald in the name of the King of heaven, bringing His commands.

(2) An ἀπόστολος, an ambassador of Christ, one who is fulfilling the office of apostle with which God charged him.

6 From the Proper Preface for Easter Day.

(3) Τῶν ἐθνῶν διδάσκαλος ["teacher of the Gentiles"], sent chiefly to teach the Gentiles and call them into the fellowship of Christ's reign, for he and Peter had agreed that he would preach among the Gentiles with Barnabas while Peter would preach among the Jews with James and John (Gal. 2:9). Still, this should not be understood exclusively but chiefly with respect to the divine call described in Acts 22:21: "Go, for I will send you far away to the Gentiles."

Verse 12.

δι' ἣν αἰτίαν καὶ ταῦτα πάσχω. ["For this reason I suffer these things also."] By "these things" he has in mind the prison that detained him and the chains that bound him. The sense is: "The reason I have been cast into this prison and these chains is because I have been appointed by God as proclaimer of the Gospel, apostle, and teacher of the Gentiles."

ἀλλ' οὐκ ἐπαισχύνομαι. ["But I am not ashamed."] "I am not ashamed of these chains that I endure because I preach the Gospel." He is thinking of v. 8, which uses the same verb (ἐπαισχυνθῇς), and means to say, "So neither should you be ashamed of the Gospel or my chains."

οἶδα γὰρ ᾧ πεπίστευκα. ["For I know whom I have believed."] He is stating the reason why he is not ashamed of the Gospel or his chains.

Some want πεπίστευκα here to mean "entrusted," since he immediately makes mention of the deposit. So the sense would be: "I know how powerful, faithful, good, and true the Lord is to whom I have entrusted my deposit for safekeeping." But it is more correct to take it in the usual sense of "believed": "I know the One in whom I had faith in my conversion. My faith does not depend on a sandy, slippery foundation but on one that is sure and unshaken."

καὶ πέπεισμαι ὅτι δυνατός ἐστιν τὴν παραθήκην μου φυλάξαι ["And I am convinced that He is able to guard my deposit."] On the verb πέπεισμαι, see v. 5.

By παραθήκην some understand the deposit God entrusted and commissioned to Paul, namely, the deposit of grace and preaching, and both those who by his efforts had been converted and those who had yet to be converted. This is nearly the sense in which the apostle John is said to have spoken about a youth whom he had entrusted to another, to which people apply Acts 20:32: "I commend (παρατίθεμαι) you to God."

But it is more correct to understand it as the deposit of life and eternal blessedness which God had laid for Paul in heaven or, in the words of [2 Tim.] 4:8, "the crown of righteousness" which God has promised to faithful preachers of the Gospel. The following interpretations agree with this one: (1) Some understand the "deposit" to be Paul's soul, salvation, and safety (cf. 1 Pet. 4:19). (2) Some understand it as good works done in the hope of the eternal reward. (3) Others understand it as the very reward of works which is said to be deposited with God insofar as one does not immediately receive the reward after doing the work but patiently awaits the time of reward which will be paid in full on the Day of Judgment.

φυλάξαι. ["To guard,"] "so that the promised glory cannot be taken away from me by the devil or the world."

ˋεἰς ἐκείνην τὴν ἡμέραν. ["Until that day."] He means the final Day of Judgment when God will distribute the rewards promised to faithful preachers of the Gospel.

Verse 13.

Ὑποτύπωσιν ἔχε ὑγιαινόντων λόγων. ["Hold to the pattern of sound words."] He now moves on to the second part of his exhortation about guarding the deposit of sound teaching.

Ὑποτύπωσιν. ["Pattern."] Some render this "expressed form"; others have it "image and sketch"; and others, "representation" [*informationem*]. It is with this last word that the Vulgate translator rendered it in 1 Tim. 1:16.

Most people understand this word to mean "a brief outline, description, and record that Timothy has before him and that he follows when teaching." To use a metaphor drawn from painters, when they are going to depict an image, they first draw a rough outline; they then follow these outlines as a guide when they are going to add in bold colors. Thus ὑποτύπωσιν is the same as σκιαγραφία ["outline"]. However, the word ὑποτύπωσιν does not only mean the form and mode of teaching but also the very foundation of the teaching.

ὑγιαινόντων λόγων. ["Of sound words."] Estius notes that "the apostle mentioned 'words' because the teaching of the Gospel is handed down more in words and speech than in writing. Thus the apostle adds 'which you heard from me.'" I respond. (1) Second Timothy was written shortly before Paul's death when the four Gospels and the apostolic Epistles had already existed in the church for some time. Therefore the teaching of the Gospel at that time had been handed down both orally and in writing. (2) What the apostles first preached orally they later handed down to us in the Scriptures by God's will so that it would be the foundation and pillar of our faith. Therefore there is no real difference[7] between the apostolic preaching and the apostolic Scriptures.

ἐν πίστει καὶ ἀγάπῃ. ["In faith and love."] This passage may be explained in three ways:

(1) Some take this with the preceding words "which you heard from me," the sense being: "which you heard from me with faith and love, not only giving your trust to my words but also adding in loving affection by which you sought not what is your own but what is Christ's."

---

7 *Reale discrimen*, that is, a distinction or difference in content.

(2) Some take this with the more distant "hold to the pattern of sound words" and explain it thus: "Hold to the pattern of sound words with faith and love that will keep you from departing from that pattern."

(3) Still others take it with the more distant words but in a different sense: "Hold to the pattern of sound words, that is, of sound teaching which has to do with faith and love, so that you will maintain the integrity of faith and the sincerity of love," for these are the two chief parts of Christian doctrine. Luther has *vom Glauben und von der Liebe* ["of faith and of the love"], which fits the text very well.

τῇ ἐν χριστῷ Ἰησοῦ. ["Which are in Christ Jesus."] The Vulgate rendered it *in Christo Iesu,* but it should not have omitted the Greek article τῇ ("*which* is in Christ Jesus"). The same translator expressed this article that way in 1 Tim. 1:14.

Verse 14.

τὴν καλὴν παραθήκην φύλαξον. ["Guard the wonderful deposit."] The word "deposit" in this passage is not used in the same sense as it was earlier in v. 12, but in the sense of 1 Tim. 6:20: "O Timothy, guard the deposit by avoiding profane novelties of words." There this word means "the teaching of the Gospel" which he had entrusted to Timothy.

Furthermore, he calls the doctrine of the Gospel about Christ "the good deposit" not only because its Author is good, or because its material and content is good, or because its end is good, but also because its effect is good, for this teaching makes men good.

Καλὴν can also be translated as the deposit that is "beautiful, outstanding, wonderful." What Paul a little earlier had called "the sound words heard from him" he now calls a "wonderful deposit."

Estius notes on this passage:

> One should use this passage against the heretics who cannot provide any such deposit, that is, teaching delivered and received from the apostles through a continuous series of successors—unless they might say that this deposit is Holy Scripture. But one cannot claim this, for it was not Holy Scripture that Paul had deposited with Timothy but the teaching he delivered verbally. Besides, what sort of deposit is it if nearly all heretical sects have it in common? Therefore Scripture, which we have also received from the apostles, is part of the deposit but is not the whole, entire deposit the Catholic Church alone preserves.

We have discussed our response to this argument in *On Scripture* [1625 *Exegesis*, Commonplace I], § 405; and *Confess. Cathol.* (bk. 1, part 2, ch. 5, argum. advers. 6).

διὰ πνεύματος ἁγίου τοῦ ἐνοικοῦντος ἐν ἡμῖν. ["Through the Holy Spirit who dwells within us."] He is pointing out the way of keeping that deposit, namely, through the grace of the Holy Spirit.

Estius thinks that "within us" applies "to the prefects of the church by whose ministry the deposit promised them through the Holy Spirit is preserved in the church." But it is more correct to take this as being about the whole church and all its true and living members, to whom the keeping of this deposit has been commended and promised by the grace of the Holy Spirit.

Verse 15.

Οἶδας τοῦτο, ὅτι ἀπεστράφησάν με πάντες οἱ ἐν τῇ Ἀσίᾳ. ["You are aware of this, that everyone in Asia turned away from me."] He recounts how many defected from him so as to encourage and console Timothy who could have been distressed upon hearing this.

Ἀπεστράφησάν is rendered by the Vulgate as *aversi sunt a me* ["were turned away from me"], but it literally means *aversati sunt me* ["turned away from me"].

Some, especially Greek commentators, understand "everyone in Asia" to be "those in Rome at the time who had come from Asia, since the apostle was imprisoned there." Thus the preposition "in" would stand for "from."

Others keep the natural meaning of the word ἐν and render it "those who were from Asia," since the apostle says indeterminately οἱ ἐν τῇ Ἀσίᾳ. They claim, then, that "the apostle is talking about those who seemed to have faith and to be following the apostle when he was preaching in Asia, but after they came to Rome and saw how he was imprisoned, they defected from him."

Others think that "the apostle is speaking about those who were in Asia at the time when the apostle was writing this." This explanation has the benefit of the prior words οἶδας τοῦτο ["you are aware of this"]. For Timothy was working in Asia and was able to know what was going on in Asia but not in Rome.

He means Asia Minor and those converted from the Jews but not from the Gentiles. He does not say whether they turned away from the faith or the person of Paul, but the latter is more probable. It seems that they were a little scared of being caught up in the danger with him. At the same time, however, a departure from the faith could easily have arisen as a result of this turning away from his person.

ὧν ἐστιν Φύγελος καὶ Ἑρμογένης. ["Among whom are Phygelus and Hermogenes."] Clearly these two were harsher and more damaging to Paul than the rest.

Tertullian (*De praescript. adv. haereticos*, ch. 3) lists Phygelus and Hermogenes as deserters of the church.

As for Phygelus, Metaphrastes relates (*Sermo de Petro et Paulo Apostolis*): "Peter appointed him bishop of Ephesus, but he later turned Jewish believers away from the faith." But the credibility of this Metaphrastes is entirely unreliable.

Tertullian wrote against Hermogenes (*Adversus Hermogenem*), but it is clear from Tertullian's own words that this was a different Hermogenes: "Neither did the apostle's Hermogenes persevere in the rule." Here he calls "the apostle's Hermogenes" the one the apostle mentioned in this Epistle.

Verse 16.

δῴη ἔλεος ὁ κύριος τῷ Ὀνησιφόρου οἴκῳ. ["May the Lord give mercy to the household of Onesiphorus."] "May God be merciful and gracious to him and grant him to find mercy."

This is an exception to the universal "everyone in Asia turned away from me," for Onesiphorus was from Asia, as we see at the end of this Epistle ([2 Tim.] 4:19): "Greet the house of Onesiphorus." More specifically, it is thought that he was an Ephesian because of what follows here in [2 Tim.] 1:18: "And you well know how much he served me in Ephesus."

ὅτι πολλάκις με ἀνέψυξεν. ["For he often refreshed me."] "He refreshed me by his kindness." Kindness and consolations shown to the godly are like a cool breeze in the dog days of summer.

καὶ τὴν ἅλυσίν μου οὐκ ἐπαισχύνθη. "He was not ashamed of my chains" as were the others from Asia.

Verse 17.

ἀλλὰ γενόμενος ἐν Ῥώμῃ, σπουδαιότερον ἐζήτησέν με καὶ εὗρεν. ["Instead, when he arrived in Rome, he kept searching for me quite zealously and found me."] "So far was he from being ashamed of my chains that, when he came to Rome and learned that I was bound in chains for preaching the Gospel, he most earnestly sought me and would not rest until he found me."

The question arises: *Why was such a search even necessary?* I respond. (1) There was not one jail but several that held people who were going to stand before Caesar's tribunal. (2) Acts 28:16: "Paul was granted permission to stay alone with a soldier guarding him."

Verse 18.

δῴη αὐτῷ ὁ κύριος εὑρεῖν ἔλεος παρὰ κυρίου ἐν ἐκείνῃ τῇ ἡμέρᾳ. ["May the Lord grant him to find mercy from the Lord on that day."] The apostle has the preceding in view. "Just as he sought and found me in Rome, so may the Lord grant him again to find mercy."

Estius thinks that the words "May the Lord grant him to find mercy" is a Hebraism, as in Gen. 19:24: "The Lord sent rain from the Lord." "So the sense is: 'May the Lord from Himself grant him to find mercy,' for the Hebrews often repeated the antecedent in place of the reflexive pronoun." I respond. (1) We are aware of this Hebraism and do not deny it, but we do deny that it applies to this passage. (2) For there is no reason that compels us to depart from the usual and natural meaning, especially since, as we claim, it greatly conforms to the analogy of the faith. (3) You see, since God the Father has made Christ Judge of the living and the dead (John 5:22; Acts 10:42), the apostle prays for Onesiphorus that God the Father may grant him to find mercy with the Lord Christ on the Day of Judgment. (4) Against Calvin and the Photinians who distort the Mosaic text of Gen. 19:24, we press the clear distinction of Jehovah the Son from Jehovah the Father, the emphatic placement of the preposition, the comparison of other passages of Scripture, the Chaldaic translation, and the consensus of Christian commentators. At the Council of Smyrna (can. 16) (says Socrates, *Hist. eccl.*, bk. 2, ch. 30), an anathema was given to Estius and all who promote this distortion of the text. See also *On the Trinity* [1625 *Exegesis*, Commonplace III], § 155.

Chrysostom and Theophylact note that "the apostle prays mercy for Onesiphorus on that Day of Judgment because even all the saints will need much mercy, and no one will be saved except through mercy." Augustine (*De [corrept.] et grat.*, ch. 13) writes: "On that day, mercy will be needed for the saints to be crowned by God."

Tertullian (*De resurr. carnis*, ch. 23) expounds on this mercy thus: "On the Day of Judgment all the elect will be freed from the misery of death and corruption through the blessed resurrection."

Most simply, "mercy" is used for "gracious favor," as happens in many passages of Scripture. Rom. 6:23: "Eternal life is the gift of God (χάρισμα τοῦ θεοῦ) in Christ."

Estius speculates that

> Onesiphorus was already dead at the time Paul wrote this (1) because the apostle does not say, "May the Lord grant mercy to Onesiphorus," but "to the house of Onesiphorus." (2) Then he says about Onesiphorus: "May the Lord grant him to find mercy from the Lord on that day"—that is, his hope for him was that which Christians usually hope for the faithful dead: rest and mercy.

He continues:

> If the apostle was praying for Onesiphorus to find mercy from the Lord when he was already dead, then this passage would be very strong proof for praying for the faithful dead. (3) At the end of this Epistle [the apostle] bids greetings for the house of Onesiphorus [2 Tim. 4:19] but not for Onesiphorus himself, as if he were no longer alive.

I respond. (1) Estius is not so bold as to claim for sure that Onesiphorus was already dead. He says, "This can be said probably." (2) He says this first:

"As for Onesiphorus, one should know that the apostle's good prayer for him was not without effect. For, as is related in the martyrologies of the Greeks and the Latins, Onesiphorus was eventually crowned with martyrdom for Christ's name at the Hellespont, if this is the same person they are commemorating." (3) Even in churches of great renown we pray blessed rest for the faithful dead, but we are still not praying for them to be released from purgatory. The sense in which such prayers are to be understood is explained in *The Apology of the Augsburg Confession.*[8]

καὶ ὅσα ἐν Ἐφέσῳ διηκόνησεν, βέλτιον σὺ γινώσκεις. ["And how much he ministered in Ephesus you know quite well."] Some explain this as "what many things," that is, "how many things." But it is more correct to take it thus: "In how many things he ministered at Ephesus," that is "How dutiful he was in ministry." This is how the editor takes it (*Addit.* in Estius, commentary on this passage).

Some codices add "for me," but this lacks the credibility not only of the best Greek copies but also of the Latin ones. This addition also goes against the context. You see, if Paul had written "for me," then he would not have said, "You know quite well," for surely Paul himself knew best the favors done for him.

8 Ap XXIV 94–96 (*Concordia*, pp. 235–36).

Chapter II

There are four parts to this chapter.

(1) An exhortation to readiness and endurance in teaching the Gospel (vv. 1–7).

(2) Consolation in response to Paul's chains and the sufferings of the godly (vv. 8–13).

(3) A general instruction on duly administering the ecclesiastical ministry (vv. 14–21).

(4) An encouragement toward certain specific virtues (vv. 22–26).

Verse 1.

Σὺ οὖν, τέκνον μου, ἐνδυναμοῦ ἐν τῇ χάριτι τῇ ἐν χριστῷ Ἰησοῦ. ["As for you, then, my child, be strengthened in the grace that is in Christ Jesus."]

Connection. Based on the above, he finds an opportunity to exhort Timothy to exercise his office manfully. The verb ἐνδυναμοῦ recalls [2 Tim.] 1:7: "God has not given us a Spirit of fear (δειλίας) but of strength (δυνάμεως)."

"Be strengthened in the grace that is in Christ Jesus," that is, in faith by which we apprehend the grace of God in Christ, or in the doctrine of the Gospel which is "the Word of grace" (Acts 14:3). Luther views it as a Hebraism and renders it *durch die Gnade* ["through the grace"]. Therefore [Paul] is encouraging Timothy to lay aside all timidity and act bravely in the office he has undertaken, and to do this relying on the help of God's grace which is given through Christ.

Verse 2.

καὶ ἃ ἤκουσας παρ' ἐμοῦ διὰ πολλῶν μαρτύρων, ταῦτα παράθου πιστοῖς ἀνθρώποις. ["And the things you have heard from us among many witnesses, entrust these things to faithful men."]

He is explaining what he had called a "deposit" in [2 Tim.] 1:14 and 1 Tim. 6:20—namely, the teaching delivered from him and entrusted to Timothy.

διὰ πολλῶν μαρτύρων. ["Among many witnesses."] Some translate this "through many witnesses," but it is more correct to render it "among many witnesses," that is, "in the presence of many witnesses." Furthermore, some understand the "witnesses" to be "presbyters in whose name and presence Paul had ordained Timothy to the ministry." But it is more correct to understand them as the hearers in whose presence his ordination occurred—or, rather, Timothy's instruction—for they were able to testify regarding the apostle's doctrine.

The apostle wanted to instruct Timothy in the presence of many witnesses: (1) So that the fruit of his teaching would benefit many. (2) So that, if anyone tried falsely to accuse [Timothy] of not passing on right teaching, there would be no lack of witnesses to prove that he was teaching nothing but what he had received from Paul.

Estius warns: "The apostle says 'what you heard from me,' not 'what I wrote or put in writing,' so that we may learn that sound teaching was usually delivered from the apostles more in word than in writing. This is no small argument in favor of unwritten traditions." I respond. The things the apostle delivered to Timothy orally are the same things he consigned to writing, as is shown more fully in its proper place.[1]

ταῦτα παράθου πιστοῖς ἀνθρώποις. ["These things entrust to faithful men."] "So that not only may you faithfully teach them but also [that you may] bestow on them the authority to teach others."

οἵτινες ἱκανοὶ ἔσονται καὶ ἑτέρους διδάξαι. ["Who will be competent to teach others also."] Theophylact notes: "This is the office of bishops and presbyters, through whom the deposit of teaching is also to be shared with others."

Verse 3.

Σὺ οὖν κακοπάθησον ὡς καλὸς στρατιώτης Ἰησοῦ χριστοῦ. ["As for you, then, suffer evil as a good soldier of Jesus Christ."] The Vulgate rendered it *labora* ["toil"], but the Greek verb properly signifies "enduring evil." "Whatever toils, griefs, hardships, dangers, etc., will come upon you for the sake of the Gospel, bear them with a strong spirit."

Verse 4.

οὐδεὶς στρατευόμενος ἐμπλέκεται ταῖς τοῦ βίου πραγματείαις. ["No soldier gets caught up in the affairs of life."] The Vulgate reads *Nemo militans DEO, implicat se negotiis saecularibus* ("No one fighting for *God* involves himself in worldly affairs"). But the Greek does not have the word "God" added, nor does it have the active "involves himself," but the passive ἐμπλέκεται ("gets caught up"). Estius notes here: "The word 'God' is not only lacking in the Greek and Syriac copies, but it is not even found in all the Latin ones; nor is it entirely

1 See *On Holy Scripture* [1625 *Exegesis*, Commonplace I], §§ 7, 394–413.

relevant here in the way Robert Bellarmine (*De Rom. pont.*, bk. 5, last ch.) learnedly commented on it, following others. And though it is found written in the text among Ambrose, Pelagius, Primasius, and Sedulius, it is still quite clear from their commentaries that it was not acknowledged by them."

The apostle is speaking about those who have been enlisted in physical military service. They must be free from the business of life in order to please the one who drafted them for military service and whom they serve. He thus draws three comparisons: (1) from military service, (2) from athletics, and (3) from farming. If a soldier bears all things and casts aside all business that can inhibit him from his purpose for the sake of earthly wages, and if an athlete does the same for a perishable crown while a farmer does it for an unguaranteed harvest—then how much more should a minister of the church, as a spiritual soldier, athlete, and farmer, lay aside all earthly business and diligently fulfill his vocation so that he may receive a heavenly and unfading share of glory (1 Cor. 9:25).

ἐμπλέκεται. "Gets involved, gets caught up in the affairs of life so that he may please τῷ στρατολογήσαντι, the one who drafted him for military service."

"The affairs of life" means the occupations that one undertakes in order to provide a living, such as the administration of the family, business, farming, and mechanical labor. Βίου signifies "life" insofar as one seeks sustenance for its support by some work, so "the affairs of life" are those things one does to make a living.

Estius notes here: "From this comparison and teaching of the apostle, the conclusion becomes readily apparent that it is not meet and right for church leaders to be secular princes and lords of cities and provinces. For it is impossible for them not to be distracted to some extent from the due exercise of spiritual power and military service by such [secular] power and jurisdiction—no matter how much they delegate it to others." However, scared of offending the bishops who are deeply immersed in secular affairs, he soon adds: "But we are not denying the need to maintain and preserve the power received from the fathers; one can excuse them. And much more is there an opportunity to preserve and guard the Catholic faith itself, and other concurrent circumstances." Obviously Estius is alluding to Bellarmine's statement (whom he had praised a little before) from *De Rom. pont.* (bk. 5, ch. 9): "Although it might be best, absolutely, for popes to handle only what is spiritual and kings what is temporal, yet, because the days are evil, experience cries out that it is not only advantageous but even necessary that many temporal principalities have been given to the pope and other bishops by the singular providence of God. For if the bishops had not been the princes in Germany, none of them would have remained in their seats to this day." I respond. (1) But what necessity can exist that would excuse the bishop from fulfilling the ecclesiastical ministry? (2) The matter speaks for itself. The fact that the bishops neglected their office and began to administer temporal principalities was the occasion for the introduction of a great darkness into the church. (3) How pathetic a religion is it if it has to rely on secular power and the arm of man?

Verse 5.

ἐὰν δὲ καὶ ἀθλῇ τις, οὐ στεφανοῦται ἐὰν μὴ νομίμως ἀθλήσῃ. ["Now, if one competes he is not crowned unless he competes lawfully."] The verb ἀθλῇ, from which we derive "athletes," means "to compete" in any kind of bodily competition, such as wrestling, racing, boxing, discus throwing, and jumping. Therefore the apostle has in mind the custom in Greek games where the victors were given a wreathed crown.

He is comparing the office of bishop to athletic competition because just as athletes must not only do much but also suffer much, so must bishops also.

Generally speaking, all the pious are being warned by this comparison both to fight well and to persevere in the contest until the end. He fights well who fights with such strength of spirit that he overcomes his foe and who diligently follows the rules of the contest begun, etc.

Augustine (*Ad fratr. in erem.*, serm. 8): "No one fights well unless he always stays in the arena of the fight until the end." Prosper of Aquitaine (*Epigramm.* 30, v. 7): "For the one who does not compete cannot hope for the crown."

Baptista Mantuanus (*De contemn. morte*, v. 143): "There must be a fight! None arrive triumphant without the strife, and the crown is only given if one competes."

Verse 6.

τὸν κοπιῶντα γεωργὸν δεῖ πρῶτον τῶν καρπῶν μεταλαμβάνειν. ["The farmer who toils must be the first to get his share of the crops."] This is the apostle's third comparison to encourage Timothy to discharge his office assiduously. Some explain it through transposition: "A farmer must first toil before getting the crops" (cf. Ps. 126:5). "So also a minister of the church must first toil and bear adversity before receiving the rewards of his toil." But the aim of the apostle shows that he is mostly discussing here the reward of toil. "Just as the farmer who has tirelessly toiled in cultivating his field receives the fruits and growths there first before all others, so also you, Timothy, if you tirelessly toil in cultivating the Lord's field (which is the church), then prior to your hearers you will receive the fruit of your toil—that is, a distinct glory and blessedness in heaven." The Syriac follows this construction and renders it *lacara' dlae' qale' leh dqadma' men pi'rawhy nesthaybar* ("It is right for the farmer who toils that he be fed first from his fruits").

Chrysostom (on 2 Timothy 2, homil. 4) interprets it generally about ministers of the Word and how it is right for them to be supported by their hearers. But the apostle's aim is to arouse Timothy by the hope of heavenly rewards for the toils of the office.

The word πρῶτον can be taken as a noun or as an adverb. The former fits the text best.

Verse 7.

νόει ἃ λέγω. ["Keep pondering what I say."] That is, "what I want you to grasp by these comparisons with the soldier, athlete, and farmer."

δῴη γάρ σοι ὁ κύριος σύνεσιν ἐν πᾶσιν. ["And may the Lord grant you understanding in all things."] The Vulgate has [the verb] in the future: *Dabit tibi Dominus intellectum* ["The Lord will give you understanding"]; but the Greek literally contains a prayer: "May the Lord give you understanding." The Syriac rendered it *netel lak maran hecmta'* ("may the Lord give you understanding"), for the verb *ntl* can be explained either way.

The apostle prays for Timothy that the Lord make him to understand not only what he has just said but also everything else that he needs to understand.

Connection. From the exhortation he now moves on to teaching the faith. This he does on account of heretics who were disparaging the resurrection of the dead by twisting this article of the faith into an allegorical sense, claiming that the resurrection had already happened [v. 18]. Therefore, in order to maintain this fundamental article of the faith, he drives home the truth of Christ's resurrection, which is the foundation of our own resurrection. He also drives home the resurrection of Christ because this glory of our Head is the foundation of all our hope and comfort in times of calamity.

Verse 8.

Μνημόνευε Ἰησοῦν χριστὸν ἐγηγερμένον ἐκ νεκρῶν. "Remember that Jesus Christ is risen from the dead." Luther has *Halt im Gedächtnis Jesum Christum, der von den Todten aufferstanden ist.*

The Vulgate added *Dominum,* but neither the Greek nor the Syriac paraphrase supports that.

ἐκ σπέρματος Δαυίδ. ["From the seed of David."] Understand: "Born [from the seed of David]," because this specification (προσδιορισμός) does not apply to the nearer ἐγηγερμένον but the more remote Ἰησοῦν χριστὸν.

The question arises: *Why does the apostle add this?* I respond. (1) Some think that the apostle wanted to say this in opposition to the lies of the Jews who attacked Christ's genealogy, as if He had not been born from David's line or from the tribe of Judah but from some other tribe and family. (2) Others claim that he was opposing the error of heretics who were undermining faith in the

Lord's incarnation by saying that He had a heavenly body or imaginary flesh; from this it followed that He really neither suffered and died nor rose again. Both opinions are possible.

κατὰ τὸ εὐαγγέλιόν μου. ["According to my Gospel."] Some claim that Paul is talking about the Gospel account which he dictated to Luke; thus [Paul] is directing Timothy back to Christ's genealogy in Luke 3[:23–38] to counter the lies of the Jews. Jerome mentions this idea (*Catalog.*, *in Luca*) but does not endorse it.

More correctly it means "preaching of the Gospel." Moreover, he calls it "my Gospel" with respect to the ministry, because Christ entrusted it to him and because it had been diligently performed by his preaching.

This specification applies to both preceding clauses, to both "from the seed of David" and to "raised from the dead." For Paul faithfully taught both in his preaching of the Gospel.

Verse 9.

ἐν ᾧ κακοπαθῶ μέχρι δεσμῶν, ὡς κακοῦργος. ["In which I am suffering evil unto chains as an evildoer."] In the words κακοπαθῶ and κακοῦργος there is an elegant play on words: "I suffer evil as an evildoer."

He adds that he is enduring persecutions for the sake of the Gospel even unto imprisonment and chains in order to confirm the veracity of the Gospel, because no sensible person would want to face endangering his reputation and life for something doubtful and uncertain.

ἀλλ᾽ ὁ λόγος τοῦ θεοῦ οὐ δέδεται. ["But the Word of God is not bound."] God's Word cannot be prevented from accomplishing its purpose and bearing fruit in the places where it is preached (Isa. 55:[11]; Phil. 1:12). But the apostle especially means that not even in jail is he wanting in his office of spreading the Gospel, whether by tongue or pen, speaking or writing.

There is an elegant wordplay and word clash (ἀντανάκλασις) in the words δεσμῶν and δέδεται: "The *chains* may have been put on me, but God's Word has not been *restrained*."

Verse 10.

διὰ τοῦτο πάντα ὑπομένω διὰ τοὺς ἐκλεκτούς. ["Because of this, I endure all things for the sake of the elect."] By διὰ τοῦτο ["because of this"] he is referring back to v. 8: "Because I firmly believe that Christ has been raised from the dead and that I, too, shall rise in His time unto eternal life and glory by the benefit of Christ's resurrection, therefore I endure all things with a patient spirit."

Some take this with the nearer [verse]: "Because of this—that is, so that the Gospel may be disseminated and spread far and wide—I endure all things patiently; I do not run away from any toil, any persecution."

διὰ τοὺς ἐκλεκτούς. ["For the sake of the elect."] Not "so that I may make satisfaction for their sins," but (1) "so that I may promote their salvation by preaching the Gospel"; and (2) "so that I may give them a living example of steadfastness and patience to build them up and strengthen them in faith" (cf. 2 Cor. 1:6).

Yes, but in the assembly of those who are called and have the Gospel preached to them, are not some also condemned? I respond. Of course. In this life the condemned are mixed in with the elect, the goats with the sheep. Hence the same services are applied to them through the ministers of the church. At the same time, however, these are not conducted for the sake of the condemned but for the sake of the elect. Augustine (*De civ. Dei*, bk. 21, ch. 24): "If the church knew who the condemned are, it would no more pray for them than for the devil."

A defense. Estius comments on this passage thus:

> If Paul endured only for the sake of the elect, then Christ also properly suffered only for the sake of the elect—and in fact much more so in His case since in suffering Christ perfectly knew who the condemned were. "I know whom I have chosen" (John 13[:18]). No more should one say that He suffered for the condemned than that He prayed for the condemned. "I am not praying for the world," He says (John 17[:9]).

I respond. (1) Estius stands apart from the more sound Papists who recognize that Christ suffered for all people. This is very common among the Scholastics, that Christ suffered for all with respect to sufficiency though not with respect to efficacy, since, by their own fault, they do not receive the benefits of His Passion. Windeck (*De efficacia mortis Christi*, ch. 14): "Christ offered the sacrifice on the altar of the cross for all the sins of all people in accordance with His and His Father's eternal purpose." [Ibid.] (class. 3): "Christ offered the sacrifice on the altar of the cross for the salvation of every single person." Maldonatus (on Matthew 20): "If you consider Christ's will, then He died for all men without exception. If you consider the benefit, then it does not reach everyone but many, because not all have been willing to receive it."

(2) Estius himself, commenting on 1 Tim. 2:6, cites an excellent statement from Prosper (*Resp. objectionum Vincentianarum*, obj. 1):

> As to the magnitude and power of the price and the single cause of humankind, Christ's blood is the redemption price of the whole world. However, those who spend this life without faith in Christ and without the Sacrament of regeneration are strangers to His redemption. So, then, we rightly say that all men have been redeemed because our Lord in truth took up the one nature of all and the one cause of all mankind, and yet not all have been released from captivity. Because of this, the actual possessing of redemption undoubtedly belongs to those for whom the prince of the world was cast out and who are no longer vessels of the devil but members of Christ.

He continues later: "The cup of immortality, which was made from our weakness and God's strength, does indeed have in itself the power to benefit all men, but if it is not drunk it does not heal." Estius acknowledges that this is consistent with the statements of the Scholastics, that "Christ redeemed all in sufficiency but not in effect." Why, then, instead of agreeing with this distinction, does Estius run off to the Calvinist distinction between "all kinds of individuals" and "every individual"?[2] Moreover, Estius himself adds a little later: "Nothing prevents some things from being done by the saints even for the sake of the condemned that they may receive certain temporal gifts of God's grace, even as they exercise themselves in faith, repentance, righteousness, and especially salvation in time by good works. For Christ merited even these gifts for them by His Passion and bestows them also through His grace." But now, if by His Passion Christ merited for the condemned that they receive certain gifts of grace, then by what semblance of truth can one say that Christ did not also suffer for the condemned? Certainly Christ also suffered for those for whom He merited gifts of grace.

(3) Christ's Passion and Paul's passion are different. Christ's Passion is a λύτρον ["ransom, atonement"] given for all because it is God's earnest purpose and will to save all [1 Tim. 2:3–4]. But Paul's passion is not a λύτρον but a μαρτύριον and δοκιμασία ["a witness and proof"].

(4) Reprobation must not be looked for in some absolute decree of God, but in His consequent and judicial will.[3] Therefore, because our heavenly Father in His antecedent will wants all to be saved and come to acknowledge the truth [1 Tim. 2:4], Christ gave the redemption price for all. Also, because Christ's will is the same as the Father's in heaven [John 5:19; 10:30; 17:11], He therefore gave Himself for all as a λύτρον ["atonement"].

(5) Therefore, though Christ knew perfectly well who the condemned were, one still cannot infer from this that He did not suffer for them. In the end, He condemned unbelievers from eternity according to His *consequent will* in unity with the Father and the Holy Spirit, but according to His *antecedent will* He earnestly desires their salvation and thus also wanted to make provision for them from His merit and the means of salvation.[4]

(6) Although in that specific intercession for the apostles and those who would believe through the apostles' word Christ does not pray for the condemned [John 17], one cannot infer from this that He never prayed in any way

---

2 The Calvinist teaching that Jesus died for all kinds of individuals (*genera singulorum*) but not every individual of all kinds (*singula generum*).

3 See *On Election and Reprobation* [Commonplace X,] §§ 93, 95, as well as Benjamin T. G. Mayes, introduction to *On Creation and Predestination* (Theological Commonplaces VIII–XI), xvii.

4 See *On Election and Reprobation* [Commonplace X], §§ 78–80.

at any time for the whole of mankind and thus also for the condemned. Indeed, He prayed for those who crucified Him [Luke 23:34], and some of them were condemned.

From this very passage Estius tries to conclude that good works are a means of salvation:

> We learn that God's certain election (by which He infallibly elected us for salvation) does not exclude the necessity of good works, so that He makes them, too, a sort of means ordained by Him to fulfill that [election], just as He fulfills this election through the actions and sufferings of His ministers who, along with Paul, must strive in all things in their ministry to this end: that those who have been elected may be saved.

I respond. (1) We do not deny that good works are necessary for those regenerated and justified by faith. What we deny is that they are necessary for salvation, that is, that they merit salvation or are a means of salvation. They are "the way of the kingdom, not the cause of the kingdom."[5]

(2) The actions of the church's ministers are to be accounted differently than their sufferings. The actions of ministers of the church (preaching the Word, administering the Sacraments according to God's institution) are means of salvation because the Gospel they preach "is the power of God unto salvation for all who believe" (Rom. 1:16). Hence Paul writes to Timothy (1 Tim. 4:16): "Pay attention to yourself and the teaching; persist in them, for by doing this you will save both yourself and those who hear you." However, the sufferings of ministers of the church do not merit salvation, nor are they means of it. Rather, they are testimonies to heavenly doctrine by which the faithful are strengthened in faith; they are examples of patience and endurance which they imitate.

(3) How much less, then, are the good works of believers means of salvation. Of course, the faithful should be fruitful in good works, even ζηλωταί ["zealous"] for them [Titus 2:14]. At the same time, however, they cannot, properly speaking, merit or cause salvation for them. Rather, "eternal life is the χάρισμα ('free gift') of God in Christ" (Rom. 6:23).

ἵνα καὶ αὐτοὶ σωτηρίας τύχωσιν. ["So that they, too, may obtain salvation."] Some people think the conjunction καὶ in the Scriptures is often redundant, especially in Paul's writings. But it is more correct to say that through it Paul is including others, so the sense is: "I endure all things for the sake of the elect, not only those who are already believers but also for the sake of the others who are going to be led by the preaching of the Gospel into Christ's flock and, consequently, to salvation."

τῆς ἐν χριστῷ Ἰησοῦ. ["Which is in Christ Jesus."] This salvation does not only come through Christ and because of Christ as the meritorious cause

5 Bernard of Clairvaux, *De grat. et lib. arbit.*, ch. 14.

and giver of salvation, but it is also in Christ because just as we are justified in Christ, so also we are saved in Christ. "God gave us eternal life, this life in His Son" (1 John 5:11). "Eternal life is the χάρισμα of God in Christ" (Rom. 6:23).

μετὰ δόξης αἰωνίου. ["Along with eternal glory."] The Vulgate rendered it *cum gloria caelesti* ["with heavenly glory"]. The Greek text and the Syriac paraphrase have "with eternal glory." Furthermore, this specification should be applied to the word σωτηρίας ["salvation"]: "So that they may obtain salvation together with eternal blessedness and glory, which they will share in Christ, through Christ, and with Christ."

Verse 11.

πιστὸς ὁ λόγος. ["The saying is trustworthy."] This applies to the previous assertion regarding the salvation of the elect, which is the reason he had said that he endures all things.

εἰ γὰρ συναπεθάνομεν, καὶ συζήσομεν. ["For if we have died together, we will also live together."] "If we have died together with Christ in this age, then we shall also live together with Him in the age to come, for we shall be raised to life not only in soul but also in body."

"To die together with Christ" is interpreted by some in regard to that spiritual, saving death wherein we die to sin through the daily putting to death of the old man (Rom. 6:2[–11]). But from the next verse it becomes clear that "to die together with Christ" here means to endure all adversities in this world and even death itself for Christ's name and to be conformed in this way to the suffering and dying Christ (2 Cor. 4:10–11). Chrysostom and the other Greek fathers follow this meaning.

Verse 12.

εἰ ὑπομένομεν, καὶ συμβασιλεύσομεν. ["If we keep enduring, we will also reign together."] The Vulgate has *si sustinebimus* ["if we will endure"], but in the Greek the verb is present tense, as the apostle's meaning demands: "If in this life we endure afflictions, insults, crosses, and death with Christ, then it will come to pass that we shall reign with Him in heaven." (Cf. Rom. 8:17.)

εἰ ἀρνούμεθα, κἀκεῖνος ἀρνήσεται ἡμᾶς. ["If we deny Him, He also will deny us."] This is the antithesis to the previous statement. He described to whom the promise of heavenly glory and reigning belong; now he is explaining who are alienated from it.

"If we deny Him and His Word from fear of death or persecution, then He also will deny us; He will not acknowledge us as His own." This is a reference to Christ's statement in Matt. 10:33 and Luke 12:9.

Verse 13.

εἰ ἀπιστοῦμεν, ἐκεῖνος πιστὸς μένει. ["If we are faithless, He remains faithful."] "If we distrust, if we refuse to have faith in Him, if we do not keep faith in Him, He still remains faithful." Christ casts aside the unbelievers, faithless, and perfidious. At the same time, He Himself remains true and constant in His promises and words. For just as He has promised eternal life to those who persevere in faith, so also He has foretold damnation to those who are unbelievers to the end. (Cf. Mark 16:16; John 3:18, 36.)

Here ἀπιστοῦμεν denotes *positive unbelief* (as it is called), which belongs to those who either refuse to receive the heavenly truth offered in the Word of the Gospel or who reject it again after having once received it.

Rom. 3:3 is a parallel to this verse: "For what if some of them have not believed? Their unbelief does not nullify the faithfulness of God, does it?"

ἀρνήσασθαι ἑαυτὸν οὐ δύναται. ["He cannot deny Himself."] He cannot back out of a word of promise or threat—that is, if there is no added condition to the promise or threat. This, too, should be understood regarding the decrees of God.

One might crassly conclude from this that God is not almighty. But the ability to sin, like the ability to die, is not an ability but rather an inability, a weakness and defect which is to be utterly removed from God who is almighty and completely perfect.

Dionysius (*De div. nom.*, ch. 8) gives this response to Elymas the magician, who asked about this true statement of Paul: "God cannot deny Himself because to deny Himself is to depart from truth. But God is truth, and thus to depart from truth is to depart from God, which is an impossibility and contradiction."

Augustine (*De symbolo*, bk. 1, ch 1): "God is almighty precisely because He cannot do those things" (sin, lie, die). "For if He could do those things, then He would not be almighty. Therefore the great power in God is the inability to lie."

Anselm (*Cur Deus homo*, bk. 3, ch. 17): "Whenever it is said that God cannot, this is not saying that He lacks an ability. Instead, it signifies a superpowerful ability and strength."

Verse 14.

Ταῦτα ὑπομίμνησκε. ["Recall these things."] "Of the things I just spoke admonish the hearers entrusted to your care frequently, and especially those who are your co-workers in preaching the Gospel, that they may patiently endure adversity and persecution in hope of blessedness and glory which will follow."

διαμαρτυρόμενος ἐνώπιον τοῦ κυρίου. ["Solemnly charging before the Lord."] "Call God as witness and judge against them if they refuse to obey your salutary admonitions." (Cf. 1 Tim. 6:13.)

This can be applied both to the preceding and to the following sentences, but it better fits the Greek text to join it to what follows.

μὴ λογομαχεῖν. ["Not to fight over words."] The Vulgate rendered it *noli contendere verbis* ["Do not fight with words"]. However, the Greek text is clear that Paul is not directly telling Timothy to refrain from controversies and fighting with words, but instead he is prescribing for Timothy what he ought to warn others about: "By God as your witness, who will come as judge and avenger, frequently admonish your συνέργους ['co-workers'] in the Gospel about these things: that they not contentiously draw the sword of their words."

Now, λογομαχεῖν means: (1) To quarrel maliciously about words though the matter itself is well established. (2) To employ a method of disputation that is contentious and argumentative. (3) To seek in disputation the prize of victory instead of truth. Augustine (*De doctr. Christ.*, bk. 4, ch. 28): "To 'fight over words' is to be concerned not that truth triumph over error but that your speech gain preference over another's."

Estius here tries to acquit Scholastic theology from the charge of logomachy leveled against it. But we showed (*Confessio Catholica*) that the sounder Papists themselves reprove Scholastic theology on these grounds.

εἰς οὐδὲν χρήσιμον, ἐπὶ καταστροφῇ τῶν ἀκουόντων. ["For no purpose, to the ruin of the hearers."] The Vulgate has *ad nihil enim utile est nisi ad subversionem audientium* ["for it serves no purpose but to ruin the hearers"]. Some take the words εἰς οὐδὲν χρήσιμον as if included in parentheses, thus: "Admonish them not to quarrel over words (which serves no purpose) to the ruin of the hearers." But they can also be rendered without parentheses thus: "Admonish them not to pursue word fights for no advantage but to ruin those who hear." The Syriac has *dla' nehwun metkhareyn bmele' dla' yutran lsukhapa' da'yleyn dsham'iyn lheyn* ("that they not fight in useless speeches to the ruin of those who hear them"). Luther has *[Das] sie nicht umb Wort zanken, welches nichts nütz ist, denn zuverkehren die da zuhören* ["that they not quarrel over words, which is useful for nothing but to mislead those who listen"].

His argument is mounting up: word fights not only lack any fruit, but they also violently harm the hearers, who are disturbed by such quarrels and start to have doubts about the things they believed, and in this way their faith is undercut.

Verse 15.

σπούδασον σεαυτὸν δόκιμον παραστῆσαι τῷ θεῷ. "Strive to present yourself approved to God."

Up to this point [Paul] has been giving Timothy directions as to how he should admonish others, especially his co-workers in the Gospel. Now he admonishes Timothy himself as to how he should conduct himself in the ministry—namely, that above all things he should present himself and his ministry to God as good and be zealous to please Him in all things.

ἐργάτην ἀνεπαίσχυντον. ["As a workman without cause for shame."] Some take this in an active sense. Augustine (*Contra Cresconium*, bk. 1, ch. 2): "Present yourself as a worker who is not ashamed." But others take it in the passive sense: "who will not be put to shame."

Most of those who favor the first sense relate it to this life, the sense being: "Take care to present yourself as such a worker who is uninhibited from ministry and work by any absurd sense of shame, so that you may freely preach the Gospel of Christ and not be ashamed of my chains." (Cf. 2 Tim. 1:8.) But it can also be applied to the Day of Judgment, the sense being: "Present yourself as such a worker who will not be confounded and who should not be put to shame when he will give an account to his Lord."

Those who favor the passive sense teach this meaning: "Present yourself as such a worker who is so faithful and industrious in his work that his Lord may not be ashamed of him but rather delight in him." This is how Erasmus explains it. But the active sense better fits the Greek word ἀνεπαίσχυντον.

ὀρθοτομοῦντα τὸν λόγον τῆς ἀληθείας. "Who cuts the Word of truth straight." Lest anyone think the apostle is giving a command about superstitiously or scrupulously dividing subtleties—or, rather, futile dichotomies—we should note that he does not say διχοτομοῦντα ["dichotomizing, cutting in twos"] but ὀρθοτομοῦντα τὸν λόγον τῆς ἀληθείας.

But what does it mean to "cut the Word of truth straight"?

(1) For the Greeks, τέμνειν ὁδὸν ["to cut a path"] is "to open the way." Καινοτομεῖν is "to cut new paths," that is, to undertake or institute something new. Therefore ὀρθοτομεῖν is "to make or undertake things rightly." Ὀρθοτομοῦντα τὸν λόγον τῆς ἀληθείας means, so to speak, "opening up the straight path of the Word of truth." The LXX translated *yashar* ("cut straight, make straight") with the verb ὀρθοτομεῖν (Prov. 3:6; 11:5). The Syriac renders it *mucre' lariytsa'iyt melta' dashrara'* ("rightly preaching the Word of truth").

(2) To "cut the Word of truth straight" is wisely to give and apply it for the hearer's use. A metaphor may be drawn from servants at a feast and the masters and arrangers of the feast. Or even closer to the truth, a metaphor may be drawn from the Old Testament priests who cut up the sacrificial victim according to the specified rite. One could also draw this comparison: just as the father of a house distributes rations to his children and servants according to the age and needs of each, so also a preacher of the Word, or minister of the church, has been appointed by God to be the distributor for His household, to give every servant "his portion at the proper time" (Luke 12:42). 1 Cor. 3:1–2: "I was unable to speak to you as to people of the Spirit but of the flesh, as to little

children in Christ. I gave you milk to drink, not solid food, for you had not been up to it." Heb. 5:12: "You have come to need milk, not solid food."

(3) By this ὀρθοτομεῖν, Timothy and every minister of the church is told to lay out the chief parts of doctrine in suitable order and to arrange the biblical text methodically, lest, when teaching, things that should go together be pulled apart or things become mixed up that should be separated.

(4) Also [they are told] by that same word [ὀρθοτομεῖν], as if by a knife, to cut out the useless, foreign, and superfluous when preaching the Word of God. So this verb may be understood to command a methodical treatment of Scripture, the distinction of Law and Gospel, a separation of the precious from the cheap. (Cf. Nicolas Fuller, *Miscellan. sacrorum*, bk. 3, ch. 16.)

Theodoret (commentary on this passage): "We praise farmers for plowing straight. So also a teacher is worthy of praise for following the straightedge of the oracles of God." Therefore, according to Theodoret, he "cuts the Word of truth straight" who gives his hearers the teaching of Christ (which is the teaching of Truth) with such faithfulness that he nowhere departs from the rule of truth, which is the Word of God. Gal. 2:14 has the same sense: ὀρθοποδεῖν πρὸς τὴν ἀλήθειαν τοῦ εὐαγγελίου ["to walk straight according to the truth of the Gospel"].

Theophylact and Oecumenius, following Chrysostom, derive a metaphor from tanners who cut out the superfluous from the hides they are preparing: "So also Timothy—and in him every minister of the church—is being told to cut off and throw away the superfluous and tainted when teaching the doctrine of truth."

Verse 16.

τὰς δὲ βεβήλους κενοφωνίας περιΐστασο. ["But flee profane empty talks."] The Vulgate inserts the copulative *et*, but this is not in the Greek nor does it fit, as seen by the parallel 1 Tim. 6:20: ἐκτρεπόμενος τὰς βεβήλους καινοφωνίας ["avoiding profane word novelties"].

There is a strong connection both in form and meaning between καινοφωνίας in 1 Tim. 6:20, which means "word novelties," and κενοφωνίας in this verse, which means "empty talks, idle speech, uproars about empty things." For novelties are usually vain, and vanities are usually new.

τὰς δὲ βεβήλους κενοφωνίας περιΐστασο. "Flee, ward off, do not allow." The sense is that a minister of the church must forbid vain empty talk and clamorous verbosity, especially that which is profane and unbecoming of God's servant who handles the mysteries of God. Luther has *Des ungeistlichen losen Geschwetzes entschlahe dich* ["Have nothing to do with the unspiritual, loose talk"].

ἐπὶ πλεῖον γὰρ προκόψουσιν ἀσεβείας. "For they will advance ungodliness all the more," that is, "they will contribute to greater impiety." Some relate this to things, the sense being: "Profane empty talk is kindling for ungodliness." But Chrysostom more correctly relates it to persons: "By this the apostle is showing that those who have willingly strayed from the truth cannot be fixed or corrected." Therefore the sense is: "Those who utter such empty talk go on all the more in ungodliness, unless, of course, they are kept from them."

This latter interpretation is supported: (1) Because he immediately moves on to persons: "and their speech spreads like cancer" [v. 17]. (2) Because προκόψουσιν ἐπὶ πλεῖον ἀσεβείας more befits men than "empty talk." (3) Because in [2 Tim.] 3:9 and 13 προκόψουσιν is used of men. Therefore the construction is to be taken according to this meaning even though no mention of men preceded it.

Verse 17.

καὶ ὁ λόγος αὐτῶν ὡς γάγγραινα νομὴν ἕξει. "Their speech will have pasture like gangrene, so that it will consume like gangrene"; that is, it will subvert the faith of many (as is explained a little later). Gangrene is the dying out and extinction of some member in the body which arises from a swelling that can neither be dispersed nor changed into pus. It then spreads its infection into the adjacent body parts, not even sparing the bones, which decay and start to die off since they have been soaked in the diseased fluid that flows out of the surrounding tissue. ([See] Galen, *De tumoribus praeter naturam* and *In aphor. Hippocr.*, comment. 7, sect. 7, art. 50; Actuarius, *Περὶ διαγνως. παθ.*, bk. 2, ch. 30; Celsus, bk. 5, ch. 26; Aegineta, bk. 4, ch. 9; Amandus Lusitanus, cent. 3, curat. 32, p. 396.)

The Vulgate translation as well as Luther, who translated it "cancer," claim that the apostle by synecdoche used a species for a kind—that is, gangrene for a disease that spreads like a cancer and devours the adjacent members of the body.

Claudius Espencaeus comments on this verse: "The Greeks and Latins understand that breast cancer, unless quickly treated, putrefies and gradually infects and corrupts all the members; and when the disease gets into the heart there is no treatment."

Many aspects of this comparison can be stated: (1) Gangrene has its origin in small beginnings. So also error seems small in the beginning. (2) Gangrene extinguishes vital heat. So also heretical error extinguishes the truth of teaching and holiness of life. (3) Gangrene daily spreads further, as does heresy. Haymo (commentary on this verse, f. 137): "Just as cancer spreads—that is, increases from member to member—so error spreads, passing from one to many." (4) Gangrene, unless treated quickly, kills people. So also heresy kills people and brings them second death.

ὧν ἐστὶν Ὑμέναιος καὶ Φιλητός. ["Among whom are Hymenaeus and Philetus."] It is not very clear who Philetus was. Of Hymenaeus the apostle says

(1 Tim. 1:20): "I handed him over to Satan along with Alexander"—that is, he excommunicated him as a recalcitrant, incorrigible heretic.

Verse 18.

οἵτινες περὶ τὴν ἀλήθειαν ἠστόχησαν. ["Who have missed the truth."] Those who have wandered away from the scope of truth have fallen into grave error, "making shipwreck of their faith" (1 Tim. 1:19). The Syriac has *haleyn dat'aw* ("who have wandered away from the truth"). Augustine (Letter 119 *ad Januar.*, ch. 3): "Who have wandered round about the truth." Ambrosiaster (commentary on this verse): "Who have wandered off from the truth."

λέγοντες τὴν ἀνάστασιν ἤδη γεγονέναι. ["Saying that the resurrection has already happened."] They ignorantly misapplied what Scripture says about the coming resurrection of bodies at the end of the age to the spiritual resurrection which happens daily through true repentance and faith. As a result, then, they denied the resurrection of bodies.

Some people say that those heretics taught that we should not expect any other resurrection besides the daily one by which men are reborn through the procreation of children and live again, so to speak, in their children. Augustine attributes such a teaching to the Seleucians (*Haeres.* 59): "They do not think there will be a resurrection but that it happens every day in the begetting of children."

At the same time, Augustine (Letter 119 *ad Januar.*) attributes the former opinion to Hymenaeus and Philetus—that what [Scripture] says about the resurrection of bodies should be understood in terms of the daily regeneration and transfer from the death of sin to the life of righteousness. One can relate to this how Tertullian recalls (*De resurr. carn.*, ch. 19) that in his day there was no lack of "those who took the resurrection of the dead so clearly proclaimed and twisted it into an imaginary resurrection, claiming that people have obtained a resurrection with the Lord by faith once they have put on Baptism." Thomas (commentary on this passage) testifies that even in his day there were heretics who took everything Scripture says about the resurrection of the dead and applied it to the resurrection of souls which has already happened within us.

καὶ ἀνατρέπουσιν τήν τινων πίστιν. "They keep corrupting" and "overturning the faith of some." That is, they turn them away from the truth of teaching. In Greek the verb is in the present tense, and by this the apostle signifies that they are not only in error, but they also persist in their perverse zeal to spread error.

The emphasis is on the word for "overturn," because to take away faith in the resurrection is to pull out the foundation of all Christianity, and then the whole building of Christianity immediately collapses into ruins (1 Cor. 15:13[–19]).

Verse 19.

ὁ μέντοι στερεὸς θεμέλιος τοῦ θεοῦ ἕστηκεν. ["Nevertheless the firm foundation of God stands."] Lest one think that he should fear the upheaval of all Christianity due to the overturning of some, the apostle adds this: "Although the faith of some has been overturned, the foundation of God still is not and cannot be overturned."

Some understand the "foundation" to be (1) the decree of election and writing in the book of life—or (what is the same) the eternal, unchanging plan of God for the salvation of the elect. (2) Others understand it to be the promises and testimonies in the Scriptures by which that plan of God is announced to us and confirmed. (3) Others understand it to be the church among His elect, whose faith cannot be overturned in the end. Even though some leave the church, she still remains among His elect. (4) Others understand it to be the faith itself of God's elect, which firmly relies upon Christ as the sole foundation for salvation and which does not allow itself to be overturned by the scoffing of heretics. Even though the faith of some is overturned (that is, of those who are πρόσκαιροί ["for a while," Mark 4:17]), the faith of the elect stands unshaken nonetheless. However, these explanations flow in logical order [*subordinatae*], and none of them are at odds with the analogy of the faith.

ἔχων τὴν σφραγῖδα ταύτην, Ἔγνω κύριος τοὺς ὄντας αὐτοῦ, καί, ἀποστήτω ἀπὸ ἀδικίας πᾶς ὁ ὀνομάζων τὸ ὄνομα χριστοῦ. ["Having this seal: 'The Lord knows those who are His' and 'Let everyone who names the name of Christ depart from iniquity.'"] Those who take "God's firm foundation" to be His decree of election in Christ also take this "seal" to be the fatherly care and providence of God. For the decree of election is confirmed though God's providence as by a seal, seeing as God not only knows those whom He elected by grace in Christ, but He also exercises His fatherly care for them. Others, however, take this "seal" to be the faith of the elect because God seals His promises through faith (as Ambrosiaster says on this passage) and because faith is a sort of mark and token by which believers are made distinct from unbelievers (as Gregory says, *Moral.*, bk. 29, ch. 2).

Moreover, those who take "God's firm foundation" to be the faith of the elect or the church among His elect then take this "seal" to signify the special love of God by which God specially loves His own whom He elected from eternity by grace in Christ and whom He guards from every evil and lapse, bringing them to eternal life. For when the apostle says, "God knows those who are His," he does not mean a theoretical but a practical knowing, that is, knowledge connected with His kind affection and love.

Some understand this "seal" to be the very act of election. They think that it is compared to a seal because it is strong and firm, for the seal affixed to contracts and promises makes them firm and strengthens them.

Chrysostom thinks that this reference is from Deuteronomy, but it is more correct to say that it is from Num. 16:5: "The Lord will make known the one who belongs to Him" or "who is His." The LXX has ἐπέγνω or, as other copies read, ἔγνω ὁ θεὸς τοὺς ὄντας αὐτοῦ ["God knows those who are His"]. So, then, just as the Lord gave a public indication there and made known whom He had chosen for leadership and priesthood, so also He chooses[6] the elect for eternal life, keeps them in faith, and in this way makes their election known by an external indication.

For the second part (ἀποστήτω ἀπὸ ἀδικίας πᾶς ὁ ὀνομάζων τὸ ὄνομα χριστοῦ) there are different readings. Most Greek copies today read χριστοῦ, but some, including the *Editio Complutensis*, read κυρίου, which is how the Syriac paraphrase reads as well. The Vulgate translated the verb ὀνομάζων with the verb *invocare* ["to call upon, invoke"], as also it translated Acts 19:13—ὀνομάζειν τὸ ὄνομα τοῦ κυρίου Ἰησοῦ ["to name the name of the Lord Jesus"]—*invocare nomen Domini* ["to call upon the name of the Lord"]. But now, (1) not all Latin copies read this way. Some have *nominat* ["names"]. (2) Ὀνομάζων can be taken in its usual meaning here: "whoever names the name of Christ"—that is, professes himself a Christian, says that he embraces Christian teaching, and wants to be a member of Christ's church.

Thomas and Cajetan make the apostle's sentence here the second part of the "seal," since the apostle alludes the same as before to Num. 16:21 and 26: "Be separated from the midst of this congregation. Depart from the tents of those ungodly people, and do not touch what belongs to them, lest you become involved in their sins." Thus the meaning would be: "Let whoever says he belongs to Christ depart from unrighteousness, and whoever keeps on doing this can firmly conclude from this mark that he is in the number of the elect."

In nearly the same way Piscator understands the "seal" to be

> those two dispositions of souls that the apostle mentions, namely, faith—by which one apprehends that "God knows those who are His," that is, He loves His own and therefore He also embraces me with His fatherly love—and, second, the earnest pursuit of piety, which speaks to everyone this axiom as if declared by the voice of God: "Let everyone who names the name of the Lord depart from unrighteousness." For everyone's soul is sealed, so to speak, by these two dispositions—that is, it is made certain about election and salvation.

Others, however, claim that the effect of the seal (that is, of eternal election) is meant by this statement, for it is through election (which belongs to those who persevere in faith in Christ) that they also depart from iniquity and

6 Reading *deligit* instead of *diligit*.

become zealous for holy living. Neither explanation, rightly understood, is at odds with the analogy of the faith.

Some understand ἀδικίας to mean "falsehood" as opposed to truth (Rom. 2:8). Some understand it as "shameful living." But it is more correct to take it as a general reference to any iniquity, since it is not enough for certainty about one's election for one to abstain from one kind of sin, but he must restrain himself from all sins against conscience.

Verse 20.

Ἐν μεγάλῃ δὲ οἰκίᾳ οὐκ ἔστιν μόνον σκεύη χρυσᾶ καὶ ἀργυρᾶ, ἀλλὰ καὶ ξύλινα καὶ ὀστράκινα. ["Now, in a great house there are not only vessels of gold and silver but also of wood and clay."] The apostle's aim is to teach that no one should think it strange that in the external society of the church nonsaints, who soon quit the faith or lead shameful and ungodly lives, are mixed in with the true believers and saints.

So far be it that one should find it strange that in the church the wicked are mixed in with the good that instead one ought to regard this as belonging to the order of God's providence. For His providence knows how to use well even the wicked for His purposes planned according to His divine goodness and wisdom, just as the father of a house has all manner of vessels in his home and knows how to use them for certain purposes.

By "vessels of gold and silver" he means "precious ones"; by "of wood and clay" he means "cheap ones."

καὶ ἃ μὲν εἰς τιμήν, ἃ δὲ εἰς ἀτιμίαν. ["The ones are for honor, but the others for dishonor."] In the words τιμήν and ἀτιμίαν there is a nice play on words. Some Latin translators have expressed it *alia ad decus, alia ad dedecus* ("the ones adapted to honorable uses, but the others to dishonorable and lowly uses").

This arrangement should be applied to both kinds of vessels with this sense: as with vessels made of gold and silver, so those of wood and clay are put to use—the ones for honorable uses, but the others for dishonorable uses.

"Great house." (1) Chrysostom and those who follow him understand this to be "the world, in which the good and bad are mixed together just as the wheat and the tares are in the field."

(2) Cyprian (Letters, bk. 3, ep. 3; bk. 4, eps. 2, 51, 52) and Augustine (*De bapt. contra Donatist.*, bk. 3, chs. 18–19; bk. 4, ch. 12; bk. 7, ch. 51; this is confirmed by the author of the commentaries on Paul's Epistles carrying the name "Ambrose," bk. 2, chs. 12 and 18, on this passage) think that it means "the church in the wide sense, in that it includes all who confess the name of Christ, be they catholics or heretics or schismatics; in this way the pagans often claim that there are many sects among the Christians."

Obviously the matter itself shows that this means the church, for no one is puzzled or bothered by the fact that wicked men exist in the world, but that they are in the church, and so much so that many forsake her on account of wickedness.

Some take the "vessels of gold and silver" to be those who are talented, eloquent, erudite, and endowed with manifold gifts of the Holy Spirit. They take the "vessels of wood and clay" to be those who have few or none of such gifts.

Others take the "vessels of gold and silver" to mean those who have been ordained in the ministry, that is, bishops, presbyters, and deacons. They explain the "vessels of wood and clay" to mean men of a lower order. They prove this explanation based on 1 Corinthians 12.

"Vessels for honor" means the elect while "vessels for dishonor" means the reprobate, an explanation proved from Rom. 9:23.

Therefore this apostolic passage proves that in the external society of the church even the hypocrites, wicked, and reprobate have a place. Chrysostom and Theophylact do not deny this, for they are using the word "church" narrowly for that portion of the church to which that name properly belongs, that is, for those who are true, living members of the church.

Verse 21.

ἐὰν οὖν τις ἐκκαθάρῃ ἑαυτὸν ἀπὸ τούτων. ["Therefore, if one cleanses himself from these things."] "These things" can refer to:

(1) The things in vv. 16 and 19 where he dealt with empty talk and unrighteousness.

(2) The people he discussed in vv. 16[–18], namely, corrupt teachers.

(3) The vessels of dishonor from v. 20. The devout should cleanse themselves of these, that is, separate themselves from them and avoid fellowship with them.

But these interpretations can be joined together in a very good way: "if anyone cleanses himself from the corruptions of doctrine and life that corrupt the vessels of dishonor." Properly speaking, it is not from men but from corruptions and vices that we are cleansing ourselves.

ἔσται σκεῦος εἰς τιμήν. ["He will be a vessel for honor."] "He demonstrates by this fact that he belongs to the number of the elect; he will be taken up for honorable use and receive the eternal life to which he was predestined before the foundation of the world."

ἡγιασμένον καὶ εὔχρηστον τῷ δεσπότῃ εἰς πᾶν ἔργον ἀγαθὸν ἡτοιμασμένον. ["Sanctified and useful to the master, prepared for every good work."] "Sanctified to the Lord" because he has been purified from the corruption of doctrine and life and has been consecrated to the Lord. "Useful to the Lord"—that is, adapted for the Lord's uses, and especially such uses as belong only to those who are truly pious and elect, namely, for the good of the neighbor and the glory of God.

Δεσπότῃ ["master"] means Christ, who is the "master" of this great house and whose purposes all the vessels serve (Heb. 3:6).

"Prepared"—both through eternal predestination (Eph. 2:10) and through the grace of rebirth and sanctification (2 Cor. 4:7). Of ourselves "we are useless" (Luke 17:10), but through God's grace He prepares us to be useful for every good work.

Connection. [The apostle] returns to his exhortation to Timothy and warns him as a youth to flee youthful lusts and passions.

Verse 22.

Τὰς δὲ νεωτερικὰς ἐπιθυμίας φεῦγε. ["So flee youthful passions."] Such "youthful passions" include craving honor, desiring to stand out and be famous, and despising others (which is usually the result of these).

Some relate this to fleeing the desires of lust and the pleasures of the flesh. However, if we would consider Timothy's person and the circumstances of his office, it will be clear that this is more correctly related to the vices of the mind to which young men raised to high office tend to be exposed. The same becomes clear from the antithesis below.

δίωκε δὲ δικαιοσύνην, πίστιν, ἀγάπην, εἰρήνην, μετὰ τῶν ἐπικαλουμένων τὸν κύριον ἐκ καθαρᾶς καρδίας. ["But pursue justice, faith, love, peace with those who call upon the Lord from a pure heart."] "Pursue justice," that you give everyone what is his and so also give "honor to whom honor is owed" (Rom. 13:7). "Faith," that you embrace the mysteries of the faith with simple assent without contentious arguing. "Love," which "is not puffed up, does not conduct itself unbecomingly, does not seek its own, but is patient and kind" (1 Cor. 13:4–5). "Peace" with those with whom you live in the church.

μετὰ τῶν ἐπικαλουμένων τὸν κύριον ἐκ καθαρᾶς καρδίας. ["With those who call upon the Lord from a pure heart."] Some explain this by the example of all the truly pious (Thomas and Cajetan): "As for you, pursue those virtues with all who call upon God, for these virtues are common to all the faithful." But it is more correct to take this thus: Timothy should have peace with all who call upon Christ, which peace is upset by empty talking and useless controversy.

This stands in contrast to Hymenaeus, Philetus, and others of their ilk [*farinae*] (or, rather, junk [*furfuris*]). Timothy should not seek peace and friendship with them, but loathe, avoid, and flee them.

Verse 23.

τὰς δὲ μωρὰς καὶ ἀπαιδεύτους ζητήσεις παραιτοῦ, εἰδὼς ὅτι γεννῶσι μάχας. ["But cast away foolish and ignorant controversies, knowing that they breed fights."] By "foolish and ignorant controversies" he means those which do nothing for faith or love; they add nothing to true Christian wisdom.

παραιτοῦ. "Cast away," that you neither introduce them before the church yourself nor allow others to stir them up.

γεννῶσι μάχας. "[They breed] fights" of words, which he called **λογομαχίας** in 1 Tim. 6:4. For it often happens that people, driven by overfervent zeal and grave emotions, argue over things that are of little importance to godliness.

Verse 24.

δοῦλον δὲ κυρίου οὐ δεῖ μάχεσθαι, ἀλλ' ἤπιον εἶναι πρὸς πάντας. ["But a servant of the Lord must not be quarrelsome but gentle toward all."] He adds the reason why Timothy and any minister of the church should refuse foolish and ignorant controversies that breed word fights: because it is improper for a servant of the Lord (that is, a minister of the church) to be contentious and to fight over things that do not matter.

He is not condemning the disputations but correcting the vices of the disputants.

By "Lord" he means Christ, who is frequently called "Lord" in the New Testament. Within this term for a teacher of the church there is a tacit confirmation of the minor [proposition] for the argument at hand: "Foolish and ignorant controversies cause word fights. But now, a minister of the church should keep away from word fights. Therefore." The rationale behind the minor proposition is: because he is a servant of that Lord who is "not a God of discord but of peace" (1 Cor. 14:33). Therefore he should imitate Him.

ἤπιον. "Gentle, calm, tender, kind toward all." *But how must he be tender toward all since sometimes church discipline demands sternness?* I respond. Although a minister of the church should sometimes be stern according to the people, time, and place, he should still temper this sternness with tenderness and always keep the disposition of tenderness fixed in his spirit.

διδακτικόν. ["Apt to teach."] The Vulgate rendered this in poor Latin as *docibilem* ["docile, teachable"]. In 1 Tim. 3:2 it rendered it *doctorem* ["teacher"]. It properly signifies "one who is endowed with gifts for teaching, apt to teach." In this verse it signifies one who would rather teach than yell and compel.

Cyprian (Letter *ad Pompeianum*) seems to take *docibilem* ["docile"] passively: "A bishop should not only teach but also learn, because he teaches all the better who daily grows and progresses by learning better." Augustine praises this quote of Cyprian's (*De bapt.*, bk. 5, ch. 26). But **διδακτικόν** is active in meaning.

ἀνεξίκακον. ["Enduring evil men."] The Vulgate rendered it *patientem* ["suffering, patient"], but the Greek properly signifies "one who endures evil men." Some take this about things, because a minister of the church should patiently endure persecutions and adversity. But the context shows that it is better to relate it to people, because he must endure evil men with equanimity, as long as there is still some hope for their conversion.

Apparent contrariety. In Rev. 2:2 the angel of the church at Ephesus is praised for being "unable to endure those who are evil." I respond. Evil men should not be endured in such a way that we try to be complaisant with their vices and look the other way, but that we overcome their impudence with gentleness, as long as there is still some hope of converting them.

Verse 25.

ἐν πρᾳότητι παιδεύοντα τοὺς ἀντιδιατιθεμένους. ["Instructing the opponents with gentleness."] Luther took ἐν πρᾳότητι with the previous verse in his German translation, but in the Greek text and in the Vulgate it goes with what follows it.

That said, the Vulgate translation rendered ἐν πρᾳότητι [as] *cum modestia* ["with restraint"] (which is how Ambrose also quotes it, *De Abraham*, bk. 2, ch. 6), but the Greek words properly signify "with gentleness."

Some render παιδεύοντα as "correcting" while others have it "instructing." Although the verb παιδεύειν means both, the latter sense fits the context better since instruction must precede correction in those who still do not know the truth.

Augustine (commentary on Galatians 6, tom. 3): "How 'with restraint'? How 'correcting,' unless while we keep tenderness in the heart we also apply some bitter medicine by a word of correction?"

τοὺς ἀντιδιατιθεμένους. ["The opponents."] Those who are committed to another religion and who disagree not from malice or obstinacy but from ignorance and human weakness; those who are afflicted by contrary thinking, who resist the truth of heavenly teaching. Ambrosiaster: "With restraint correcting those who think differently." Augustine also reads it thus (*De corrept. et grat.*, ch. 5).

The Vulgate adds *veritati* ["to the truth"] from [2 Tim.] 3:8, where it says, "Those who are opposed to the truth." But this addition is not found in the Greek or the Syriac.

μήποτε δῷ αὐτοῖς ὁ θεὸς μετάνοιαν. ["Someday God may grant them repentance."] The Vulgate has *ne quando det illis Dominus paenitentiam* ["Lest God ever grant them repentance."] But the Greek μήποτε sometimes means *si quando* ["someday"]. This is how Ambrosiaster has it in his text, and this meaning best fits the context. A negation, however, clearly does not fit.

The sense is this: "Even if their conversion does not seem to follow after instructing them once, one should still bear with them in gentleness and keep instructing them while praying for and expecting God's help so that they may be brought to repentance through this teaching and correction."

(1) Chrysostom, Theophylact, and Oecumenius rightly conclude from this passage that the conversion of a sinner is God's doing.

(2) Still, however, God does not want to work this conversion apart from means but uses the work of the ecclesiastical ministry to effect it.

(3) At the same time, this external ministry of the Word, teaching, and correction is in vain unless God works inwardly through grace.

εἰς ἐπίγνωσιν τῆς ἀληθείας. ["Unto a recognition of the truth."] Some claim that the preposition εἰς is a Hebraism for ἐν or διὰ: "through a recognition of the truth," "when a change of mind arises from a recognition of the truth." So the sense is: "Someday God may grant them to recognize the truth and repent." However, the usual meaning of the preposition εἰς can also stand, so the sense would be: "Someday God may grant them such a change of mind that, when a messenger is sent to address their errors, they will recognize and embrace the truth."

Estius comments on this passage: "In the justification of man, faith is prior to repentance." I respond. There must be a distinction between historical faith, which includes only knowledge and assent, and justifying faith, which includes a trusting apprehension of Christ's merit. Taken in the former sense, faith is prior to repentance (Jon. 3:5), but in the latter sense faith is the second essential part of repentance. [Faith], along with contrition, completes [repentance] (Mark 1:15).

Verse 26.

καὶ ἀνανήψωσιν ἐκ τῆς τοῦ διαβόλου παγίδος. ["And they may come to their senses, [released] from the snare of the devil."] "They may return to sobriety, to a more sound mind, through the enlightening of the Holy Spirit, after being in error and sin for some time, as if they were drunk." Luther has *dass sie wieder nüchtern würden* ["that they become sober again"].

ἐκ τῆς τοῦ διαβόλου παγίδος. "From the snare of the devil." Understand: "released." The Vulgate rendered it in the plural: *ex laqueis Diaboli* ["from the snares of the devil"], because the devil keeps the unrepentant trapped with more than one kind of snare.

From this passage the following description of true repentance can be deduced: it is the conversion of the will, which was formerly obedient to the devil because of a spiritual drunkenness of the mind, to yield to God with the mind as if brought to sobriety.

ἐζωγρημένοι ὑπ' αὐτοῦ. ["Having been captured by him."] The Vulgate has *a quo captivi tenentur* ["by whom they are held captives"]. Some codices read *capti* ["captured"], which better fits the Greek text, for ἐζωγρημένοι properly means "to be caught alive," as when hunting something alive as in trapping or fowling. Thus does the devil, that hellish hunter, capture men alive when he traps them in the nets of his temptations.

εἰς τὸ ἐκείνου θέλημα. "To obey his will." Some take the pronoun **ἐκείνου** to the remoter "God," who was mentioned earlier in v. 25. In this way this specification would apply to the verb ἀνανήψωσιν ["come to their senses"]. However, it is more aptly related to the nearer "devil," and thus this specification depends on the participle ἐζωγρημένοι ["having been captured"].

Note: Sinners are held captive under the power of the devil until a stronger One comes, undoes the traps, and restores the captives to freedom.

Theophylact takes this specification with the word ἐζωγρημένοι, but he still understands τὸ ἐκείνου θέλημα ["that one's will"] to be God's will and not the devil's, the sense being:

> The opponents of heavenly truth are held captive by the devil according to God's will, that is, by the just judgment of God and as long as God wants, for not even the devil himself can resist His will. Accordingly, even though the devil resists and fights back, they can be freed from those snares of the devil through the ministry of the Word, through the teaching and correction of faithful ministers of the church. This should encourage ministers of the church to keep on teaching and correcting them, for someday God may work repentance in their hearts and loose the bonds of their long-standing captivity.

This interpretation is strengthened by the fact that the Greek does not read **αὐτοῦ** ("his") but **ἐκείνου** ("that one's"). This demonstrative, according to Greek usage, should refer not to the nearer but to the farther.

That said, the first explanation (that "the will of that one" refers to the devil) is simpler, and even Theophylact mentions it. Also, there are many places where **ἐκείνου** also refers to nearer [referents] (Matt. 17:27; Mark 16:20; John 1:8, 18).

Chrysostom (on Matthew, hom. 37):

> Before we sin, all men do indeed have free choice as to whether we will follow the devil's will or not. But once we sin we bind ourselves to his works, and now we cannot escape by our own strength. Instead, just as a ship with a broken rudder is driven where the storm wills, so also man, having lost the help of God's grace through sin, does not do what he wants but what the devil wants. And unless God releases him by His strong hand for His mercy's sake, he will remain in the bonds of his sins unto death, (etc.). We see this also in the kings of this world. No one can make himself king, but the people create for themselves a king whom they elect. But once the king has been crowned and sits on the throne, he now has authority over men, and the people cannot cast his yoke off their neck. For at first it is within the people's power to make a king for themselves of anyone they

want. But it is not in their power to take him off the throne now that he has been made king, and thus their will turns into compulsion. So it is with man. Before he sins he has free choice as to whether he will live under the devil's kingdom or not. But once he hands himself over to his kingdom by sinning, now he cannot escape [the devil's] power, but his primary will turns into compulsion.

Chapter III

There are three parts to this chapter.

(1) The apostle's prophetic prediction about the state of the end times (vv. 1–9).

(2) An illustration of the apostle's example in showing patience, set forth to be imitated (vv. 10–12).

(3) An earnest forewarning against deceivers and an exhortation to read Holy Scripture diligently (vv. [13]–17).

Verse 1.

Τοῦτο δὲ γίνωσκε. ["Now know this."] Lest Timothy or anyone else be astonished or offended that evil men and hypocrites multiply in the church, he forewarns that this will happen.

ὅτι ἐν ἐσχάταις ἡμέραις ἐνστήσονται καιροὶ χαλεποί. ["That in the last days there will be hard times."] By ἐσχάταις ἡμέραις ["last days"] he means the entire time from Christ's first coming until His second coming. Thus his prediction applies even to Timothy's times, for he adds "avoid these also" [v. 5]. Therefore he means the entire time following the apostolic age (cf. 1 Tim. 4:1).

καιροὶ χαλεποί. ["Hard times."] The Vulgate rendered this *tempora periculosa* ["dangerous times"], but in Greek it is literally "hard times" in which it is hard to decide how one should act in relation to those men. It can also be translated "troublesome times," because nothing more troublesome can befall a pious man than to have to fight with such men. Luther rendered it *greuliche Zeiten* ["dreadful times"]. It can also be translated *beschwerliche Zeiten* ["burdensome times"].

Such times can be considered by metonymy on account of the things that happen in time, especially on account of the ways and pursuits of the men who will live in those times. Note, then, that the apostle does not place the difficulties of the times in external evils (war, famine, plague, etc.), but in the wicked ways of men.

Verse 2.

ἔσονται γὰρ οἱ ἄνθρωποι φίλαυτοι. ["For people will be lovers of the self."] The Vulgate has *seipsos amantes, sui amantes* ["loving themselves, lovers of self"]. Augustine marvelously explains the force of this word (on John, tract. 123): "In an inexplicable way, anyone who loves himself and not God does not love himself; but anyone who loves God but not himself, he is the one who loves himself. For one who cannot live of himself surely dies by loving himself. Therefore he does not love himself who loves himself to death. However, when one loves Him from whom is life, by not loving himself he loves more, who therefore does not love himself so that he may love Him from whom he lives."

The apostle listed this vice first because it is the source and origin of the others. Augustine (ibid.): "When the apostle said, 'People will be lovers of themselves,' he continued by adding 'lovers of money, arrogant, proud, blasphemers,'" (etc.). "All these evils flow from the one he listed first as from a spring: 'loving themselves.'" Again (beginning of *De civ. Dei*): "The love of self built the city of the devil, just as the love of God built the city of God."

Theophylact (on this verse, "loving themselves"): "He immediately brought the cause of all evils to the forefront—that everyone looks out for his own good more than for his neighbor's. For one who is governed only by love of himself often ends up not even loving himself."

Apparent contrariety. *Eph. 5:[29]: "No one ever hated his own flesh." But here he lists love of self among the most grievous of vices.* I respond. One must distinguish between the ordinate love of self (of which there is mention in "You shall love your neighbor as yourself" [Matt. 19:19]) and the inordinate or perverse (which is mentioned in this verse). Those who are lovers of the self are those who seek what is theirs, who take pains only for their own good.

φιλάργυροι. ["Lovers of money."] The Vulgate has *cupidi* ["desirous"]. The Greek properly means "lovers of money, desirous of riches"; so also φίλαυτοι is "desirous of honor."

ἀλαζόνες. ["Proud."] The Vulgate has *elati* ["puffed up"]. Ambrosiaster has *insolentes* ["arrogant"]. The Greek word properly means "boaster, braggart, show-off." Luther has *ruhmretig* ["boastful"]. The grammarians derive it from ἄλη ["wandering"] and ζωή ["life"], so that it properly means "one who wanders for a living," like those called ἀγύρται, that is, "vagabonds," and as a result a "boaster, show-off, braggart." Xenophon (*Paed.*, bk. 2): Ὁ μὲν γὰρ ἀλαζὼν ἔμοιγε δοκεῖ ὄνομα κεῖσθαι ἐπὶ τοῖς προσποιουμένοις καὶ πλουσιωτέροις εἶναι ἢ εἰσὶ καὶ ἀνδρειοτέροις καὶ ποιήσειν ἃ μὴ ἱκανοί εἰσιν ὑπισχνουμένοις. ("For it seems to me that the word ἀλαζὼν has been given to those who present themselves richer and more vigorous than they are, who make promises they cannot keep.") Ulpian, expounder of Demosthenes, says that ἀλαζονεία is characteristic "of men who promise more than they can keep."

ὑπερήφανοι. "Haughty." Those who despise the humble and lowly. *Übersichtige*, ἀλαζονεία, arrogance arises in words and actions from a ὑπερηφανία, haughtiness hiding in one's spirit.

βλάσφημοι. "Slanderous." Some explain this as being slanderous toward God, but the Greek word is general and denotes those who injure the reputation of others so that they alone can stand out. Luther has *Lästerer*.

γονεῦσιν ἀπειθεῖς. "Disobedient to parents." The Greek properly signifies those who do not allow themselves to be convinced that they owe obedience to their parents. The Syriac rendered it *la'nashayhun la' mettpiysiyn* ("not obeying their own men").

ἀχάριστοι. ["Thankless."] The disobedient and the thankless are connected because the former arises from the latter.

ἀνόσιοι. ["Profane."] The Vulgate has *scelesti* ["scoundrels"], but the Greek properly signifies "the profane, impious, despisers of religion and the sacred." They have no regard for what is holy and right to keep them from daring to commit crimes. Luther has *ungeistliche*.

Verse 3.

ἄστοργοι. ["Heartless."] Those who utterly lack natural affections toward parents, children, and brothers. Luther has *störrige*. The Vulgate has *sine affectione*—those who are not touched by any affection of love toward their neighbor, not even toward those whom nature especially tends to drive us to love.

ἄσπονδοι. "Perfidious, faithless." Σπονδή signifies familiarity and friendship, hence the ἄσπονδοι are those who break oaths or who are unappeasable and refuse reconciliation. Ambrosiater has *sine fide* ["without credibility"]. The Vulgate has here *sine pace* ["without peace"] and, in Rom. 1:31, *sine foedere* ["without agreement"]. Luther has *unversöhnliche*.

διάβολοι. "False accusers," those who suppress the innocence of others by lies and fictitious accusations. The Vulgate has *criminatores*. Luther has *schänder*.

ἀκρατεῖς. "Uncontrolled," those who wallow in the pleasures of the flesh. Luther has *unkeusch*; the Vulgate, *intemperantes*.

ἀνήμεροι. "Savage," those given to behave like animals. The Vulgate has *immites*; Luther, *wilde*.

ἀφιλάγαθοι. ["Not loving good."] This can be taken with reference to people and things, those who love neither what is good nor those who are good. Ambrosiaster: "enemies of the good." The Syriac has *sanyay tabata'* ("haters of the good"). Luther has *ungütige*. It is more probable to take it with reference to people so that it signifies those who flee from friendship with good men and hate them on account of their disparate behavior.

Verse 4.

προδόται. "Treacherous, deserters of friendship," those who toss well-deserving friends to the perils of life.

προπετεῖς. "Reckless, rash," those who follow the impulses of their desires without reason or counsel. The Vulgate has *protervi*; Luther, *Freveler.*

τετυφωμένοι. "Puffed up with arrogance," those who are full of themselves and teeming with derisiveness. The Vulgate has *tumidi*; Luther, *auffgeblasene.*

φιλήδονοι μᾶλλον ἢ φιλόθεοι. "Loving pleasure more than God." There is an elegant play on words in the Greek.

Moreover, because here the apostle is not only discussing evil men but also false teachers, Augustine (on John, tract. 123) elegantly applies all these things to false teachers:

> Let those who feed Christ's sheep not be "lovers of self" nor feed them as their own but as His. For they want to profit from them, as "lovers of money," and to lord it over them, as "haughty"; to boast about the honors they receive from them, as "braggarts"; to go so far as to cause divisions, as "blasphemers." They fail to give deference to the holy fathers, as "those who do not obey their parents." They repay evil for good to those who seek to correct them because they do not want them to perish, as "unthankful." They murder souls—both their own and those of others—as "wicked." They demolish the motherly womb of the church, as "irreligious," and fail to suffer with the weak, as "those without feeling." They try to tarnish the reputation of the saints, as "detractors," and fail to check the worst of lusts, as "those without self-control." They bring lawsuits, as "harsh," and they do not know how to help, as "those lacking kindness." To the enemies of the faithful they point out what they know should be kept hidden, as "traitors." They disturb proper modesty by shameless agitation, as "insolent." They neither understand what they are saying nor about what they are making assertions, as "blind." They prefer carnal pleasures to spiritual joys, as "those who love pleasure more than God." These vices and ones like them—whether they all rule in one man, or some of them in these, others in those—they all bring corruption from the same root: when men are "lovers of self." And this vice must especially be guarded against by those who feed Christ's sheep.

Verse 5.

ἔχοντες μόρφωσιν εὐσεβείας, τὴν δὲ δύναμιν αὐτῆς ἠρνημένοι. ["Having the shaping of godliness but having denied its power."] The Vulgate has *habentes speciem quidem pietatis, virtutem autem eius abnegantes.* ["Although they have the appearance of godliness, they deny its power."]

The Greek word μόρφωσιν properly signifies "shaping." Ambrosiater reads *formam* ["shape"]. (1) Some understand this as "the appearance, image, likeness of godliness," so that it speaks against hypocrites, the sense being: "By their external words and actions they carry godliness before themselves, but in truth they do not have it—actually, they are so far from it that it seems they have denied it and sworn against it." (2) Others think it means that they are being reproved as those who are good at teaching others what must be done, but they still hardly do it themselves (cf. Matt. 23:3). For μόρφωσιν signifies the method of teaching and shaping, as when a teacher teaches a student how he should speak or act (cf. Rom. 2:20). However, both explanations can be united. For those who teach others the rules of godliness but do not keep them themselves have the μόρφωσιν of godliness.

The "power of godliness" consists in true faith in Christ, which "purifies the heart" (Acts 15:9); in spiritual, inner obedience of the heart (1 Tim. 1:5); and in genuine, sincere love for God and neighbor. This, then, is "to live piously in Christ" ([2 Tim. 3:]12).

Some want "power" to stand for "truth," for the truth of anything in nature is grasped from its power and working.

Ἠρνημένοι is a participle not of the present tense (as the Vulgate rendered it) but of the past: "having denied."

καὶ τούτους ἀποτρέπου. ["Turn away from these people also."] The Vulgate has *devita* ["avoid"], but the Greek properly signifies "to turn away from them" by (1) not consenting or approving, (2) removing one's self from them, (3) and not being yoked with them.

Based on this apostolic admonition, we may conclude that Paul is speaking about future circumstances in such a way that he may still show that there will be no lack of such people even in Timothy's day, otherwise it would not have been worthwhile to urge Timothy to turn away from them.

Verse 6.

Ἐκ τούτων γάρ εἰσιν οἱ ἐνδύνοντες [εἰς] τὰς οἰκίας. ["For among these are those who press into houses."] The Vulgate has *ex his enim sunt qui penetrant domos*. The Greek ἐνδύνοντες is the same here as καταδύνειν ("enter thoroughly or deeply; betake one's self into the inner recesses"). Hence Hesychius generically explains καταδύνειν as τοὺς λαθρίους τόπους καὶ βαθεῖς ("[to enter] hidden and deep places"). Suidas specifically and distinctly explains them as φωλεοὺς, ὑπονόμους, πήλαια ("dens or lairs, holes or underground passages, and caves"). Therefore it does not only denote their secret entrance into homes but especially how they were invading the full depths, so to speak, seeking the most hidden inner things and searching and acquainting themselves with every intimate detail.

Ambrosiaster reads *qui irrepunt in domos* ["who creep into homes"]. A parallel passage is found in Titus 1:11: οἵτινες ὅλους οἴκους ἀνατρέπουσιν, διδάσκοντες ἃ μὴ δεῖ, αἰσχροῦ κέρδους χάριν ["They are overturning entire houses by teaching what they should not, for the sake of shameful gain"].

καὶ αἰχμαλωτεύοντες τὰ γυναικάρια. "Utterly subjecting naïve women to themselves." They either inflict empty fear upon them or deceive them with their charm; they make them so compliant that, like captives, they can seemingly be led in any direction. In the prior case [the apostle] had chided the impudence of the false teachers, but here he chides these men's fraud whereby they insinuate themselves upon the sex that is not as strong in discernment and reason. He uses the diminutive to signify that he is talking about those women who are quite naïve and fickle.

σεσωρευμένα ἁμαρτίαις. ["Burdened with sins."] That is, burdened and overwhelmed by a heap of sins. The Scriptures often compare sins to a most burdensome weight that presses man down. Ps. 38:4: "My iniquities came over my head; like a heavy weight they weighed me down." Lam. 1:14: "The yoke of my iniquities was tied on; by His hand they were tied up and placed upon my neck."

Furthermore, they are called "burdened with sins," either because, seduced by the false teachers themselves, they were burdened with this yoke or because they put this burden on themselves because previously they had led a dishonorable life stained by sins of the flesh. Chrysostom follows the latter.

ἀγόμενα ἐπιθυμίαις ποικίλαις. "Who are driven by various passions," namely, detestable passions of vice. The Vulgate renders it *quae ducuntur* ["who are led"], but the Greek properly signifies *aguntur* ["driven"], because these naïve women, like beasts, allow themselves to be driven into various sins by their depraved desires and perverse affections. Luther has *sie fahren mit mancherlei Lüsten* ["they go on with various desires"].

Verse 7.

πάντοτε μανθάνοντα, καὶ μηδέποτε εἰς ἐπίγνωσιν ἀληθείας ἐλθεῖν δυνάμενα. "Always learning but never able to arrive at a knowledge of the truth," since they are fickle and always look for something new.

Some Latin commentators relate this to the false teachers, but it is clear from the Greek text that it should refer to the naïve women.

It says that "they cannot arrive at the truth" (1) because they were taking in errors and not truth from these teachers; or (2) because they were not content with the teaching given from the apostles. Because of their curiosity and fickle minds, they kept seeking new teachings, ones that corresponded to their cravings (cf. 2 Tim. 4:3).

Verse 8.

ὃν τρόπον δὲ Ἰαννῆς καὶ Ἰαμβρῆς ἀντέστησαν Μωϋσεῖ. ["And in this way Jannes and Jambres opposed Moses."] The apostle uses this example to teach that it is nothing strange if true teachers still today suffer bitter enemies of the truth, for Moses and the prophets suffered their own opponents long ago. The Vulgate reads *Iannes et Mambres,* but the Greek text and also the Syriac paraphrase do not have "Mambres" but "Jambres."

In defense of the Vulgate's reading, Estius presses the fact that in the Hebrew Talmud (*Tract. de oblationibus*, in ch. *Omnes oblations*) it says "Mambres" and that "this is also how Rabbi Nathan [reads it], according to Genebrardus (*Chronol.*, bk. 1)." I respond:

(1) Various changes occur when proper names are translated into another language.

(2) Jerome (*Hebraicorum nominum interpretatione*) gives both "Jambres" and "Mambres," and he does it as if there were no difference between them.

(3) Chrysostom (on 2 Timothy 3, homil. 8, f. 1673) reads the Greek "Jannes and Jambres." The Syriac has *yaniys wyanbaris* ("Janis and Janbaris").

But who were Jannes and Jambres? The name Jannes is extant even with Pliny (bk. 30, ch. 1). Most commentators take it as a reference to the Egyptian magicians who stood against Moses before Pharaoh and fought him with their miracles (Exod. [7:11]). Mornaeus (*De verit. rel. Christ.*, ch. 26) relates from Numenius of Apamea, a Pythagorean philosopher from Syria, that when the magicians tried to copy him, Moses fought with miracles against Jannes and Mambres. (The passage from Numenius, *Περὶ Τἀγαθοῦ*, bk. 3, is extant in Eusebius, *De praeparat. evang.*, bk. 9, ch. 8, f. 241.) In the Talmud (*In Sanhedrin*) it says: "Juhani and Mamre, chief magicians of Pharaoh, said to Moses: 'You bring straw to Aphraiim.'" ("You are like one importing straw to Aphraiim," which was a fertile city rich in straw, which it exported to many places. That is to say, "You are carrying water into the Nile, for Egypt abounds in magicians.") Chrysostom (on this passage): "Who are Jannes and Jambres? They are magicians who lived in Moses' day."

Palladius (*Vita Macarii*) relates from the apocryphal book called *Poenitentia Iamnis et Mambris* that

> Jannes and Mamre were brothers because they excelled in the art of magic before Pharaoh and the Egyptians, holding authority and power at that time. While they were living, they built for themselves a grave out of four-foot stones among some gardens in a secluded place in Egypt. There they buried a lot of gold, planted all kinds of trees, and dug out a huge well in the hope that after their death they would enjoy the luxuries of this paradise (etc.). St. Macarius of Alexandria once journeyed long and hard to see this grave, to the chagrin of demons.

(Cf. Camerarius, *Horar. subseciv.*, centur. 3, ch. 9.) But Palladius cites many things that are fable in this "history" of his.

Aretius (commentary on this passage) thinks that

> Jannes and Jambres refer to Jewish rebels such as Dathan and Abiram, rather than Egyptian magicians, because the issue here is domestic enemies and hypocrites—those who wanted to be and be considered Christian, even to be considered Christian teachers. The magicians, however, though they opposed Moses, still did so as overt enemies. They were different from him in terms of their religious profession and their manner of life and studies.

It may further be asked: *Where did Paul get the names of these magicians?* Chrysostom responds (on this passage): "Paul probably taught this from tradition or from the Holy Spirit." Estius thinks that "the latter is unlikely, since knowing the names of those magicians is unimportant. Paul thought he should list the names because Timothy, to whom he was writing, was a Jew who had learned the unwritten traditions of the Hebrews along with the sacred writings." But now, (1) the apostles not only know the teachings but also the histories of the prophets by the revelation of the Holy Spirit. (2) Paul, as with everything else, put even the names of these magicians into writing by the inspiration of the Holy Spirit. So why is it unlikely that he also knew it by the revelation of the Holy Spirit?

A defense. Estius comments on this passage thus: "This passage teaches that, even from antiquity, among the Jews there existed, apart from Holy Scripture, certain true traditions that were acknowledged and received by the faithful. How much more credibility the church has, since it brings forth traditions received from Christ or the apostles."

I respond. (1) It has not yet been proven for sure that Paul got these names from traditions, for it is just as likely that he knew them by the Holy Spirit's revelation.

(2) By no means do we reject traditions about history that do not oppose the articles of the faith as revealed in Scripture. This is a tradition about history, not dogma.

οὕτως καὶ οὗτοι ἀνθίστανται τῇ ἀληθείᾳ. ["So these also oppose the truth."] The order of speech seems to require [the apostle] to say: "Just as Jannes and Jambres opposed Moses, so these also oppose us." However, he turns his pen and says more emphatically "they oppose the truth," to show that their resistance is not so much against men preaching the truth of the Gospel but against truth itself, and therefore against God who is primary Truth [*prima veritas*] and at whose bidding they are preaching the truth.

ἄνθρωποι κατεφθαρμένοι τὸν νοῦν. ["Men who have been corrupted in mind."] Their mind has been clouded and corrupted by affections for vice so that they cannot bear judgment that is sound and right.

ἀδόκιμοι περὶ τὴν πίστιν. ["Unfit as regards the faith."] In matters of faith they understand nothing nor can they make right judgments. In the same way

Titus 1:16 says men who are unfit for bearing the fruit of good works are πρὸς πᾶν ἔργον ἀγαθὸν ἀδόκιμοι ["unfit for every good work"]. So also men are called "unfit for or as regards the faith" who have cut themselves off from the way to a right and sound faith because of the corrupted judgment of their mind and obstinacy in their spirit.

Verse 9.

ἀλλ᾽ οὐ προκόψουσιν ἐπὶ πλεῖον. "But they will not get far," for God will confound their wickedness and perversity. He is talking about the seductive spirits who were disturbing the church at that time. He adds this comfort so that Timothy and other preachers of the truth will not lose heart because they suffer such grievous opponents.

Apparent contrariety. How do these words—"they will not get far"—fit with what he says in [2 Tim.] 2:16, that the promoters of profane teachings will go on to much ungodliness; and also with what he says here in [2 Tim.] 3:13, that evil men and deceivers will go on erring even worse and sending [others] into errors?

I respond. (1) Some reconcile them thus: the deceivers themselves will go on getting worse, but they will not harm others anymore because their foolishness will be made evident to all. However, the apostle expressly says, "They will go on erring even worse and sending others into error."

(2) Some say the words "but they will not go on for the worse" pertain to Judgment Day. At that time their ungodliness will be made evident to all the world. However, it seems pointless to say that evil teachers will not continue on at the day of retribution.

(3) Cajetan explains it thus: "They will not get farther than deceiving naïve women, for this evil will not progress to prudent women and men."

(4) Others explain it thus: they will not go on to something good, but will go from one error to another.

(5) To put it in the simplest way, the apostle's meaning is this: They will not progress in such a way as to avoid having their errors and fraud uncovered by true teachers, so that their folly will be exposed openly and everywhere, and many will recognize the error and turn back from them. At the same time, however, they will continue to murder others with the poison of their false teaching. This is how the Greek commentators explain it.

(6) This explanation agrees with the following one, which some use to explain the apostle's meaning: they will indeed progress with respect to spreading the contagion so as to deceive many, but they will not progress to the point of overturning the church, against which not even the gates of hell can prevail [Matt. 16:18].

ἡ γὰρ ἄνοια αὐτῶν ἔκδηλος ἔσται πᾶσιν, ὡς καὶ ἡ ἐκείνων ἐγένετο. ["For their folly will be evident to all, as was that of those men."] By ἄνοια he means the stupidity of the false teachers, their errors and deceits, which he foretells will be exposed to the light.

By ἐκείνων ["of those men"] he means Jannes and Jambres (v. 8), who were convicted of stupidity and weakness when "Aaron's staff swallowed up their staffs" (Exod. 7:12); when, in their failure at the third sign, they said, "This is the finger of God" (Exod. 8:19); and when, at the sixth sign, "they could not stand before Moses because of their bursting sores" (Exod. 9:9[–11]).

Verse 10.

Σὺ δὲ παρηκολούθηκάς μου τῇ διδασκαλίᾳ, τῇ ἀγωγῇ, τῇ προθέσει. ["But you, you have been following my teaching, manner, purpose."] He sets his own example in opposition to the heretics' corrupt teachings and ways, and by the same urges Timothy to carry on his duty steadfastly: "But you, you have followed and know full well my teaching, manner, and purpose; that is, since you were an inseparable companion on my journey and associate in my works, you therefore well know and understand all about me."

Some think ἀγωγῇ means his method of instruction since (according to Aristotle, *Rhetoric.*, bk. 1) ἀγωγῇ signifies "a leading and understanding of principle, when an instructor and teacher leads, so to speak, the student who needs instruction to an understanding of something." Others relate it to his manner of life and way of living. Both meanings can be conjoined.

By προθέσει he means the purpose and aim of his apostolic works, namely, that in all the actions of his ministry his purpose was not his own glory or good but the glory of God [and] the good of the neighbor.

τῇ πίστει, τῇ μακροθυμίᾳ, τῇ ἀγάπῃ, τῇ ὑπομονῇ. ["My faith, gentleness, love, endurance."] Some understand "faith" as steadfastness of spirit, but it is more correct to take it as the assurance of faith which shows itself through strength and steadfastness of spirit.

By μακροθυμίᾳ he means gentleness of spirit and moderation toward persecutors and enemies of the truth.

By ἀγάπῃ he means Christian love toward all men.

By ὑπομονῇ he means endurance in bearing hardships and persecutions.

Verse 11.

τοῖς διωγμοῖς, τοῖς παθήμασιν. ["My persecutions, sufferings."] He recalls the persecutions and sufferings he has endured for the sake of the Gospel in order to arouse and encourage Timothy to do likewise.

οἷά μοι ἐγένετο ἐν Ἀντιοχείᾳ, ἐν Ἰκονίῳ, ἐν Λύστροις. ["Such as happened to me at Antioch, Iconium, and Lystra."] He names three cities that know of his sufferings: (1) Antioch (of Pisidia, not Syria), (2) Iconium, (3) and Lystra. He specifically mentions these because "Timothy well knew what Paul had suffered in those places, since Timothy had come from Lystra, and the other two cities are nearby" (say Theodoret and Theophylact). Or it was because the persecutions of these places were instigated by the Jews, as seen in Acts 13–14.

οἵους διωγμοὺς ὑπήνεγκα. ["Such persecutions I endured."] He has in view either the persecutions he endured in the cities just mentioned or other persecutions, because Timothy had seen many other persecutions of Paul.

καὶ ἐκ πάντων με ἐρρύσατο ὁ κύριος. ["And from them all the Lord delivered me."] He adds this to comfort Timothy. Moreover, God does not rescue us from adversity in just one way. Sometimes He removes adversity, sometimes He eases it, but through the suffering He is always at work in the hearts of the faithful and gives them a blessed issue—if not in life, then through death.

[Verse 12.]

καὶ πάντες δὲ οἱ θέλοντες εὐσεβῶς ζῆν ἐν χριστῷ Ἰησοῦ διωχθήσονται. ["Indeed, all who desire to live piously in Christ Jesus will be persecuted."] That is to say: "If persecutions and adversities come upon you too, this is nothing strange or unusual, because this is common to all those who are truly pious."

The question arises: *Why does he add "in Christ Jesus," since one can only "live piously" in Christ?* I respond. [He includes this] to show the means through which alone we can live piously: by faith in Christ.

Gregory (Letter 27, bk. 6): "I say with confidence that you are not living so piously if you have hardly endured persecution."

Verse 13.

πονηροὶ δὲ ἄνθρωποι καὶ γόητες προκόψουσιν ἐπὶ τὸ χεῖρον. ["But evil men and deceivers will keep getting worse."] It is not the case that persecutions will cease in this age, as we might hope, because evil men and deceivers always get worse. Hence arise persecutions against the faithful.

Γόητες properly signifies "sorcerers and magicians," and hence is generally used for "imposters and deceivers."

The words "will keep getting worse" recall what the apostle said earlier in v. 9: "They will not get far." Moreover, they send us back to the just judgment of God, according to which the false teachers and their hearers are being struck blind (Rom. 1:28).

πλανῶντες καὶ πλανώμενοι. An elegant polyptoton:[1] "Deceiving and being deceived." Erasmus: "While they lead others into error, they err themselves."

The Vulgate translation changed the word order since the natural order of things is to err prior to leading others into error. But there is no reason forcing us to seek refuge in a [rhetorical] case of the last coming before the first. The

1 Repeating the same word in a different form.

meaning is: "As they are deceiving others they themselves are suffering by God's just judgment so that they subsequently fall into graver errors."

Verse 14.

Σὺ δὲ μένε ἐν οἷς ἔμαθες καὶ ἐπιστώθης. ["But as for you, remain in the things you have learned and firmly trusted."] "But as for you, separate yourself from those false teachers and remain in those things you once were taught."

καὶ ἐπιστώθης. Most translate this: "Remain in those things which were entrusted or committed to you." That is how the Vulgate translation reads, as if the Greek were ἐπιστεύθης (cf. Rom 3:2; Gal. 2:7; 1 Tim. 1:11). In this way this exhortation would be the same as the previous one in 1 Tim. 6:20 and 2 Tim. 1:14. Others explain it thus: "Remain in the things which were believed by you," that is, "which you believed and received in full faith."

However, the apostle does not say ἐπιστεύθης ["entrusted"] or ἃ ἐπίστευσας ["which you believed"] but ἐν οἷς ἐπιστώθης ["in which you trusted"]—that is ἐπείθης, ἐπληροφορήθης ["in which you were persuaded, came to full assurance of"], as Hesychius interpreted it in a way very much in line with Paul's statement and usual manner of speaking. For to "firmly trust" or "to be certain of" is greater than to "have learned" generally. Therefore it should be translated thus: "And of which your trust was made firm" or "full." As the Syriac rendered it: "About which you were made sure" or "firm" (ἐβεβαιώθης).

εἰδὼς παρὰ τίνος ἔμαθες. "Knowing from whom you learned," namely, "from me, an apostle of Christ, having infallible testimony from the Holy Spirit."

Verse 15.

καὶ ὅτι ἀπὸ βρέφους τὰ ἱερὰ γράμματα οἶδας. ["And that from infancy you have known the Sacred Scriptures."] Estius gives the following logical sequence for the apostle's giving two reasons why Timothy should remain in the teaching he had received: "The first reason is the main one and the foundation for the second. 'Steadfastly,' he says, 'retain what you learned since you know from what teacher you learned it, namely, from me, an apostle of Christ. For you this should be as if Christ Himself had been your teacher.'" The second but accessory reason for why Timothy should not depart from the teaching he once received is this: that he knows—that is, he should consider—that he has been endowed with the meaning of the Scriptures in no small way, for he began learning them from early childhood. From these points Estius concludes: "You see how the authority of the teacher is necessary; otherwise Timothy could have said, 'What does it matter from whom I learned, since I have the Scriptures from which I can learn and have the Holy Spirit as my teacher?' This is how the arrogant heretics speak today as they assert their own dreams apart from the teacher."

I respond. (1) Timothy's teacher was the apostle Paul, who was endowed with the gift of infallibility, but today it is not given us to have such blessed teachers, since there is no man living today who has been given the gift of infallibility.

(2) Estius is pointlessly enticing us toward the Roman pontiff, but it can be shown by many proofs—and obvious ones at that—that he is liable to the danger of error.

(3) Today the sole infallibility must be sought in Holy Scripture as the voice of the Holy Spirit. Pronouncements of a teacher of the church are to be examined according to the norm laid out in Scripture.

(4) We have nothing in common with heretics asserting their own dreams, but in all things we appeal singularly to Scripture.

(5) Although the apostles were endowed with the gift of infallibility, they still proved their teaching on the basis of Scripture. How much more should the Roman pontiff confirm his teachings from the Scriptures.

"'From infancy,' that is, 'from the prime of life,'" says Chrysostom (commentary on this passage).

By τὰ ἱερὰ γράμματα he means "Holy Scripture," as is clear from the following verse where he calls it γραφὴν θεόπνευστον ["a God-breathed writing"]. Moreover, he calls it "sacred" (1) from its principal cause,[2] which is God, the Holy of holies; (2) from its instrumental cause,[3] which is "the holy men of God" (2 Pet. 1:21); (3) from the material, because it treats sacred things; (4) from its end purpose and effect, because the Holy Spirit sanctifies man through the reading, hearing, and meditation of Scripture; (5) from its opposite, to distinguish it from all other human writings, not only the secular but also the ecclesiastical.

τὰ δυνάμενά σε σοφίσαι εἰς σωτηρίαν. ["Which are able to make you wise unto salvation."] The Vulgate rendered it *instruere* ["instruct"], but the Greek σοφίσαι is more emphatic. It means "to make wise." Bullinger objects that "σοφίσαι is the same as 'to instruct.'"

I respond. (1) The etymology itself shows that σοφίσαι, since it comes from σοφός ["wise"], means "to make wise."

(2) *Glossarium vetus:* "Σοφίσαι is to display wisdom." Phavorinus: "Σοφίζομαι ὑπό τινος stands for 'I become wise.'" 1 Kings 4:31: Solomon ἐσοφίσατο ὑπὲρ πάντας ἀνθρώπους ("became wiser than all men"). Gregory Nazianzen: Σοφισάμενος περισσὰ ὑπὲρ πάντας ("He excelled everyone in wisdom").

2 Also called a "primary cause." In producing an effect, the principal cause is not an instrument of some cause that is higher or more primary in its class or genus.

3 See above, p. 104 n. 5.

(3) Estius himself comments on this passage: "The Greek σοφίσαι means 'to make wise or learned.' "

(4) "To instruct" is a secondary meaning of σοφίσαι.

Note, the apostle does not say "which have made you wise unto salvation," but "which are able to make you wise," if you continue to apply yourself in reading them. Therefore he is implicitly urging him to study Holy Scripture. (Cf. 1 Tim. 4:13: "Attend to the reading.")

Furthermore, this purpose of reading and this use of Holy Scripture is shared by all members of the church. The latter [purpose and use], which he discusses in the following verses, properly and principally belongs to the teachers of the church.

διὰ πίστεως τῆς ἐν χριστῷ Ἰησοῦ. ["Through faith which is in Christ Jesus."] Because it is from the Holy Scriptures that we can learn faith in Christ, therefore the Holy Scriptures are able to make us wise unto salvation.

Estius thinks that

> the apostle added this specification to show that no one can draw sound, uncorrupted doctrine out of the Holy Scriptures because of their obscurity and because of the blindness and weakness of our understanding and the depravity of the affections under which we labor—unless, that is, he has been armed beforehand by the faith of Christ and uses that as a guide to understand them. Only then will reading Scripture increase one's faith and bring salvation.

I respond. (1) On the contrary, Scripture is so clear on the teachings that are necessary to know for salvation that we can learn faith in Christ from it. John 20:31: "These things are written that you may believe that Jesus is the Christ."

(2) Therefore Scripture's purpose and use is twofold: that from reading it we receive faith in Christ as well as that we strengthen our faith from the same.

(3) It is enough to approach the reading of Scripture with a mind ready to learn, not bewitched by preconceived opinions, not resisting the Holy Spirit, even if faith in Christ is not actually present yet.

(4) It is entirely the same Word of God whether one reads in Scripture or hears it from the mouth of a teacher. But now, faith can be received from the mouth of one teaching the Word. Therefore also from reading Holy Scripture.

Verse 16.

πᾶσα γραφὴ θεόπνευστος. ["All Scripture is God-breathed."] Understand ἔστι ["is"]. Because he had urged Timothy to read Scripture, he embellishes the same with eminent praise, and a twofold praise at that. First, from its authorship; second, from its usefulness.

πᾶσα γραφὴ. Some take the word πᾶσα distributively: "every (Holy) Scripture." But Dionysius Carthusianus teaches: "It is more correct to take this collectively so that πᾶσα γραφὴ is the same as 'the whole of Scripture.'" Πᾶσα is used for ὅλη ["whole"] in 1 Cor. 13:2; Matt. 3:5; and Col. 2:9. For here such things are said about Holy Scripture which do not equally apply to each individual verse of Scripture but to the whole system of Scripture. Hence the rule of logic applies here: "The size of the attribute indicates the size of the subject." Chrysostom (on 2 Timothy, homil. 9): "What, then, is 'all,' which one? 'The one I was speaking about,' he says, 'all the sacred one.' This is what he was discussing. He spoke these things about that which he said, 'You have known the sacred writings from infancy.'"

θεόπνευστος. "Divinely inspired, written at the Holy Spirit's dictation." The Syriac has: *brukha' etctev* ("written through the Holy Spirit"), so that not only the meaning but also each word, the word order, and the entire arrangement is from God.

καὶ ὠφέλιμος πρὸς διδασκαλίαν, πρὸς ἔλεγχον, πρὸς ἐπανόρθωσιν, πρὸς παιδείαν τὴν ἐν δικαιοσύνῃ. ["And is useful for teaching, for refutation, for correction, for training in righteousness."] He lists the four chief duties of a teacher of the church which Scripture sufficiently prepares him to carry out rightly. The first is διδασκαλίαν, which means instruction in the articles of the faith and in all of Christian doctrine. The second is ἔλεγχον, which means refutation of errors at odds with orthodoxy. Luther translates it *Straffe* ["chastisement"], but it is better rendered *Widerlegung* or *Überweisung* ["refutation"]. The third is ἐπανόρθωσιν, which means the correction of life and morals that happens through admonitions, chastisements, and reproaches. The fourth is παιδείαν τὴν ἐν δικαιοσύνῃ, which means exhortation unto a righteous and holy way of living.

Rom. 15:4 adds παράκλησις ("consolation"), but this can be included here under "teaching" or "instruction," for whoever consoles someone teaches him about the wisdom of God in governing the elect and instructs him about his duty in bearing persecutions.[4]

Verse 17.

ἵνα ἄρτιος ᾖ ὁ τοῦ θεοῦ ἄνθρωπος. ["So that the man of God may be complete."] Cajetan understands "man of God" to mean "a man wholly dedicated to God," but this is not very apt. It is better to say that here "man of God" means

4 For a further discussion of this verse as it relates to the teaching office, see Johann Gerhard, *Method of Theological Study*, part 3, section 4, ch. 2 (included in Johann Gerhard, *On Interpreting Sacred Scripture and Method of Theological Study*, trans. Joshua J. Hayes, Theological Commonplaces I–II [St. Louis: Concordia, 2017]).

"teacher of the church," to whose office belongs "the teaching, the refutation, the correction, and the training." The same can be concluded from the aim of this Epistle, which is to instruct a minister of the church. He is called "a man of God" because he presides over the people in God's name and with the things of God (1 Tim. 6:11; 1 Cor. 4:1). The apostle likely has in mind the fact that, in the Old Testament, prophets were uniquely called "men of God" (1 Sam. 9:6; 1 Kings 17:18; 2 Kings 4:7).

Ἄρτιος signifies something that is "whole, absolute, and complete." Suidas: "Ἄρτιος means the suitable, complete, and sound." Estius: "He calls him ἄρτιος who maintains all the aspects of his office, for something is whole when it has all its parts."

πρὸς πᾶν ἔργον ἀγαθὸν ἐξηρτισμένος. ["Prepared for every good work."] From ἄρτιος comes the verb ἀρτίζω and its compound ἐξαρτίζω, which means the same as "to perfect, to render complete and absolute" or "to instruct and prepare perfectly." Thus it is the same as its cognate καταρτίζω, examples of which occur in Matt. 21:16; Heb. 11:3; Luke 6:40; Eph. 4:12; 2 Cor. 13:9; and 1 Thess. 3:10. There one is ἄρτιος and ἐξηρτισμένος who has been sufficiently prepared to fulfill all the aspects of his office. The Syriac has the word *gamiyr*, which means "perfect and absolute." Oecumenius explains it as πεπληρωμένος ["made complete"].

Instead of ἐξηρτισμένος, some codices read ἐρηξτυμένος. But now, (1) this is a recent reading and, (2) according to Suidas, this is the same as "made complete."

The "good work" is mentioned in relation to "the man of God"—that is, a teacher of the church. For him such work is "teaching, refutation," etc. Thus the apostle means that from diligent reading and meditation of Scripture the teacher of the church can become sufficiently prepared duly to perform all aspects of his office.

This is the standard passage [*locus classicus*] for demonstrating Scripture's perfection against the Papists. For if a teacher of the church can become sufficiently prepared for all aspects of his office by the study of Scripture, then surely Scripture is perfect, that is, it contains everything one needs to know for salvation. The logical sequence is demonstrated in that the purpose of the ecclesiastical ministry is the salvation of men. Hence in v. 15 the apostle says: "The sacred writings are able to make us wise unto salvation."

Estius objects:

> (1) If one can conclude from this passage that Scripture is perfect, then it would follow that only the Old Testament Scripture is sufficient, and there is no need for the four Gospels or the other books of the New Testament. Clearly Paul is speaking here about the Old Testament Scripture, because the New Testament Scripture was not yet attached to the canon of the sacred

> books—indeed, it was yet partially unwritten. This is also clear because he mentioned before that [Timothy] "knew the sacred writings from infancy." But Timothy could not have known the books of the New Testament from infancy, for they did not yet exist during his infancy or childhood.

I respond. (1) In every time and age the books then extant provided a sufficient canon for the state of the church of those times. Thus the five Books of Moses were perfect by themselves when the other books of the Scripture did not yet exist. Therefore the books of the Old Testament which existed while Timothy was young contained a sufficient canon.

(2) Nevertheless it does not follow from this that today in New Testament times the Old Testament Scripture is sufficient by itself and that there is no need for the New Testament books. The New Testament books were added to the canon by God's will. They teach us that the Messiah promised in the Old Testament has come in the New, and that Jesus is this promised Messiah. They also expound the articles of the faith more clearly and shed more light on the prophecies. Therefore these books utterly belong to the integrity of the canon and are necessary for it on the assumption of God's will.

(3) Therefore we may invert the argument. If Paul rightly and deservedly says this about the books of the Old Testament that were extant while Timothy was a boy—namely, that they are able to make the man of God complete and well-prepared to fulfill all aspects of the office—then how much more is such praise for Scripture's perfection to be given now that so many [New Testament] books have entered into the canon.

(4) When Paul wrote this, most of the books of the New Testament were already extant: the three Gospels of Matthew, Mark, and Luke; Acts; and nearly all of the apostolic Epistles except the ones penned by John. Indeed, Timothy added his own greeting to the Epistle to the Romans [16:21]. He had delivered 1 Corinthians. He had subscribed to 2 Corinthians, 1 and 2 Thessalonians, Philippians, Colossians, and Philemon. He had read 1 Timothy, which was sent to him. Therefore the apostle has in mind the entire system of canonical Scripture, which he had said was known to Timothy from childhood. He declares this praise about the books that belonged to the canon of Scripture and which were extant in it at the time.

(5) "From infancy" denotes Timothy's childhood so that it also includes the entire time period that passed from Timothy's childhood to the present. Within this time period many of the New Testament Scriptures had been published. They were never unknown to Timothy or neglected by him.

[Estius further objects:]

> (2) When the apostle says "for every good work," by this universal signifier he does not mean to include all works of all kinds, but kinds of specific works. This is clear from the preceding where he listed only the kinds of

> good works that belong to the episcopal office. This, then, is what he says: Scripture is useful partly to teach, partly to refute, partly to correct, and partly to train in righteousness. Of these, the first kind applies to teaching; the second, to refuting and uprooting errors; the third, to correcting vices; and the fourth, to teaching the life ordered according to the Law of God. The other duties of the man of God can easily be listed under these four kinds. Therefore the result of this is that by reading and studying Holy Scripture the man of God becomes complete with respect to his office, especially prepared for every kind of work that belongs to his office.

I respond. (1) Although the word "all" sometimes is used only about kinds of specifics, it still does not follow that it is being used thus in this passage. (2) Indeed, the apostle says beforehand that "Scripture makes us wise unto salvation" [v. 15]. Therefore it prepares us not only for kinds of specific works but also for all works of all kinds, "in every good work." (3) That it is generally useful for teaching, refuting, correcting, and training in righteousness is one thing. It is another thing that it is useful for teaching, refuting, correcting, and training in righteousness so that "the man of God may be complete"—that is, so that completeness is connected with its usefulness. The apostle ascribes usefulness to Scripture not only of the first kind but also of the second kind—usefulness combined with completeness. Therefore he is defining this usefulness not only with respect to all kinds of specifics but also to all specifics of all kinds. (4) Yes, the apostle lists only kinds [of works] for the episcopal office. Nevertheless, since he claims that a bishop can be sufficiently prepared for those kinds [of works] belonging to his office, he clearly also asserts that Scripture is sufficient for all works of all kinds.

Chapter IV

There are three parts to this chapter.

(1) An earnest exhortation to fulfill the office faithfully (vv. 1–5).

(2) An illustration of the exhortation drawn from Paul's own example (vv. 6–8).

(3) A list of some personal instructions (vv. 9–18).

Following these parts come mutual greetings and the apostolic prayer [*votum*] (vv. 19–22).

Verse 1.

Διαμαρτύρομαι οὖν ἐγὼ ἐνώπιον τοῦ θεοῦ, καὶ τοῦ κυρίου Ἰησοῦ χριστοῦ. "I therefore charge [you] before God and the Lord Jesus Christ."

Connection. This is now the third time he prescribes a certain rule of the episcopal office for Timothy with God as his witness. He had already done this twice before (1 Tim. 5:21; 6:13).

Διαμαρτύρομαι. ["I charge."] "I say and command to you these things before the greatest witnesses of all, who will also be the judges for violating the charge and will demand an account of how the ministers of the church administered their office."

τοῦ μέλλοντος κρίνειν ζῶντας καὶ νεκρούς κατὰ τὴν ἐπιφάνειαν αὐτοῦ καὶ τὴν βασιλεῖαν αὐτοῦ. ["Who is going to come to judge the living and the dead according to His appearing and His kingdom."] That this power of administering the judgment has been given to Christ according to His human nature is clearly seen from John 5:22; Acts 10:42; 17:31.

How will Christ judge the living and the dead since the final judgment will happen after the universal resurrection of the dead? I respond. (1) Theophylact mentions that "some understand 'the living and the dead' to mean 'souls and bodies.'" But the apostle is speaking about judging persons, not parts of persons. (2) Some interpret "the living" as "the righteous" and "the dead" as "sinners." (3) Most of the Greek fathers understand "the living" to be those whom the Lord will find alive when He comes for judgment so that they will have no need of a resurrection from the dead; "the dead," however, are those whom He will find dead at His coming and hence will need to be raised to life. (Cf. 1 Thess. 4:17.)

κατὰ τὴν ἐπιφάνειαν αὐτοῦ. ["According to His appearing."] Some relate this specification to the verb διαμαρτύρομαι, so that the charge is by the coming and kingdom of Christ as by an event most earnestly desired by all the faithful. But it is more correct to take it with the nearer referent—"who is going to come to judge the living and the dead"—so that the sense is: "Christ will judge the living and the dead at the time when He shall come openly for judgment and reign in glory openly, having already subjected all things to Himself." For (1) the Greek does not have the preposition διὰ, which tends to be used in such charges (Rom. 12:1; 1 Cor. 1:10), but κατὰ, which, combined with the accusative, serves to indicate time. (2) "According to His appearing" is [the same as] "at His appearing." (3) The Syriac also rendered it this way: *bgelyana' dmalcuteh* ("at the appearance of His kingdom").

Verse 2.

κήρυξον τὸν λόγον. ["Preach the Word."] The connection is that he is laying out his purpose for such a serious, grave charge—namely, that Timothy diligently discharge the office of preaching and the other duties of the ecclesiastical ministry.

ἐπίστηθι εὐκαίρως, ἀκαίρως. ["Be ready in season and out."] Some people always have this apostolic dictum in their mouths as they rail against sins at times and places they should not:[1] "Stick to the work, constantly do what must be done," in such a way that this is related back to the preceding verb "preach" and to those that follow: "refute, rebuke, encourage." But this is not the apostle's meaning.

(1) Theophylact explains it thus: "at whatever time—peaceful or perilous."

(2) Some explain it thus: "Whether the hearers think it good or not." The context shows that the apostle is talking about preaching the Word. The sense, then, is: "Preach the Word, even if some say that it is inconvenient for them to hear it. The Word must be offered to those who are willing to hear it; it must be thrust upon those who despise it."

(3) Augustine's statement applies here (commentary on Galatians 6): "Urge it at an opportune time, but if you make no progress in this way, then at an inopportune time. Although the man who hears you unwillingly may think you inopportune, you should still know that what you say to him is opportune for him; you should keep loving and caring for his salvation with a gentle, calm,

1 Gerhard is speaking against those who understand this to mean "at appropriate times and inappropriate times."

and fraternal spirit." Again (*Enarrat. Ps.* 128): "Let him sound the Word. To the willing, opportunely; to the unwilling, inopportunely."

(4) Some take this with "rebuke," saying, "The apostle himself adds παρακάλεσον, ἐν πάσῃ μακροθυμίᾳ ['encourage with all patience'], that is, 'When you think it necessary, when you find out that someone has transgressed and not stopped after being rebuked,' then apply inopportune severity as you continue to correct him." But the context shows that the apostle is not dealing with rebuke yet but with preaching the Word.

Apparent contrarieties. (1) *In this passage the apostle says, "Be ready in season and out," but Christ says in the parable (Luke 12:42) that the housefather should give food* ἐν καιρῷ *["at the proper time"].* I respond. Christ has in mind the spiritual prudence of a housefather, that he should discuss different areas of teaching for his different hearers. Paul has in mind the temper of men to whom the teaching is given, to whom it never seems timely to have the threats of the Law urged and forced upon them.

(2) *"Be ready in season and out." To the contrary, the wise king says (Prov. 15:23): "An opportune word is best." [Prov.] 25:11: "Golden apples in a silver sculpture is one who speaks a word in its time." Eccl. 3:7: "A time to keep silent and a time to speak."* I respond. That which is done advantageously for the salvation of others is always opportune and timely, even if the one for whose sake such a thing is done thinks it untimely.

Some think [the apostle said this] with respect to Timothy himself and, under his person, to all preachers of the Word. The sense would be: "Keep at the work, be it a good and suitable time for you or an inopportune, untimely, and inconvenient time, so that you even abstain from time for sleep and refreshment so as to take pains for the salvation of your neighbors." But it is more correct to take this with respect to hearers.

ἔλεγξον, ἐπιτίμησον, παρακάλεσον. Although in the Greek this means "refute, rebuke, exhort," the Vulgate reordered the words *argue, obsecra, increpa* ["refute, exhort, rebuke"].

The apostle is reiterating the four aspects of the episcopal office, and even in the same order in which he had listed them above [2 Tim. 3:16]. He says (1) κήρυξον ["preach"], which is διδασκαλία ("teaching and instruction"); (2) ἔλεγξον ["refute"], which is ἔλεγχος ("the refutation of false teaching"); (3) ἐπιτίμησον ["rebuke"], which is ἐπανόρθωσις ("the correction of depraved morals"); (4) παρακάλεσον ["exhort"], which is παιδεία ἡ ἐν δικαιοσύνῃ ("exhorting to pure and holy living").

ἐν πάσῃ μακροθυμίᾳ καὶ διδαχῇ. ["With all patience and teaching."] Earlier he put it thus (2 Tim. 2:25): ἐν πρᾳότητι παιδεύοντα ["correcting with gentleness"]. Theophylact takes this clarification with all four aspects of the episcopal office just listed. However, μακροθυμίᾳ ["patience"] mainly pertains to rebuke and correction, seeing as rebukes and censures get nowhere unless coupled with a gentle, calm spirit. Διδαχῇ ["teaching"] mainly pertains to refutation, since one who is to be called out of error must be correctly taught sound teaching.

Gregory (bk. 2, Letter 52) concludes from this passage:

> A bishop should teach with words, not whips. You, brethren, well know what the canons say about bishops who seek respect at the end of the whip. For we have been made pastors, not punchers. The famous preacher says (2 Tim. 4[:2]): "Refute, exhort, rebuke with all patience and teaching." It is a novel and unheard-of preaching which compels faithfulness by the whip.

This saying is quoted in [*Ius canonicum*,] c. *Quid autem*, dist. 45.[2]

Verse 3.

Ἔσται γὰρ καιρὸς ὅτε τῆς ὑγιαινούσης διδασκαλίας οὐκ ἀνέξονται. ["For the time will come when they will not endure sound teaching."] He is laying out the reason why he exhorted him with such a grave charge to perform his office zealously: he knows by the revelation of the Spirit that many will not only abandon the pure faith but also not even endure hearing sound teaching. They will still want to appear to be members of the church, but they will refuse to bear the preaching of the truth.

ἀλλὰ κατὰ τὰς ἐπιθυμίας τὰς ἰδίας ἑαυτοῖς ἐπισωρεύσουσιν διδασκάλους. ["But they will accumulate for themselves teachers in accordance with their own desires."] They will not be content with one or two false teachers, but they will accumulate for themselves many false teachers. They will pile on more and more as if to pile up a heap of teachers just as their depraved desires will drive and lead them. For since they are given to gluttony and lust, they also will seek such teachers who will teach them what fits their carnal lusts.

Estius says: "In our day such are the Lutherans and nearly all the new teachers who have emerged after Luther, especially those who, with one voice, despise the prescribed fasts of the church, monastic vows, and all the pious observances and laws of the church."

I respond. (1) On the contrary, the Papists foster the wicked lusts of men in their teaching. They allow priests to fornicate [*concubinatum*]; they sell indulgences for money; they tolerate public whorehouses; they decree fasts only by distinguishing foods. (Cf. *Disput. de labefacto per Pontificias corruptelas pietatis studio*.) (2) We reject neither public nor private fasts undertaken at the church's suggestion or by private devotion. Neither do we despise church laws. Instead, we reject the evil goal of fasting, that it is done to gain merit and satisfaction for sins. Also, we say that human traditions must not be held equal to the Word of

2 *Decretum Gratiani* 1.45.1, in Aemelius Friedberg, ed., *Corpus Iuris Canonici* (Graz: Akademische Druck- u. Verlagsanstalt, 1959), vol. 1, col. 160.

God. (3) That monastic vows are a snare for consciences is shown in its own place.[3] (4) We teach the mortification of the flesh and patience in persecution for those undivided in their share of the confession of the Gospel.

A defense. In the same place, Estius writes thus: "Here the Greeks studiously note how pernicious it is for the church when bishops and pastors are elected by the votes of the common crowd. 'For the crowd,' says Theophylact, 'does nothing according to reason, but chooses those who suit their desires. They elect and promote those who say and do everything in a way that pleases and charms them.'"

I respond. (1) We do not give the election of ministers of the church to the people alone, but to the whole church which encompasses three orders: the ecclesiastical ministry, the political magistracy, and the people or the order of citizens. (2) The people cannot be nor should they be excluded from giving their votes in calling ministers of the church. This has been proven in many ways in its own place.[4] (3) There must be a distinction between a faulty accident[5] and the salutary use of a thing. We do not deny that sometimes the people's election has some faulty accidents. Nevertheless the salutary use of the election through the people's votes remains. (4) Bellarmine himself concedes that "the election of pastors through the votes of the people was commonplace in the primitive church."

κνηθόμενοι τὴν ἀκοήν. ["Having itching ears."] This is the second reason why they will pile up false teachers for themselves: because they have ears itching to hear novelty. Some think this is to be taken with respect to a desire to hear what is welcome and pleasing.

Verse 4.

καὶ ἀπὸ μὲν τῆς ἀληθείας τὴν ἀκοὴν ἀποστρέψουσιν, ἐπὶ δὲ τοὺς μύθους ἐκτραπήσονται. ["And they will turn away from hearing the truth and turn aside to fables."] By "truth" he means the soundness of true, salutary teaching which checks and restrains the desires of the flesh. From this, he says, those men will turn away and instead turn to hearing fables.

By "fables" (1) some understand "Jewish fables" (Titus 1:14). In 1 Tim. 1:4 fables and genealogies are connected. (2) Others understand "fables of heretics, especially the Simonians" [Acts 8:9–24]. (3) But these can be understood generally as any silly fable, be it of Jewish, Gentile, or heretical origin.

---

3 See *On the Ecclesiastical Ministry* [Commonplace XXVI/1], § 336 (last paragraph), where there is further reference to *On Marriage, Celibacy, and Similar Topics* [Commonplace XXVIII], §§ 513–515.

4 See *On the Ecclesiastical Ministry* [Commonplace XXVI/1], §§ 85–107.

5 That is, a misuse, a fault that does not belong to the substance of the thing.

Verse 5.

Σὺ δὲ νῆφε ἐν πᾶσιν. "Be prudent, vigilant, [in all things]." Some take the addition of "in all things" as relating to the following, but it is more correct to take it with the preceding: "Diligently perform all aspects of the office."

κακοπάθησον. "Suffer evil, bear affliction, hold out in afflictions and labors."

ἔργον ποίησον εὐαγγελιστοῦ. ["Do the work of an evangelist."] Some interpret "evangelist" generally as "a preacher of the Gospel," but it is more correct to understand it specifically as those who accompanied the apostles as they fulfilled their office (Acts 21:8; Eph. 4:11).

τὴν διακονίαν σου πληροφόρησον. "Completely fulfill your ministry." "Fulfill your ministry with full confidence of spirit, and by doing that show how you are a true and faithful minister of Christ. Engage in your office and ministry in such a way that you never omit anything that is rightly demanded of a faithful minister of the Gospel." Luther has *Richte dein Ampt redlich aus* ["perform your office rightly"].

The Vulgate translation adds here *sobrius esto* ["be sober"], but Estius himself admits that this is out of place. He comments thus:

> The Greek does not have this part, and neither do the Syriac or Ambrosian translations know of it. Furthermore, it is not in all the Latin manuscripts. Finally, since Pelagius and Haymo do not discuss it, they show that they did not read it. It is more than likely that it was added in, because instead of "but you be vigilant" a Latin version had "but you be sober," as it reads according to the older editions of the Ambrosian text.

He continues later: "Also, there was no need to exhort Timothy to sobriety at this point since in 1 Timothy he had advised him about not drinking water [1 Tim. 5:23]."

[Verse 6.]

Ἐγὼ γὰρ ἤδη σπένδομαι. ["For already I am being poured out as a drink offering."] "I am being immolated and made a libation as a sacrifice." The metaphor is drawn from the sacrifices of the Old Testament to which libations were once added.

At the same time, he is alluding to the fruit of the suffering he will have to bear, which is a sign of the truth of the Gospel. For he says, "I am being poured out," that is, he will be poured out; his blood will be poured out to confirm the truth of the teaching of the Gospel. Just so, covenants were ratified by libations, that is, the pouring out of wine which the contracting parties had first "libated," that is, tasted on the front of their lips.

We see clearly that our death is a sacrifice we offer to God, but this sacrifice should be voluntary. So when the hour of our death comes, we follow our Lord not unwillingly or sadly but with a ready spirit.

There is a parallel passage to this one in Phil. 2:17: Ἀλλ᾽ εἰ καὶ σπένδομαι ἐπὶ τῇ θυσίᾳ καὶ λειτουργίᾳ τῆς πίστεως ὑμῶν, χαίρω ["Even if I am to be poured out as a libation upon the sacrifice and service of your faith, I rejoice"].

The word ἤδη means "happening soon." Soon he will be pulled into suffering and seal the truth of the Gospel by pouring out his blood.

καὶ ὁ καιρὸς τῆς ἐμῆς ἀναλύσεως ἐφέστηκεν. "And the time of my release (from bodily chains) has come." Cyprian seems to have read "the time of my assumption (ἀνάληψις)." Some say the reason for the phrase is "because through death the body is dissolved into ashes." But the truer reason for the phrase was given a little earlier: because through death is loosed the chain by which the soul is tied to the body.

There is a parallel passage in Phil. 1:23: ἐπιθυμίαν ἔχων εἰς τὸ ἀναλῦσαι καὶ σὺν χριστῷ εἶναι ["I have the desire to be released and be with Christ"].

Most commentators conclude from this passage that "this Epistle was the last of all of Paul's Epistles, written by the apostle before his imminent death" (Eusebius, *Hist. eccles.*, bk. 2, ch. 22). Estius speaks against this idea (commentary on the argument of this Epistle), claiming that "this Epistle was written first or second among those sent from Rome, many years before Paul's death, that is, in the third or fourth year of Nero's reign, while his martyrdom occurred in the thirteenth year of Nero's reign." He proves this by the following arguments:

(1) Since Paul had recently arrived in Rome, he wanted to inform his dearest disciple Timothy about his affairs, namely, as to the success of his first defense before Nero. This he does at the end of the Epistle (2 Tim. 4:16).

(2) This Epistle contains some things which clearly argue for his recent arrival in Rome. [2 Tim.] 4:13: "When you come, bring with you the cloak I left in Troas." Verse 20: "Erastus stayed in Corinth, but I left Trophimus sick in Miletus."

(3) In this Epistle he indicates that he is still being kept to fulfill the office of preaching among the Gentiles ([2 Tim.] 4:17): "The Lord was with me and strengthened me so that through me the preaching might be fulfilled and all Gentiles hear."

(4) Is the Epistle to Philemon, wherein he asks for a guest room [Phlm. 22] as if for one soon to be released from prison, much later than this one?

In his commentary on [2 Tim.] 4:13, [Estius] confirms the same with another argument: "If Paul sensed that the day of his death was already near as he wrote this letter, why, if they already would be of no future use to him, would he ask for the cloak or the box or the books he left at Troas nearly ten years ago?"

As concerns the present passage, [he] answers: "The apostle did not sense that he was already about to be dragged off into martyrdom. He only means this: that he, though uncertain about the time of his death, is being prepared little by little for sacrifice through chains and tribunals." But this explanation does not fit the emphasis of the apostle's words, and the strength of the arguments Baronius and Estius adduce is weak.

Verse 7.

τὸν ἀγῶνα τὸν καλὸν ἠγώνισμαι, τὸν δρόμον τετέλεκα, τὴν πίστιν τετήρηκα. ["I have fought the good fight, I have finished the race, I have kept the faith."] This is a flowery and triumphant, so to speak, construction with asyndeton[6] wherein he highlights the course of his life by three illustrative metaphors.

The first of these comes from a strong athlete: "I have fought the good fight," that is, one that is beautiful, outstanding, and distinguished. Some want to understand the "fight" here as one that happens in a race, since he immediately adds: "I have finished the race." But it is more correct to say the metaphor is drawn specifically from a wrestling fight—a metaphor he also uses in 1 Cor. 9:25.

The second metaphor comes from the tireless runner. By "I have finished the race," he compares himself to those who run in the stadium—a metaphor he also uses in 1 Cor. 9:24 and 26, where he also connects it to the above metaphor of an athlete. Some claim the metaphor comes from the long-distance traveler, but the earlier explanation fits the text better.

The third metaphor comes from the honorable soldier: "I have kept the faith." By "faith" he not only means the trusting apprehension of Christ's merit but also the good faith of his office, or faithfulness with respect to the office and which is owed to God and promised by God. He is comparing himself to a soldier who has given his word [*fidem*] to the emperor or military general and who keeps it. 1 Cor. 4:2: "This is required among stewards, that one be found faithful."

Therefore Paul's life consisted in (1) *the good fight*, because by the power of Christ who strengthened him he came out victorious on the battlefront against sin, the world, the flesh, the devil, heretics, false apostles, and the enemies of Christ, both Jewish and Gentile.

(2) *Tireless running*, for he did not tire in the middle or lack faithfulness in the course of the public ministry and private life in which he had thus far run and sweated, but he finished the race victoriously.

(3) *The continual exercise of faith*, because he remained faithful to his general, Christ, unto the last breath of his life and kept his word to Him.

"He says that 'he has fought the fight, finished the race, kept the faith' even though the end of his suffering and death still remained, because he was approaching the finish of the race and had a sure confidence in the Lord about

6 The omission or absence of a conjunction between parts of a sentence.

the remaining part of the course to be run" (Augustine, *De peccat. merit.*, bk. 2, ch. 16).

Verse 8.

λοιπόν, ἀπόκειταί μοι ὁ τῆς δικαιοσύνης στέφανος. ["Henceforth there is laid up for me the crown of righteousness."] Ambrose rendered the Greek λοιπόν as *quod reliquum est* ["that which is left"].

He continues with the metaphor and calls the reward of the fight, race, and military service conducted with honor a "crown," because crowns were often given to contestants, runners, and soldiers.

Also, he calls the blessedness and glory of eternal life "the crown of righteousness"—not Paul's, but God's. This righteousness of God, moreover, is not understood as the righteousness which judges according to the merits of works, but as the righteousness according to which God is faithful in His promises and which gives the wages not of merit but of His gracious promise.

Therefore [it is called] "the crown of righteousness": (1) Because Christ earned it for us by His perfect obedience and righteousness. (2) Because God faithfully promised it to those who serve Him and are zealous for holiness and righteousness (1 Cor. 9:25; James 1:12; 1 Pet. 5:4). With respect to the former, it is the merit of righteousness; but with respect to the latter, it is only what follows. (3) It can also be called "the crown of righteousness" because on that day Paul and all the elect will plainly and perfectly be transferred into that life where there is righteousness without sin. In this sense it is called "the crown of life" (James 1:12), "the crown of beauty" (Ezek. 16:12), and "the crown of glory" (Isa. [28:5]; 1 Pet. 5:4), etc.

Estius asks: "How can it be called 'the crown of righteousness' since it is 'the crown of mercy' in Ps. 103:4?" He responds:

> These are not any less compatible than the fact that Scripture sometimes calls eternal life a reward and sometimes a gift. It is a reward because it is given for the merits of good works; it is a gift since these merits are themselves gifts of God. So also the very same eternal life is "the crown of righteousness" because it is owed to him who competes lawfully; it is "the crown of mercy" because one could not compete lawfully unless God granted it, nor could he reach the crown unless the Lord also mercifully pardoned him for his falls and errors committed while competing.

He continues later:

> If Christ as righteous judge will render to Paul and all the elect the crown of righteousness for keeping the faith and finishing the race, then there is in these works an accounting of merit with respect to the same crown. Catholics do not add these merits of works against the grace of Christ (etc.). For they teach that God's kindness toward us is so great that He wishes

> those merits which are His gifts to be ours, and He will give eternal rewards for these things which He Himself graciously bestowed.

I respond. (1) It is not eternal life itself, which is the essential reward, that is called a "reward" (Matt. 5:12), but the nonessential rewards within eternal life. Luke 6:23: "Your reward will be rich in heaven." Here there is a notable distinction between heaven itself—or eternal life—and "the reward in heaven." So also 1 Tim. 4:8 says that "piety has promises for the present and future life"—that is, [promises] of rewards in the present and future life. (2) If Scripture sometimes calls eternal life "a reward" and sometimes "a gift," then it is not the reward for merit but the reward of grace. Consequently, it is not given for the merits of good works but by grace. Rom. 11:6: "If from grace, then no longer from works." (3) When the fathers call the good works of the faithful "merits"—and those such as owe their origin to the gift and grace of God—then they are using the word "merit" in its broader sense and outside of its proper meaning. This has been demonstrated clearly in its own place.[7] (4) We concede that eternal life is called "the crown of righteousness" because it is given to the one who competes lawfully. However, it does not follow from this that the contest is meritorious for eternal life and that eternal life is the merited reward, owed because of such a contest. You see, it is one thing to ask to whom the crown of eternal life is given. To this it is correct to say "to those who compete lawfully." But it is another thing to ask on what account it is given. The former question is about the subject; the latter, about the meritorious cause. (5) Something owed with respect to righteousness, properly so called, is the opposite of a reward of grace. But something owed with respect to a gracious promise, so called apart from its usual meaning, does not exclude grace nor is it opposed to it. The fathers (but never Scripture) call the reward of good works "owed" with respect to the promise, but with the promise it becomes purely gratuitous (Isa. [45:13]; Rom. 11:35). Hence it is called something "owed" outside of the word's proper sense. Augustine (on Psalm 109): "God is faithful, for He makes Himself our debtor, not by receiving anything from us but by promising us such great things. Whatever He promised, He promised it to those who are unworthy, so that the wages were not promised as to the works, but grace was given freely by His name." (6) If man could not compete lawfully unless God granted it, then surely the contest cannot be the meritorious cause for the crown of glory or eternal life. The reason is this: If the ability to compete lawfully is given by God, then man thereby is more in God's debt than that God should then owe him anything. If good works are the gifts of God, then properly speaking we can merit nothing by them. (7) If man could not attain the crown unless God mercifully pardoned his falls and errors committed while competing, then surely the contest cannot

7 See *On Good Works* [Commonplace XX], §§ 87–133.

be the meritorious cause of eternal life. The reason for the logical sequence is this: the contest is not full, perfect, and blameless in all respects. But now, for works to be meritorious, they must be perfect, pure, and entirely clean of every sinful stain.

Moreover, the apostle says that the crown of righteousness has been laid up for him, naturally with God, from whom he most confidently expected it to be given him. 2 Tim. 1:12: "I am sure that He is able to keep my deposit." Hence he immediately adds:

ὃν ἀποδώσει μοι ὁ κύριος ἐν ἐκείνῃ τῇ ἡμέρᾳ, ὁ δίκαιος κριτής. ["Which the Lord, the righteous Judge, will render to me on that day."] Estius highlights the fact that "Paul does not say 'He will give it,' but 'He will render it,' as if something owed and entrusted or deposited, a thing which must be rendered by right, as Theophylact and Oecumenius say."

I respond. (1) The verb ἀποδώσει refers to the gracious promise, for that which God has promised of His grace He will faithfully keep. Therefore it is owed not [because] of our righteousness but [because] of His promise. Basil (on Psalm 17, hom. 2, in Psalm 7, p. 68) teaches: "Scripture has the habit of saying ἀνταπόδοσις ['reward'] for δόσις ['gift'] and ἀνταποδοῦναι ['to give back'] for δοῦναι ['to give'], even as it otherwise uses composite words instead the simple." (2) Col. 3:24 calls the rewards of good works ἀνταπόδοσις τῆς κληρονομίας ("the repayment of the inheritance"). Just as a son is born an heir and has no need to then merit it by works, so the faithful have been born from God as beloved sons of God in Christ; and if they are sons, then surely they are heirs [cf. Gal. 4:4–7]. At the same time, however, even as a rich inheritance is also the reward of filial obedience, so also the rewards of heavenly life far and most richly outweigh the works and sufferings of the faithful beyond what they deserve.

By "the Lord" he means "Christ," whom he calls "the righteous Judge," to whom "the Father has given all judgment" (John 5:22). Of Him the apostle notably says that He will give the crown to him and to all who love His coming. This is clear proof that the power to judge has been given to Him as a man.

Estius raises an objection: "Christ will not present the elect with heavenly bliss in a way other than how He will award to the apostle Paul and the others the crown owed to them only by giving the verdict, for to beatify a creature efficiently and properly belongs only to His uncreated power." I respond. On the contrary, the uncreated, infinite power to beatify a creature was given in time to Christ as man through and because of the personal union. Accordingly, He will not only proclaim His judicial verdict by His external, audible voice, but He also will demonstrate His omniscience by revealing all things, even the most hidden things (1 Cor. 4:5). He will demonstrate His omnipotence by raising the dead prior to the judgment, by summoning and gathering all men before His judicial tribunal, and by effectively carrying out His judicial verdict. To accomplish every one of these works He must truly have divine power and glory, which is why Scripture frequently says that Christ will come to judge in glory, strength, and power that is truly divine.

By "on that day" he means the Day of Judgment, otherwise called "the Day of the Lord."

Apparent contrariety. *Paul received the crown of righteousness immediately after death according to his soul, so why does he say that Christ will finally give it to him on the Day of Judgment?* I respond. He is talking about the fullest and most perfect beatification that will be given not to the soul but to the [entire] person, who consists of a body and a soul.

From this we conclude that the apostle was certain regarding his salvation. Estius objects:

> Here Paul does not simply affirm what will happen, but either his talk is one of good confidence—that is, "I hope for the crown from the Lord with a certain hope"—or a condition is implied: "If I persevere unto death." Furthermore, what he writes in his Epistle to the Philippians (written after this) speaks against certainty of salvation (Phil. 3:11): "If somehow I may attain to the resurrection which is from the dead."

I respond. (1) The words of the text show quite clearly that the apostle was fully certain about receiving the crown of glory from Christ the Judge. In fact, he says that the crown of glory has been laid up for him with the Lord and will be given on that Day of Judgment. He does not use verbs in the optative mood but the indicative.

(2) Many Papists concede that the apostle was certain about his salvation, but they add that his certainty came from unique revelation (Duraeus, *Contra Witaker.*, bk. 8, f. 259; Pistorius, *Hodeget.*, p. 201).

(3) The words of Rom. 8:38—"I am sure that neither death nor life," etc.—are not merely words of good confidence but also of immovable certainty and most certain conviction. The words in the present text agree with these words most precisely.

(4) True, a condition of perseverance is implied, but the apostle was certain about that very perseverance based on the kindness, faithfulness, and power of God, as has been shown in its own place.[8]

(5) The particle εἴ πως ["if somehow"] in Phil. 3:11 does not express doubt but signifies the difficulty and afflictions which beset the faithful in this life.

He is called "the righteous Judge" because He will judge "with righteousness" (Acts 17:31) and execute that righteous judgment of God which Paul describes thus (2 Thess. 1:6–7): "It is righteous with God to repay with affliction

8 See above, pp. 117–18, the discussion of 2 Tim. 1:5, point (1).

those who afflict you, and to repay you who bear affliction with rest along with us at the revealing of the Lord Jesus from heaven," etc.

οὐ μόνον δὲ ἐμοί, ἀλλὰ καὶ πᾶσι τοῖς ἠγαπηκόσιν τὴν ἐπιφάνειαν αὐτοῦ. ["And not only for me but also for all who have loved His appearing."] They love Christ's coming who await their Savior with longing and vigilance, who daily prepare themselves for Christ's coming, who by the earnest pursuit of piety demonstrate that they love Him and are yearning for His coming.

Estius conjectures that "the distributive πᾶσι is an addition in the Greek text because: (1) Hentenius does not translate it in Oecumenius. (2) The Ambrosian text and other Latin fathers do not read it. (3) The Syriac translator did not find it in his Greek text. (4) It is easier to add this small word than to omit it because the sense seems to require it." I respond. (1) The main reason why Estius moves to claim that this particle is an addition is because it is not in the Vulgate version the Council of Trent declared authoritative. (2) And what does this mean for the same fathers of Trent who expressly included ["all"] when they quoted this verse (sess. 6, ch. 16)? (3) Estius himself admits that "the sense seems to require it." Therefore it is more likely that it was dropped in the Latin than added in the Greek, especially since other examples of omissions of this sort are present in the Vulgate. (4) Oecumenius's Greek text explicitly has it, and Hentenius's translation cannot be used as a prior basis to judge it. In fact, Oecumenius draws a useful observation from this particle: "Here [the apostle] is also encouraging Timothy, for he says: 'He shall render it to you too. For if He will give the crown to all who love His coming, then how much more will He give it to you.'" (5) The Ambrosian text and the other Latin fathers followed the Vulgate translation which, as can be confirmed from several examples, sometimes also followed the Syriac translation and overlooked the Greek text.

Verse 9.

Σπούδασον ἐλθεῖν πρός με ταχέως. "Make an earnest effort to come to me quickly."

But why does he summon him to Rome if he had made him bishop[9] *over the churches of Asia?* I respond. From what follows we may conclude that the apostle wanted to use his ministry to promote the cause of Christ, since he had obviously been abandoned by his other assistants.

A little later (v. 21) he explains "quickly" as "before winter," that is, that he not delay his departure another year.

Estius concludes from this passage that "bishops can be away from their churches temporarily for grave reasons." I respond. (1) Temporarily, (2) for grave reasons, they can be away, this we concede. (3) However, this in no way defends those bishops who are never with their flock and never fulfill their

9 Reading *episcopum* instead of *epistolam*.

teaching office but instead exercise political rule. One may see how great the disputes were in the Council of Trent over the residency of bishops from Petrus Suavis (*Historia Concilii Tridentini*).

Verse 10.

Δημᾶς γάρ με ἐγκατέλιπεν, ἀγαπήσας τὸν νῦν αἰῶνα. ["For Demas has abandoned me, having loved the present age."] Estius, in order to preserve his thesis (that this Epistle was the first or second among all those Paul wrote in Rome ten years before his death), thinks that

> these words do not mean that Demas abandoned the faith of Christ but that he left Paul in captivity only temporarily out of fear of danger and thinking of his own safety and rest. He was driven by the love of the goods of this life to care more for his personal advantage than Paul's or the Gospel's. Nevertheless he later returned to him and gave him his help.

As proof of this, he cites that "Colossians [4:14] and Philemon [24], written after this Epistle to Timothy, list Demas among those sending their greetings, and in the latter instance as a fellow worker of Paul. Jerome" (he says) "subscribes to this opinion in his commentary on Philemon." In this respect he is following Baronius, who says (*Annal.*, tom. 1, *ann. Christi* 61, p. 588): "Demas did not abandon the faith of Christ. One can clearly love his age without apostasy. Demas could have later thought better of it and returned after recoiling from Paul out of the fear of affliction." I respond. (1) To say that "Colossians and Philemon were written after this Epistle to Timothy" is begging the question. (2) That Demas is said "to have loved the present age" stands in contrast to the description of the faithful "who have loved Christ's coming." Therefore the meaning is that Demas refused to be a sharer of suffering but sought to have good days in this life and live free from the fear of persecution. This can scarcely hold sway without apostasy from the faith. (3) "To love the world and the things in the world" is the same as "to love the present age." But now, the former is attributed to carnal and worldly people who set their minds on worldly things (1 John 2:15). (4) Dorotheus (*Synopsis*) recalls that he was a worshiper of images and was made a priest among the Thessalonians after he abandoned Paul. Epiphanius (*Haeres.* 51) recalls that "Demas abandoned the way of truth and became a heretic who agreed with Cerinthus, the Ebionites, and others who claimed that Christ was merely a man." Baronius and Estius repudiate both, but we can as easily receive them as they repudiate them. (5) Also, it is pure conjecture when Estius surmises that "this Demas is the same one Ignatius mentions in his letter *Ad Magnesianos* as their bishop 'worthy of God.'"

καὶ ἐπορεύθη εἰς Θεσσαλονίκην. ["And left for Thessalonica,"] either because this was his homeland or to be far away from danger.

Κρήσκης εἰς Γαλατίαν. ["Crescens to Galatia."] Understand: "left," which must be supplied again from the preceding. But Crescens did not leave from love of this age but either because Paul sent him there for the sake of the Gospel or because of some other good reason.

Epiphanius (*Haeres.* 51) finds fault with this reading as having been introduced by mistake and claims that it should read Γαλλίαν ["Gaul"] instead of Γαλατίαν ["Galatia"]. Theodoret, in fact, reads "Galatia" but translates it "Gaul." However: (1) All Greek copies read Γαλατίαν. (2) "Galatia" in the Scriptures is often used for the region of Asia Minor, but never for Gaul. (3) Martyrologies say that Crescens was sent by Paul into Galatia, the region of Asia Minor, crossed over into Gaul, and preached the Gospel there. Finally, he returned to Galatia and there finished his life with martyrdom. Perhaps because of this Epiphanius took opportunity to argue that it should read "Gaul" instead of "Galatia."

Τίτος εἰς Δαλματίαν. ["Titus to Dalmatia."] Dalmatia is in the region of Illyricum. Undoubtedly Titus set out for there for the sake of the Gospel, according to Paul's wishes, for in Rom. 15:19 the apostle writes that he has "fulfilled all things for the Gospel of Christ, from Jerusalem all the way around to Illyricum."

Verse 11.

Λουκᾶς ἐστὶν μόνος μετ' ἐμοῦ. ["Luke alone is with me."] This is he who wrote down the third Gospel account and the Acts of the Apostles. Jerome (*Catalog.*) calls him "a follower of the apostle Paul and an inseparable companion in all his journeys."

Μάρκον ἀναλαβὼν ἄγε μετὰ σεαυτοῦ. ["Get Mark and bring him with you."] This is not Mark the evangelist who wrote the second Gospel account, for he was Peter's companion and follower. This is John Mark, the cousin of Barnabas (Acts 12:25; 15:37). In Colossians and Philemon this Mark is listed among those sending greetings, but Timothy is included with Paul in the title.

ἔστι γάρ μοι εὔχρηστος εἰς διακονίαν. ["For he is very useful to me for ministry."] He means the ministry of the Gospel, for which he at one time did not seem useful. For in Acts 15:37 there was a disagreement over him between Barnabas and Paul. Barnabas wanted to take him along as a companion for the work of the Gospel, but Paul said he should not be taken because he had deserted them during their first Gospel expedition [vv. 38–39]. But later he was corrected and deemed useful by Paul—in fact, "very useful for the ministry of the Gospel"—and is summoned to Rome for that work along with Timothy.

Verse 12.

Τυχικὸν δὲ ἀπέστειλα εἰς Ἔφεσον. ["But Tychicus I have sent to Ephesus."] This heads off an unspoken objection. Timothy could have said, "Whom shall I leave in Ephesus to fulfill the episcopal office in my place if I am to bring Mark with me?" The apostle responds that he has sent Tychicus to Ephesus, namely, to replace Timothy while he is gone.

Baronius thinks that the past tense should be explained through the present: "I have sent Tychicus," that is, "I am sending Tychicus to Ephesus." Based on this he concludes that "this very Epistle was sent with Tychicus along with the Epistle to the Ephesians." Others make claims to the contrary: that each Epistle was sent at different times, though they disagree as to which was sent first and which later. Some think that the past tense refers to the time when Timothy was going to read this Epistle, since the apostle uses the same verb tense in Philemon, saying about Onesimus "whom I have sent," though he sent that same letter by Onesimus.

Verse 13.

τὸν φελόνην ὃν ἀπέλιπον ἐν Τρῳάδι παρὰ Κάρπῳ, ἐρχόμενος φέρε. ["Bring the cloak I left in Troas with Carpus when you come."] Some copies read φελόνην and others φαιλόνην. There are various opinions for the meaning of this [word]: (1) Some explain this as a consular cloak, but the word does not mean this nor does it fit with Paul's person. (2) The Ambrosian text interprets it as the attire of a senator, but this opinion is refuted by the same arguments. (3) Chrysostom explains it as a crate or book box, that is, a little chest in which writings were kept. In Hebrew fashion the Syriac calls this a *beyt ctabe'* ("a house of writings"), and this explanation is strengthened by the fact that the mention of books and parchments is later connected with it. (4) Some have translated the Greek word *volumen* ["volume"]. Hence Jerome, in writing to Damasius (Letter 125, q. 2) says, "I am unrolling a volume, which Paul calls a φελόνην as some do." Moreover, Jerome is talking about the Hebrew volume of the Old Testament. This explanation is strengthened by the fact that φελλός means "bark" [*librum*], as in the bark of a tree from which volumes used to be made. It is noteworthy that the books of the Old Testament used to be written down in such a way that they could be rolled up into volumes—that is, in a way that one can still observe today in Jewish synagogues. (5) Some interpret it as a cloak, the sacred vestment the Latins call a *planeta* or, more commonly, a *casula* ["chasuble"]. But the Greeks do not call that vestment a φελόνην but a φαινόλησν. (6) Most people take it as reference to a cloak in the other sense of the word, for a "cloak" [*paenula*] to the Romans was a garment suitable for resisting rain and the cold. Jerome (*Dial. 3 contra Pelag.*) translates it *lacerna* ("a raincoat"). Some object to this explanation, saying that it seems strange for Paul to tell him to bring a garment from so far away when there were people in Rome who made and sold such clothes; and that it seems preposterous for him to have left his traveling coat behind when he was beginning his journey and then to ask for it once the journey was over.

Troas was a city in Asia Minor, made famous by association with Troy, which the Greeks besieged for ten years. We read that Paul went there three times: first in Acts 16:8; second, in 2 Cor. 2:12; and third, in Acts 20:6. On this last visit he left his cloak there (says Estius).

Carpus hosted Paul in Troas and was considered worthy for the apostle even to entrust his possessions to him. He is not the same as Carpus of Crete, also praised as being a good host, and of whom Dionysius left some published recollection in his Letter *ad Demophilum*.

καὶ τὰ βιβλία, μάλιστα τὰς μεμβράνας. ["And the scrolls, especially the parchments."] (1) Those who take the φελόνην to be a book box take this part as a supplement and explanation of the preceding, so that the sense is: "When you come, bring with you the box, or bookcase, along with the scrolls and parchments stored in it." (2) Those who interpret the φελόνην as a volume of Scripture—or the Old Testament—interpret τὰ βιβλία ["the scrolls"] to be other works written on paper.

Τὰς μεμβράνας means "skin parchments" on which Paul had jotted down things worth knowing to aid his memory. This is why he expresses unique concern about them, saying "especially the parchments." The Syriac rendered it *ceraca' damgale'* ("a bundle of books") because the ancients used parchments as we use paper for writing. Pliny (*Nat. hist.*, bk. 13, ch. 11): "The parchment [*membrana*] is a writing material made from animal skins."

From this passage we conclude: (1) What the apostle's implements were, that is, for clothing and writing.

(2) How necessary bishops should consider reading Scripture to be, for Paul was taught the mysteries of Christianity in the third heaven, yet throughout all the many years of his apostolic ministry he longed to read books.

Verse 14.

Ἀλέξανδρος ὁ χαλκεὺς πολλά μοι κακὰ ἐνεδείξατο. ["Alexander the coppersmith exhibited many evils against me."] Χαλκεὺς means "a coppersmith."

He had also discussed this Alexander in 1 Tim. 1:20, where he had excommunicated him as a heretic. In response he grew angry and resisted both sound teaching and Paul all the more.

"Exhibited many evils against me," that is, "he did them, displayed them, committed them, afflicted me with many evils." It is a Hebrew way of speaking. Undoubtedly this Alexander stirred up the charge for Paul's captivity among the friends of Nero on the grounds that [Paul] was seditious, spreading strange dogmas, and destroying the ancient Jewish religion which was allowed in Rome.

Still, there are some who doubt whether this Alexander is the same as the one mentioned in 1 Tim. 1:20.

ἀποδῴη αὐτῷ ὁ κύριος κατὰ τὰ ἔργα αὐτοῦ. ["May the Lord repay him according to his works."] The Vulgate translates it in the future tense: *reddet* ["He will repay"], so as to soften the curse and turn it into a prediction. But the Greek has ἀποδῴη ("may He repay"). This reading is found in: (1) No few Latin manuscripts, as Estius himself admits. (2) Ancient commentaries of Ambrosiaster, Pelagius, Primasius, and Sedulius. (3) Also Jerome (*Dial. contra Pelag.*, bk. 3, ch. 1; and in his commentary on Ecclesiastes 8). Also Gregory (or whoever the author is of *Concordia locorum scripturae*, final question).

Of course, Augustine (*Contra Faustum*, bk. 16, ch. 22; and *De serm. Domini in monte*, bk. 1, ch. 37) reads it in the future: "He will repay." In the latter work he comments: "He does not say 'May He repay,' but 'The Lord will repay him according to his works.' This verb is one of prediction, not cursing." But Estius correctly reminds us that in the former work it should read "May He repay," "because there Augustine is teaching how such curses should be understood, and in the latter work he was using a faulty manuscript."

But how does such a curse fit with the apostle's tenderness? I respond. Paul is speaking out of his apostolic zeal. By the Spirit of prophecy he foretells and curses the evils against one who had deserted him willfully and purposely. On the other hand, he prays for the rest who deserted him out of weakness and fear of danger (v. 16). Justin (q. 125, p. 368): "This is not a curse and an insult, but a prediction befitting an apostolic man; he is not treating him unjustly, but giving place to wrath." Therefore this imprecation was not an indication of impatience or ill-will. It should be understood either that he pronounced these evils upon him in the Spirit of prophecy, with the approval of God's justice, or he prayed God's vengeance upon him, insofar as it is just, since he gave no hope of amendment by continuing to sin out of intentional malice.

Verse 15.

ὃν καὶ σὺ φυλάσσου. ["Beware of him yourself."] "Keep an eye on him and watch out for him yourself," for he was going about stirring up Jews against those who confessed the Gospel (Acts 21:[27]).

λίαν γὰρ ἀνθέστηκε τοῖς ἡμετέροις λόγοις. ["For he vehemently opposed our words."] He had accused Alexander of afflicting him with many evils, but he passes over this crime and says that Timothy should beware of him because he was vehemently against his teaching.

Verse 16.

Ἐν τῇ πρώτῃ μου ἀπολογίᾳ οὐδείς μοι συμπαρεγένετο. ["In my first defense no one was with me."] "The first time I stood before Nero and defended myself against the accusations of the Jews, no one came to my help or defense."

Based on this, Estius tries to prove his opinion that "this Epistle was written right away in the first year when Paul had arrived in Rome, when martyrdom was not threatening him yet. Surely he would not inform Timothy of what happened at his first defense after so many years had passed, especially since it is clear from his other Epistles that he had been with Paul in Rome since then." But Cajetan responds: "Paul is not referring to the first of all his defenses but to the first one after his second arrival in Rome."

ἀλλὰ πάντες με ἐγκατέλιπον. "[But] everyone left me," stuck in woes and immersed in adversity, for this is the force of the verb ἐγκατέλιπον: "I was bereft of help from friends and supporters."

It seems that the universal particle ["all"] should be understood with qualification. "Everyone," that is, "nearly everyone." It is unlikely that even Luke abandoned him.

μὴ αὐτοῖς λογισθείη. "May it not be credited against them"—that is, as culpability before God. "May God forgive them for this transgression (παράπτωμα) and not punish them for it" (cf. Acts 7:60).

Verse 17.

ὁ δὲ κύριός μοι παρέστη, καὶ ἐνεδυνάμωσέν με. ["But the Lord stood by me and strengthened me."] "Even though I was abandoned by everyone and bereft of their comfort and help, Christ the Lord still stood by me with His gracious presence and strengthened me so that I did not succumb at my defense."

Erasmus and others think that the verb παρέστη should be rendered *adfuit* ["was present"], but it is more accurate to translate it *astitit* ["stood by"]. It is, after all, a different verb from the one used in v. 16: οὐδείς μοι συμπαρεγένετο. Also, it is the same verb as in Acts 27:23: "The angel of the Lord stood by me (παρέστη) this night."

Compare the parallel passage of Acts 23:11: "The following night the Lord, standing by him (ἐπιστὰς), said, 'Be steadfast.'" All this shows that Paul here is not only talking about the presence of God's help but also about a unique appearance of Christ before him by which he was greatly strengthened in peril.

Therefore one may conclude from this passage that Christ the Lord is also present on the earth with His body and is able to present Himself so as to be seen where and when He wills. To this some people say, "Christ only stood by Paul according to His divine nature." Some say, "The Lord appeared to him through an angel, not through Himself." Still others say, "It was a vision of an image." None of these statements follows the emphasis of the text.

ἵνα δι' ἐμοῦ τὸ κήρυγμα πληροφορηθῇ, καὶ ἀκούσῃ πάντα τὰ ἔθνη. ["So that through me the preaching might be fulfilled and all the Gentiles hear."] He is explaining the purpose for why the Lord stood by him and strengthened him—namely, that the preaching of the Gospel about Christ might be set forth in full assurance, that is, through his free, public confession before Caesar. For the Spirit of God was working extraordinarily in Paul's solemn confession so that the hearts of those who already believed were strengthened and those who did not yet believe were moved. Luther has *auff daß durch mich die Predigt bestettigt würde, und alle Heyden höreten* ["so that through me the preaching might be confirmed and all the Gentiles might hear"].

In comparison to Acts 23:11 and 27:23 some deduce that these are the words of one explaining what the Lord said to him through revelation, words similar to: "Be steadfast. Do not fear. For it still must be that through you the preaching of the Gospel be set forth with full assurance and all the Gentiles hear."

The meaning is: "So that with full assurance I might preach the Gospel and the Gentiles hear it from my mouth."

καὶ ἐρρύσθην ἐκ στόματος λέοντος. ["And I was snatched out from the lion's mouth."] By "lion" he means Nero. He calls him that due to his power and cruelty, for he persecuted the Christians horrendously.

Some want this to be a proverbial expression that signifies "the magnitude of the danger from which he was saved by God's help, since it is unlikely that Paul would have spoken his case before Nero himself at that time." But even if he tried his case before a lower judge, everything was being conducted by Nero's authority, and so he is quite right to say that he was snatched out of the lion's mouth.

Ἐρρύσθην does not properly mean *liberatus sum* ["I was freed"] (as the Vulgate rendered it) but *ereptus sum* ["I was snatched out"]. You see, it does not mean that he was set free from his chains—since he wrote this Epistle from imprisonment—but that he was snatched out of the current danger he feared at that time.

Verse 18.

Καὶ ῥύσεταί με ὁ κύριος ἀπὸ παντὸς ἔργου πονηροῦ. ["And the Lord will snatch me away from every evil work."] The Vulgate rendered it in the past: *liberavit me* ["He freed me"]. However: (1) The Greek has ῥύσεταί ("He will snatch[10] me away"). (2) The Ambrosian copy and some copies of Latin manuscripts read future: *liberabit me* ["He will free me"]. (3) The following verb σώσει ["He will save"] demands the future tense, and even the Vulgate translated it future: *salvum faciet* ["He will save me"].

The sense is this: "Not only was I snatched from the lion's mouth and imminent danger to my life, but I also have sure confidence that the Lord will again preserve me in goodness henceforth, lest I act in any way contrary to God's will or my office." This can also be understood as about his liberation from all evils

10 Read *eripiet* instead of *eripit*.

through death, as Luther rendered it: *Er wird mich erlösen von allem Ubel* ["He will deliver me from all evil"]. "Even if I will not be free from persecutions and dangers in this life, Christ the Lord will still give me steadfastness in faith and a final departure (ἔκβασις). He will snatch me away from all evils and dangers."

καὶ σώσει εἰς τὴν βασιλείαν αὐτοῦ τὴν ἐπουράνιον. ["And He will save [me] into His heavenly kingdom."] "Even if I should have to die for confessing the Gospel, the Lord will still bring me through death into His heavenly kingdom, where I shall enjoy eternal life and blessing with Him."

ᾧ ἡ δόξα εἰς τοὺς αἰῶνας τῶν αἰώνων. Ἀμήν. ["To whom be the glory unto the ages of the ages. Amen."] He inserts a doxology, as he does elsewhere. Moreover, since, by "the Lord" he means Christ, a proof for affirming Christ's divinity can be drawn from this doxology.

Verse 19.

Ἄσπασαι Πρίσκαν καὶ Ἀκύλαν. ["Greet Prisca and Aquila."] Acts 18:2 discusses Prisca and Aquila. Some Latin copies read "Priscilla," but in the Greek copies here it reads Πρίσκαν. Acts 18:2 has the diminutive "Priscilla." Prisca, then, was Aquila's wife, and hence some commentators raise the question: *Why does he name the wife first?* Lyranus says the reason is that "she first believed, and the order of grace comes before the order of nature." Chrysostom (on 2 Timothy, hom. 10) thinks that "this happened because of the outstanding zeal for advancing the Gospel that was in Prisca." Others say the reason is that "she was more famous and well-known among the faithful."

Note, however, that it is not always the case that Prisca comes first, for in 1 Cor. 16:19 her husband's name comes first.

Prisca and Aquila were spouses, both Jewish (though Aquila was from Pontus). They were tentmakers but were uncommonly well educated in Christianity as those who had enjoyed Paul as their home teacher.

καὶ τὸν Ὀνησιφόρου οἶκον. ["And the household of Onesiphorus."] Onesiphorus was discussed in 2 Tim. 1:16, where the apostle commends his faithfulness and kindness.

Verse 20.

Ἔραστος ἔμεινεν ἐν Κορίνθῳ. ["Erastus stayed in Corinth."] This Erastus was one of those who ministered to Paul in Acts 19:22. In Rom. 16:23 he is also called "steward of the city," meaning of Corinth. Undoubtedly he stayed in Corinth because the public business of his office detained him.

Τρόφιμον δὲ ἀπέλιπον ἐν Μιλήτῳ ἀσθενοῦντα. ["But Trophimus I left sick in Miletus."] This Trophimus was also one of Paul's companions (Acts 20:4), where he is called "from Asia." In Acts 21:29 he is called "from Ephesus."

Melita[11] is the island for which Paul made on a raft when he set out for Rome (Acts [28]:1). There he rescued the father of the ruler of the island from a disease and there cared for all the sick. On Crete there was a city called Miletus, as some prove from Homer's *Iliad.* ([bk.] 2)[12] and Strabo (bk. 12). Trophimus could have been left sick there when Paul was captive and sailed for Crete (Acts 27:7).

Here the question arises: *How could Paul have left Trophimus sick at Miletus when it is clear from Acts 20:17 and 21:29 that he left Miletus with Paul and arrived at Jerusalem? It does not say that Paul later returned to Miletus, but that he was arrested in Jerusalem and taken to Rome by a very different route.* I respond. (1) Baronius (*Annal.*, tom. 1, *anno Christi* 58, n. 144) thinks it should read "in Melita" instead of "in Miletus." (2) But since none of the Greek copies support this conjecture, it is more correct to say that Trophimus returned to Miletus from Jerusalem and became ill there while Paul was taken to Rome. (3) Some want Paul to have called "Melite" "Miletus" by transposing the vowels, as sometimes happens.

Trophimus did not die from this illness but later recovered, and "Paul appointed him bishop of Arles, and from here as from a spring all Gaul received the streams of faith," says Pope Zosimus.

Verse 21.

Σπούδασον πρὸ χειμῶνος ἐλθεῖν. "Take pains to come to me before winter," [that is], "since your work is thoroughly necessary for me now that I have been abandoned by the other partners of the Gospel."

Ἀσπάζεταί σε Εὔβουλος, καὶ Πούδης, καὶ Λῖνος, καὶ Κλαυδία, καὶ οἱ ἀδελφοὶ πάντες. ["Eubulus and Pudens and Linus and Claudia and all the brothers greet you."]

There is no other mention of Eubulus.

Pudens was a man of senatorial rank among the Romans, the father of Praxedes and Pudentiana, according to the martyrologies.

People claim that Linus followed Peter as bishop of Rome.

People claim that Claudia was the wife of Pudens.

By "brothers" he means the faithful, Christians who were in Rome.

Verse 22.

Ὁ κύριος Ἰησοῦς χριστὸς μετὰ τοῦ πνεύματός σου. "The Lord Jesus Christ be with your spirit," [that is,] "preserve and keep your soul" (cf. Phlm. 25). "May He be with you through His grace."

---

11 Known now as Malta.

12 Homer, *The Iliad* 2.647 (LCL 170 [1924], pp. 108–9).

ἡ χάρις μεθ' ὑμῶν. Ἀμήν. ["Grace be with you. Amen."] The commentaries of the Greeks read μεθ' ἡμῶν ["with us"] and expound upon it studiously. They say that Paul is also praying God's grace for himself here. But the Greek copies we have now consistently read μεθ' ὑμῶν ["with you"], which is how the Epistle to Titus ends too.

The subscription after the end of the Epistle reads: Πρὸς Τιμόθεον δευτέρα τῆς Ἐφεσίων ἐκκλησίας πρῶτον ἐπίσκοπον χειροτονηθέντα, ἐγράφη ἀπὸ Ρώμης, ὅτε ἐκ δευτέρου παρέστη Παῦλος τῷ Καίσαρι Νέρωνι. ["The Second [Epistle] to Timothy, appointed first bishop of the church of Ephesus, written from Rome when Paul stood before Caesar Nero the second time."]

Person Index

Scripture Index

2 Timothy

Works Cited

This list is organized by the authors that Gerhard cites or, when the author is unknown, by the short title for the work as referenced in the text. The works by a particular author are further organized by the abbreviation of the work that Gerhard cites. The entry includes the full title and publication information of an edition that Gerhard could have cited. In instances where we are able (such as for the collected works of an author), we provide a modern edition as well. When possible, an English translation concludes the entry for the specific cited work.

We have tried to cite the latest edition of a cited work prior to the publication of this volume. Not all the works Gerhard cites could be located. Some of the entries below are printed in bold text. This means the book was in the Gerhard library, as found in Johann Anselm Steiger, ed., *Bibliotheca Gerhardina: Rekonstruktion der Gelehrten- und Leihbibliothek Johann Gerhards (1582–1637) und seines Sohnes Johann Ernst Gerhard (1621–1668)* (Stuttgart-Bad Cannstatt: Frommann-holzboog, 2002). However, because this library was collected not only by Johann Gerhard but also by his son Johann Ernst Gerhard, and because we do not know when he acquired these books or whether he preferred to use a borrowed book, care should be taken in drawing conclusions from this data.

Authors are generally alphabetized by family name. Since the last name of some authors is not a family name but the name of a location (e.g., Thomas Aquinas), readers should check to see whether the author is alphabetized by a name other than the last name.

The key below corresponds to the abbreviations employed in the annotations of this book as well as in the entries on the following pages. Also included is a list of abbreviations commonly found in the citations and in the footnotes in this volume.

Abbreviation	**Full Title**
ACW	*Ancient Christian Writers: The Works of the Fathers in Translation*. Westminster, MD: Newman, 1946–89; New York: Paulist, 1990–

AE	*Luther's Works*. American Edition. Volumes 1–30 edited by Jaroslav Pelikan. Volumes 31–55 edited by Helmut T. Lehmann. Volumes 56–82 edited by Christopher Boyd Brown and Benjamin T. G. Mayes. St. Louis: Concordia, 1955–. Philadelphia: Muhlenberg/Fortress, 1957–86
ANF	*Ante-Nicene Fathers*. Edited by A. Roberts. Reprint: Grand Rapids: Eerdmans, 1950–51
Ap	Apology of the Augsburg Confession
BSLK	*Die Bekenntnisschriften der evangelisch-lutherischen Kirche*. 12th edition. Göttingen: Vandenhoeck & Ruprecht, 1998
CCSL	*Corpus Christianorum: Series latina*. Turnhout: Brepols, 1953–
Concordia	*Concordia: The Lutheran Confessions*. 2nd edition. Edited by Paul T. McCain et al. St. Louis: Concordia, 2006
CSEL	*Corpus scriptorum ecclesiasticorum latinorum*. Vienna: Austrian Academy of Sciences, 1866–
CWE	*Collected Works of Erasmus*. Toronto: University of Toronto Press, 1974–
FC	*The Fathers of the Church*. Edited by R. J. Deferrari. New York, 1947ff.
GCS	*Die griechischen christlichen Schriftsteller*. Leipzig, 1897ff.
LCC	Library of Christian Classics. Edited by J. Baillie, J. T. McNeill, H. P. van Dusen. Philadelphia, 1953ff.
LCL	Loeb Classical Library. London: Heinemann; Cambridge, MA: Harvard University Press, 1912–
LFC	*Library of the Fathers of the Holy Catholic Church*. Edited by Pusey, Ekble, and Newman. Oxford: John Henry Parker, 1800–1881
LXX	Septuagint
NPNF^{1}	*A Select Library of Nicene and Post-Nicene Fathers of the Christian Church*. Series 1. 14 volumes. Edited by Ph. Schaff and H. Wace. Reprint, Grand Rapids: Eerdmans, 1952
NPNF^{2}	*A Select Library of Nicene and Post-Nicene Fathers of the Christian Church*. Series 2. 14 volumes. Edited by Ph. Schaff and H. Wace. Reprint, Grand Rapids: Eerdmans, 1952
PG	*Patrologiae cursus completus: Series graeca*. Edited by J.-P. Migne. Paris: Migne, 1857–66
PL	*Patrologiae cursus completus: Series latina*. Edited by J.-P. Migne. Paris: Garnier, 1844–65
SA	Smalcald Articles
SC	Small Catechism
Triglotta	*Triglot Concordia: The Symbolical Books of the Ev. Lutheran Church, German-Latin-English*. St. Louis: Concordia, 1921

TTH	*Translated Texts for Historians*. Liverpool: Liverpool University Press, 1989–
WA	*D. Martin Luthers Werke: Kritische Gesamtausgabe*. 73 volumes. in 85. Weimar: Hermann Böhlau, 1883–
WA DB	*D. Martin Luthers Werke: Deutsche Bibel*. 12 volumes. in 15. Weimar: H. Böhlau, 1906–
WSA	*The Works of Saint Augustine: A Translation for the 21st Century*. Edited by J. E. Rotelle. New York: New City Press, 1990–

admon.	admonition	n.	number
annot.	annotation	obj.	objection
argum. advers.	opposing argument	p.	page
art.	article	pl.	plural
bk.	book	pp.	pages
c. *or* can.	canon	prov.	saying
cent.	century	q.	question
cf.	confer	s.d.	without a date
ch.	chapter	sect.	section
chs.	chapters	serm.	sermon
class.	classification	sess.	session
col.	column	sing.	singular
comment.	commentary	s.l.	without a place
conc.	conclusion	s.n.	without a name
d.	died	tom.	tome
disp.	disputation	tr. *or* tract.	treatise
dist.	distinction	ult.	ultimate, i.e., final
ep.	epistle (letter)	v.	verse
eps.	epistles (letters)	vol.	volume
f.	folio	vols.	volumes
hom. *or* homil.	homily	vv.	verses
ibid.	*ibidem* (in the same place)	§	paragraph
lect.	reading	§§	paragraphs

Actuarius, Johannes

Περὶ διαγνως. παθ. • *De actionibus et afectibus spiritus animalis, eiusque victu.* Paris: Goupyl, 1557

Aegineta (Paul of Aegina)

Opera. Transated by Johann Winter. Lugduni, 1589 • *The Medical Works of Paulus Aegineta, the Greek Physician.* Translated by Francis Adams. London: Welsh, Treuttel, Würtz, 1834

Ambrose of Milan (Ambrosius)

Collected works • ***Omnia Qvotqvot Extant D. Ambrosii Episcopi Mediolanensis Opera, Primvm Per Des. Erasmvm Roterodamvm, Mox Per Sig. Gelenivm, deinde per alios eruditos uiros diligenter castigata: nunc uero postremum per Ioannem Costerium . . . emendata.* Basileae: Episcopius, 1567**

1 Timothy • *See* Pauline Epistles

2 Timothy • *See* Pauline Epistles

De Abel et Cain • See *De Caino et Abel*

De Abraham (PL 14) • *On Abraham.* Translated by Theodosia Tomkinson. Etna, CA: Center for Traditionalist Orthodox Studies, 2000

De Caino et Abel (PL 14; CSEL 32/1) • *Cain and Abel* (FC 42)

De dignitate sacerdotali (PL 17)

De sacramentis (CSEL 73) • *On the Sacraments.* Translated by J. H. Srawley. London: SPCK, 1950

Letters • *Epistulae* (PL 16; CSEL 82) • *Letters* (NPNF[2] 10)

Pauline Epistles • Ambrosiaster, *Commentarius in epistulas Paulinas* (CSEL 81/1–3) • *Commentaries on Romans and 1–2 Corinthians.* Translated by G. L. Bray. Downers Grove, IL: InterVarsity Press, 2009; *Commentaries on Galatians–Philemon.* Translated by G. L. Bray. Downers Grove, IL: InterVarsity Press, 2009

Ambrosiaster. *See* Ambrose of Milan

Ambrosius. *See* Ambrose of Milan

Anselm of Canterbury

Collected works • ***Opera omnia quatuor tomis comprehensa.* Cologne: Peter Cholinus, 1612**

1 Timothy • *See* Pauline Epistles

Cur Deus homo (PL 158) • *Cur Deus homo.* In Anselm, *Basic Writings.* Translated and edited by Thomas Williams. Indianapolis: Hackett, 2007

Oper. • *See* Collected works

Pauline Epistles • *In omnes Pauli Apostoli Epistolas enarrationes.* Coloniae: Gennepaeum, 1545

Apology of the Augsburg Confession

Die Apologie des Augsburger Bekenntnisses (*BSLK*) • The Defense of the Augsburg Confession (*Concordia*)

Aquila

Greek translation of Old Testament • in fragments of Origen, *Hexapla* (PG 15–16)

Aretius, Benedictus

2 Timothy • *See* Pauline Epistles

Aretius, Benedictus, cont'd.

Pauline Epistles • *Commentarii In Omnes Epistolas D. Pavli, Et Canonicas, itemque in Apocalypsin D. Ioannis.* [Geneva:] Jean LePreux, 1589

Arias Montanus, Benedictus (Benito Arias Montano)

Exemplar regium • *Biblia Sacra hebraice, chaldaice, graece, et latine.* Antwerp: Plantinus, 1569–72

Aristotle

Collected works • ***Operum . . . Graecè & Latinè.*** **[Geneva:] Guillaume Laimarie, 1597**

Metaphysics • ***Duodecim libri methaphisice.*** **Leipzig: Martin Landsberg, 1499** • *Metaphysics* (LCL 271, 287)

Rhetoric. • ***De Arte Rhetorica. Libri Tres.*** **Rostock: Jakob Lucius, 1577;** ***Rhetoricorum Libri Tres . . . in eosdem libros Commentarij.*** **Basel: Bartholomäus Westheimer, 1545** (LCL 193) • *Art of Rhetoric* (LCL 193)

Athanasius

Collected works, Commelin. edition • ***Του Εν Αγιοις Πατρος Ημων Αθανασιου Αρχιεπισκοπου Αλεξανδρειας Τα Ευρισκομενα Απαντα . . . B. Athanasii Archiepiscopi Alexandrini Opera Qvae Reperivntvr Omnia, In Dvos Tomos Tribvta. Graece nunc primùm (ex Mss. Codd. Basil. Cantabrig. Palatt. & baliis) in lucem data, cum interpretatione Latina Petri Nannii Alemariani, & aliorum vbi illa desiderabatur.*** **2 volumes. [Heidelberg]: Hieronymus Commelinus, 1601**

Disp. contra Arium • *Athanasii Episcopi Alexandrini Sanctissima, Eloqventissimaqve Opera Commentarij in epistolas Pauli Contra Gentiles Liber vnus De incarnatione Verbi . . . Disputatio contra Arrium. In vim Psalmorum opusculum. Exhortatio ad Monachos. De passione Imaginis domini nostri Libellus. Epistolae nonnullae Romanorum Pontificum ad Athanasium, et Atanasij ad eosdem. Quae omnia olim iam latina facta Christophoro Porsena, Ambrosio Monacho, Angelo Politiano interpretibus, vna cum doctissima Erasmi Roterodani ad pium lectorem paraclesi.* Parisiis: Parvus, 1519

Synop. • "Synopsis totius scripturae." In *Athanasii Magni Alexandrini Episcopi, Graviss. Scriptoris, Et Sanctiss. Martyris, Opera.* Volume 4. Basel: Froben, 1556

Athenaeus

Deipnosophistae (LCL 204, 208, 224, 235, 274, 327, 345) • *The Learned Banqueters* (LCL 204, 208, 224, 235, 274, 327, 345)

Augustine of Hippo

Collected works • ***Omnivm Opervm Primvs Tomvs [–Decimvs].*** **Paris: Claude Chevallon, 1531;** ***Primvs [–Decimvs] Tomvs . . . D. Avrelii Avgvstini . . . Cvivs Praestantissima In Omni Genere monimenta.*** **Basel: Froben, 1569**

Ad fratres in eremo, serm. 8 (PL 39)

Confess. • *Confessiones* (CCSL 27) • *Confessions* (NPNF[1] 1)

Contra Cresconium • *Ad Cresconium grammaticum partis Donati* (CSEL 52) • *To Cresconius, a Donatist Grammarian* (WSA 1/22)

Contra Donatistas post conlationem (CSEL 53)

Contra duas epist. Pelagi. • *Contra duas epistolas Pelagianorum, ad Bonifacium Romanae ecclesiae episcopum* (PL 44) • *A Treatise against Two Letters of the Pelagians* (NPNF[1] 5)

Contra epistulam Parmeniani (CSEL 51) • *Against the Letter of Parmenian* (WSA 1/21)

Contra Faustum Manichaeum (CSEL 25/1) • *Against Faustus, a Manichee* (NPNF[1] 4)

Contra litteras Petiliani Donatisti Cirtensis Episcopi (CSEL 52) • *In Answer to the Letters of Petilian, the Donatist, Bishop of Cirta* (NPNF[1] 4)

Augustine of Hippo, cont'd.

Contra Maximinum Arianum (PL 42) • *Against Maximinus, an Arian* (WSA 1/18)

De bapt. contra Donatist. • *De baptismo* (CSEL 51) • *On Baptism* (NPNF[1] 4)

De civ. Dei • *De civitate Dei* (CCSL 47–48) • *The City of God* (FC 8, 14, 24)

De cognit. verae vitae • Honorius Augustodunensis, *De verae vitae cognitione* (PL 40)

De correptione et gratia (PL 44) • *On Admonition and Grace* (FC 2)

De doctrina Christiana (CCSL 32) • *On Christian Teaching* (WSA 1/11; NPNF[1] 2)

De Genes. ad lit. • *De Genesi ad litteram* (CSEL 28/1) • *On the Literal Interpretation of Genesis* (ACW 41–42)

De gratia et libero arbitrio (PL 44) • *On Grace and Free Choice* (NPNF[1] 5)

De haeresibus (CCSL 46) • *On Heresies* (WSA 1/18)

De lib. arbitr. • See *De gratia et libero arbitrio*

De natura et gratia (CSEL 60) • *On Nature and Grace* (NPNF[1] 5)

De peccatorum meritis et remissione et de baptismo parvulorum (PL 44; CSEL 60) • *On the Merits and Forgiveness of Sins and on Infant Baptism* (NPNF[1] 5)

De serm. Domini in monte (PL 34) • *Our Lord's Sermon on the Mount* (NPNF[1] 6)

De Spiritu et littera (CSEL 60) • *On the Spirit and the Letter* (LCC 8)

De symbolo ad catechumenos (CCSL 46) • *On the Creed, to Catechumens* (FC 27)

Enarrat. Ps. • *See* Psalms

Enchir. • *Enchiridion ad Laurentium, de fide, spe et caritate* (CCSL 46) • *A Handbook on Faith, Hope, and Love* (ACW 3)

Galatians • *Expositio epistulae ad Galatas* (CSEL 84) • *Augustine's Commentary on Galatians.* Translated by Eric Plumer. Oxford Early Christian Studies. Oxford: Oxford University Press, 2003

Haeres. • See *De haeresibus*

John • *In Johannis evangelium tractatus* (CCSL 36) • *Tractates on the Gospel of John* (NPNF[1] 4)

Letters • *Epistulae* (CCSL 34, 44, 57, 58, 88) • *Epistles* (NPNF[1] 1)

Psalms • *Enarrationes in Psalmos* (CCSL 38–40) • *Explanations of the Psalms* (ACW 29–30)

Q • See *Quaest.*

Quaest. • *Quaestiones in Heptateuchum* (PL 34; CCSL 33) • *Questions on the Heptateuch* (WSA 1/15)

Sermon 9 *de verb. apost.* • *Sermo 175* (PL 38:945–49)

Sermon 10 *de verb. apost.* • *Sermo 176* (PL 38:949–53)

Sermon 11 on Psalm 118 • *See* Psalms

Balduin, Friedrich

De casib. consc. • *Tractatus Luculentus, Posthumus, Toti Reipublicae Christianae Utilissimus de Materia rarissime antehac enucleata, Casibus nimirum Conscientiae.* Wittenberg: Helwigius, 1628

Baptista Mantuanus, Johannes

De contemnenda morte. Liptzk: Thanner, 1504

Ecl. • *Bucolica seu adolescentia: in decem aeglogas diuisa.* [Strasbourg:] Prüs, 1514 • *Adulescentia: The Eclogues of Mantuan.* Translated by Lee Piepho. New York: Garland, 1989

Baronius (Cesare Baronio)

***Annales ecclesiastici*. 12 volumes. Cologne, 1609–13**

Basil of Caesarea

Collected works • ***Απαντα Τα . . . Βασιλειου . . . Opera Graeca quae ad nos extant omnia*. Basel: Hieronymus Froben, 1551; *Opera . . . Omnia: Iam recens per Wolfgangvm Mvscvlvm partim locis aliquot castigata, partim luculentis accessionibus aucta*. Basel: Johann Oporinus, 1565** (PG 29–32)

De vera virginitatis integritate (PG 30)

Psalms • *Homiliae super Psalmos* (PG 29)

Bede (Beda Venerabilis)

Collected works • ***Opera . . . omnia*. Cologne: Gymnich & Hierat, 1612;** *Opera Bedae Venerabilis Presbyteri Anglosaxonis: Viri In Divinis Atque Humanis literis exercitatissimi: omnia in octo Tomos distincta*. Basileae: Herwagen, 1563

1 Timothy • *See* Collected works, volume 3

Bellarmine, Robert (Roberto Bellarmino)

Collected works • *Opera omnia: nunc postremo ab ipso authore recogn. et in 7 tomos distributa*. Coloniae Agrippinae: Gualterus, 1617–20

De grat. et lib. • "De gratia et libero arbitrio," in *Disputationes de controversiis*

De Rom. pont. • "De Summo Pontifice," in *Disputationes de controversiis*. Or *Tractatvs De Potestate Svmmi Pontificis In Rebvs Temporalibvs: Aduersus Gvlielmvm Barclaivm*. Coloniae Agrippinae: Gualtherus, 1611

De sacram. matrimon. • "De sacramento matrimonii," in *Disputationes de controversiis*

De sacr. ordin. • "De sacramento ordinis," in *Disputationes de controversiis*

Disputationes de controversiis • ***Disputationum de controversiis christianae fidei, adversus huius temporis haereticos opus*. Ingolstadii: Sartorius, 1601** (Justinus Fèvre, ed. *Ven. Cardinalis Roberti Bellarmini Politiani S. J. Opera Omnia*. Parisiis: Ludovicus Vivès, 1870–73)

Bernard of Clairvaux

Collected works • ***Opera . . . omnia*. Basel: Johann Herwagen, 1552** (PL 182–85; *Sancti Bernardi Opera*. Edited by J. Leclercq. Romae: Ed. Cistercienses, 1957–98)

De conversion S. Pauli • *Sermones in Conversione Sancti Pauli* (PL 183)

De Gratia Et Libero Arbitrio Tractatus (PL 182) • *On Grace and Free Choice*. Translated by Daniel O'Donovan. Kalamazoo: Cistercian, 1977

Song of Songs • *Sermones in Cantica canticorum* (PL 183) • *On the Song of Songs*. Translated by Kilian Walsh. Kalamazoo: Cistercian, 1971–80

Beza, Theodore

Gloss. margin. • ***Testamentvm Novvm, Sive Nouum Foedus Iesu Christi*. [Paris: Henri Estienne], 1588**

Resp. ad colloq. Mampelg. • ***Ad Acta Colloqui Montisbelgardensis . . . Responsionis, Pars prior [–Altera]*. Geneva: Jean LePreux, 1589**

Tractatio De Polygamia, Et Divortiis. Geneva: Crispinus, 1571

Budaeus, Guilielmus (Guillaume Budé)

***Commentarii linguae Graecae*. Parisiis: Stephanus, 1548**

Bullinger, Heinrich

2 Timothy • *See* Pauline Epistles

Bullinger, Heinrich, cont'd.

Pauline Epistles • *Commentarii In omnes Pauli Apostoli Epistolas, atque etiam in Epistolam ad Hebraeos, Adiunximus Eiusdem Authoris Commentarios in omnes Epistolas Canonicas.* Tiguri: Cambierus, 1603

Cajetan, Thomas (Thomas de Vio Caietanus)

Collected works • *Opuscula omnia Thomae de Vio Caietani . . . in tres distincta tomos.* Lugduni, 1581

1 Timothy • *See* Pauline Epistles

2 Timothy • *See* Pauline Epistles

Pauline Epistles • *Epistolae Pauli et aliorum apostolorum.* [Paris], 1588

Calvin, John

Collected works • *Opuscula omnia in unum volumen collecta.* Geneva: Gerardus, 1552

1 Timothy • *Commentarii in utranque Pauli Epistolam ad Timotheum.* Genevae: Gerardus, 1548. Or *Commentarii in omnes Pauli Apostoli Epistolas, atque etiam in Epistolam ad Hebraeos.* Geneva: Crispinus, 1557 • *Calvin's Commentaries.* 23 volumes. Grand Rapids: Baker, 1989

Camerarius, Joachim

New Testament • *Jesu Christi D.N. Novum Testamentum, Theodoro Beza interprete. Additae sunt summae brevis doctrinae in Evangelistas, et Acta Apostolorum: Item, methodus apostolicarum epistolarum ab eodem authore, cum brevi phraseon, et locorum difficiliorum expositione, ex ipsius authoris maioribus annotationibus desumpta: paucis etiam additis ex Joach. Camerarii notationibus in Evangelistas et Acta.* [Geneva:] Eustache Vignon, 1575

Camerarius, Philipp

Horar. subseciv. • ***Operae Horarum Svbcisivarvm, Sive Meditationes Historicae.* Frankfurt am Main: Peter Kopf, 1601**

canon law. See *Ius canonicum*

Carthusianus, Dionysius. *See* Dionysius Carthusianus

Cassian, John (Cassianus)

Collat. • *Conlationes XXIV* (CSEL 13) • *The Conferences* (NPNF[2] 11)

Catharinus, Ambrosius (Lancelotto Politi)

1 Timothy • *See* Pauline Epistles

Pauline Epistles • *In omnes divi Pauli apostoli, et alias septem canonicas epistolas . . . commentaria.* Paris. Ald.: N. Chesneau, 1566

Celsus, Aulus Cornelius

De medicina (LCL 292, 304, 336) • *On Medicine* (LCL 292, 304, 336)

Chaldaic translation or paraphrase. *See* Arias Montanus, Benedictus; *Editio Complutensis*; Fagius, Paul; Targum

Chamierus, Daniel

Panopl. • *Panstratiae catholicae sive controversiarum de religione adversus pontificos corpus.* 1627, 1629

tom. 3 • See *Panopl.*

Chemnitz, Martin

***Examinis Concilii Tridentini . . . opus integrum*. Frankfurt am Main: s.n., 1599** • *Examination of the Council of Trent*. Translated by Fred Kramer. Chemnitz's Works 1–4. St. Louis: Concordia, 2009

Loci • *Loci theologici*. Wittenberg: Meisnerus, Bergerus, Schûrerus, 1615 • *Loci Theologici*. Translated by J. A. O. Preus. Chemnitz's Works 7–8. St. Louis: Concordia, 2009

Chrysostom (John Chrysostom)

Collected works • ***Opera . . . tomus primus* [*–quintus*]. Basel: Hieronymus Froben & Nikolaus Episcopius, 1558**

1 Timothy • *In epistulam I. ad Timotheum argumentum et homiliae* (PG 62) • *Homilies on 1 Timothy* (NPNF[1] 13)

2 Timothy • *In Epistulam II ad Timotheum homiliae 10* (PG 62) • *Homilies on the Epistles to Timothy, Titus and Philemon* (NPNF[1] 13)

Homil. on 2 Timothy • *See* 2 Timothy

Matthew • *In Matthaeum homiliae* (PG 57–58) • *Homilies on the Gospel of St. Matthew* (NPNF[1] 10)

Titus • *In Epistolam ad Titum Commentarium* (PG 62) • *Homilies on Titus* (NPNF[1] 13)

tom. 3, homil. ult. • *See* Collected works

Concil.

***Concilia Generalia, Et Provincialia, Graeca Et Latina Quotquot Reperiri Potuerunt, Item Epistolae Decrtales Et Romanor. Pontific. vitae.* [*Tomus I–II*]. Cologne: Anton Hierat, 1618; *Tomus Tertius* [*–Quartus*]. Cologne: Anton Hierat & Johann Gymnich, 1606**

Costerus, Franciscus (François de Coster)

Enchiridion Controversiarum Praecipuarum Nostri Temporis, De Religione. Coloniae Agrippinae: Mylius, 1608

Council of Smyrna. See *Concil.*

Council of Trent

See *Concil.* • *Decrees of the Ecumenical Councils*. Edited by Norman P. Tanner. Volume 2. London: Sheed & Ward, 1990

Cyprian (Thascius Caecilius Cyprianus)

Collected works • ***Opera . . . unà cum annotationunculis*. Basel: Johann Froben, 1520**

Ad Quirinum: testimoniorum libri III (CSEL 3/1) • *To Quirinus: Three Books of Testimonies* (ANF 5)

Letters • *Epistolae* (PL 4; CSEL 3/2) • (ANF 5)

Cyril of Alexandria

Collected works • ***Opera . . . In Tomos Qvinqve digesta*. Basel, 1566**

Thesaurus de sancta et consubstantiali Trinitate. In ***Opus . . . Thesaurus nuncupatus, quatuordecim libros complectens: et de consubstantialitate filii & spiritus sancti cum patre, contra hereticos luculentur disserens*. [Paris: Wolfgang Hopyl], 1514** (PG 75)

Damascenus (John of Damascus)

Collected works • ***Ιωαννου Του Δαμασκηνου Εργα . . . Ioannis Damasceni Opera Omnia . . . Item, Ioannis Cassiani eremitae non prorsus Dissimilis Argvmenti Libri Aliqvot*. Basel: [Sixtus & Sebastian Henricpetri, 1575]**

Damascenus (John of Damascus), cont'd.

De orth. fid. • See *Orth. fid.*

Orth. fid. • *Expositio fidei orthodoxae* (PG 94) • *Exposition of the Orthodox Faith* (FC 37; NPNF[2] 9)

Demosthenes

Oration 58 • *Private Cases* (LCL 351)

Dionysius Carthusianus (Dionysius Carthusiensis)

1 Timothy • *See* Pauline Epistles

2 Timothy • *See* Pauline Epistles

Pauline Epistles • ***IN OMNES beati Pauli epistolas commentaria.*** **Cologne: Peter Quentel, 1538**

Dionysius the Areopagite, Pseudo-

De div. nom. • "De divinis nominibus." In *Dionysii Areopagitae episcopi Atheniensis libri duo.* Venetiis: Zanetti, 1538/1539 (PG 3) • *On the Divine Names and the Mystical Theology.* Translated by C. E. Rolt. New York: Macmillan, 1920

Letter *ad Demophilum* (PG 3:1085)

Disput. de labefacto per Pontificias corruptelas pietatis studio

Dorotheus of Tyre

Synopsis • *Sulpitii Seueri Sacrae Historiae à Mundi exordio ad sua usque tempora deductae, libri II: Item Dorothei Episcopi Tyri . . . De vita Prophetarum et Apostolorum Synopsis.* Coloniae Agrippinae: apud Jo. Gymnicum, 1573

Drusius, Johannes

Adag. Hebr. • *Proverbia Ben-Sirae Autoris antiquissimi, qui creditur fuisse nepos Jeremiae prophetae Opera J. Drvsii in Latinam linguam conuersa scholijsq[ue] aut potius commentario illustrata; Accesserunt Adagiorum Ebraicorum Decuriae aliquot nunquam antehac editae.* Franekerae: Radaeus, 1597

Duraeus, Joannes (John Dury or Durie)

Contra Witaker. • *Confutatio, responsionis Gulielmi Whitakeri in Academia Cantabrigensi Professoris regij, ad Rationes decem, quibus fretus Edmundus Campianus Anglus . . . certamen Anglicanae Ecclesiae Ministris obtulit in causa fidei.* Parisiis: Thomas Brumennius, 1582

Editio Complutensis

[*Biblia complutensis*] *Vetus testamentum multiplici lingua nunc primo impressum; Secunda [–Quarta] pars Veteris testamenti; Nouum testamentum grece et latine in academia complutensi nouiter impressum; Vocabularium hebraicum atque chaldaicum totius veteris testamenti cum alijs tractatibus prout infra in prefatione continetur in academia complutensi nouiter impressum.* [Complutentia: Brocario, 1514–17]

Epiphanius of Salamis

Haeres. • ***Contra Octoaginta Haereses Opvs, Panarivm, Sive Arcvla, Avt Capsula Medica appellatum.*** **Basel: Robert Winter, 1543** (PG 41–42) • *The Panarion of Epiphanius of Salamis.* Translated by Frank Williams. Leiden: Brill, 1987, 1994

Erasmus, Desiderius

1 Timothy • *See* Apostolic Epistles

2 Timothy • *See* Apostolic Epistles

Erasmus, Desiderius, cont'd.

Annot. • ***In Novvm Testamentvm . . . Annotationes.* Basel: Johann Froben, 1519** • *Annotations on the New Testament* (CWE 42–44)

Apostolic Epistles • ***In Epistolas Apostolicas Paraphrasis.* Lyon: Sébastian Gryphius, 1544** • *Paraphrases on the Epistles to Timothy, Titus, and Philemon, the Epistles of Peter and Jude, the Epistles of James, the Epistle of John, the Epistle to the Hebrews* (CWE 44)

Paraphrasis • *See* Apostlic Epistles

Espencaeus, Claudius (Claude d'Espence)

Collected works • ***Opera omnia.* Paris: Claude Morel, 1619**

2 Timothy • *In posteriorem D. Pauli apostoli ad Timotheum epistolam commentarius, cum digressionibus XXXIII . . . bona ex parte ad hodiernas in religione controversias spectantibus, inter quas peculiaris est tractatus de uno Dei atque hominum mediatore Deo homine Jesu Christo.* Paris, 1564

Estius, Guilielmus (Willem van Est)

1 Timothy • *See* Pauline Epistles

2 Timothy • *See* Pauline Epistles

Pauline Epistles • *In omnes beati Pauli et aliorum apostolorum epistolas commentaria.* Paris, 1623

Eusebius of Caesarea (Eusebius Pamphili)

Collected works • *Historiae Ecclesiasticae Scriptores Graeci, Nempe, Eusebii, cognomento Pamphili, Caesareae Palaestinae Episcopi, historiae Ecclesiasticae libri X; Eiusdem de vita Constantini Magni lib. IV. Constantini Magni oratis ad sanctorum coetum Eiusdem Eusebii oratio in laudem Constantini Magni . . . Nunc primùm Graecè in lucem missa. Socratis Scholastici Constantinopolitani historiae Eccles. lib. VII. Theodoriti Cyrensis Episcopi lib. V. Theodori Lectoris collectaneorum lib. II. Hermiae Sozomeni Salaminij lib. IX. Euagrij Scholastici Epiphanensis lib. VI. Graecolatine nunc primùm editi, ex interpretatione Joannis Christophorsoni.* Coloniae Altobrogum, 1612

Chronicon (GCS 47)

De praeparat. evang. • ***De Evangelica praeparatione* [Venice: Ottaviano Scoto II., 1500]** (PG 21) • *Preparation for the Gospel.* Translated by Edwin Hamilton Gifford. Oxford: Clarendon, 1903

Demonstrat. evang. • *Demonstratio evangelica* (GCS 23; PG 22) • *The Proof of the Gospel.* Translated by William John Ferrar. London: SPCK, 1920

Hist. eccles. • ***Eusebii Pamphili, Ruffini, Socratis, Theodoriti, Sozomeni, Theodori, Evagrii, et Dorothei ecclesiastica historia, sex propè seculorum res gestas complectens . . . chronographia insuper & lectionis sacrae historiae luculenta methodo exornata.* Basel: Episcopius, 1570;** *Eusebii Pamphili Episcopi Caesariae Palaestinae, Ecclesiasticae historiae lib. X, Wolfgango Musculo interprete.* Basel: Froben et Episcopius, 1557; *Historiae Ecclesiasticae libri decem, partim Ruffino in nouem prioribus libris, partim Ioanne Christophorsono, libri ultimi, interpret.* Basileae: Petrinus, 1579 (GCS 9) • *The Ecclesiastical History* (FC 19)

Exemplar regium. See Arias Montanus, Benedictus

Faber Stapulensis, Jacobus (Jacques LeFèvre D'Étaples)

1 Timothy • *See* Pauline Epistles

Pauline Epistles • *In omnes D. Pauli epistolas commentariorum libri XIIII.* Köln: Cervicornus, Eucharius, 1531

Fagius, Paul

Annotat. ad paraph. Chaldaic • *See* Chaldaic paraphrase

Chaldaic paraphrase • *Thargum, hoc est, paraphrasis Onkeli Chaldaica in Sacra Biblia.* Argentorati: Machaeropoeus, 1546

Fuller, Nicolaus (Nickolas Fuller)

Miscellan. sacrorum • ***MISCELLANEORUM Theologicorum. QVIBVS NON MODO SCRIPTVRAE DIVINAE, SED ET ALIORUM Classicorum Auctorum plurima monumenta explicantur atque illustrantur; LIBRI TRES.*** **Heidelberg: Lazarus Zetzner, 1612**

Gagnaeus, Johannes (Jean de Gagny)

1 Timothy • *See* Pauline Epistles

Pauline Epistles • *In omnes D. Pauli Epp. Scholia.* Antverp., 1564

Galen (Galenus)

Collected works • **[*Opera quae extant omnia*]. Basel: Hieronymus Froben & Nikolaus Episcopius I., 1562**

De Tumoribus Praeter Naturam: A Critical Edition with Translation and Indices. Edited by Jeremiah Reedy. Dissertation, University of Michigan, 1968

In aphor. Hippocr. • *In aphorismos Hippocratis commentarii* • *See* Collected works

Genebrardus of Paris (Gilbert Génébrard)

Chronol. • *Chronogr. ad Arnoldum Pontanum* • *CHRONOGRAPHIAE LIBRI QVATVOR. PRIORES DVO SVNT DE REBVS veteris populi, & praecipuis quatuor millium annorum gestis. Posteriores, è D. Arnaldi Pontaci Vasatensis Episcopi Chronographia aucti, recentes historias reliquorum annorum complectuntur.* Coloniae Agrippinae: Gymnich, Johann III., 1581

Gerhard, Johann

Confessionis Catholicae, in qua Doctrina Catholica Et Evangelica, Quam Ecclesiae Augustanae Confessioni addictae profitentur, ex Romano-Catholicorum Scriptorum suffragiis confirmatur . . . Lib[ri]. 4 volumes. Jena: Steinmann, 1634–37

Glossa ordinaria

Textus biblie: Cum glosa ordinaria, Cum Nicolai de lyra postilla, Cum moralitatibus eiusdem, Cum Pauli Burgensis additionibus, Cum Matthie Thoring replicis Prima [–Sexta] pars. **[Basel: Johann Amerbach, 1508]**

Glossarium vetus

[*Etymologicum Magnus Graecae Linguae.* Venetiis, 1549]

Gregory Nazianzen. *See* Nazianzen, Gregory

Gregory the Great (pope)

Collected works • ***Opera . . . In Tomos Sex Distributa.*** **Paris, 1605**

Concordia locorum scripturae • *Concordia quorundam locorum sacrae scripturae.* Paris, 1572

Hom. 37 *in evangel.* • See *Homil. in evangel.*

Homil. 21 inter 50 • *See* penitential psalms

Homil. in evangel. • *Homiliae xl in Euangelia* (PL 76) • *Forty Gospel Homilies.* Kalamazoo, MI: Cistercian, 1990

Letters • *Registrum epistularum* (PL 77, 84) • *Letters* (NPNF^2 12)

Gregory the Great, cont'd.

Moralium • *Expositio in Librum Job, sive Moralium libri XXV* (PL 75) • *Morals on the Book of Job* (LFC 18, 21, 23, 31)

Pastoral. • *Regulae Pastoralis Liber* (PL 77) • *The Book of Pastoral Rule* (NPNF² 12)

penitential psalms • *In Septem Psalmos Poenitentiales Expositio* (PL 79)

Greifswald, ministers of

De vocat. ministrorum • *De Vocatione, Ordinatione, Institvtione, Dimissione Pastorvm Et Ministrorvm Evangelii. Et De Ivrisdictione Svper Personas Ecclesiasticas In Pomerania. Confessio Svperintendentis, Pastorvm Et Ministrorvm Verbi Dei Gryphisvvaldiae Et In Vicinis Ecclesiis. Adiecta Svnt Academiarum puriorum quarundam de his Articulis Iudicia.* Gryphiswaldiae: Ferberus, 1594

Haymo of Halberstadt (Haimo Halberstadiensis)

Collected works • *Haymonis Halberstatensis episcopi opera omnia.* Paris, 1852

1 Timothy • *See* Pauline Epistles

2 Timothy • *See* Pauline Epistles

Pauline Epistles • ***In diui Pauli epistolas cum breuis tum perlucida expositio.* Strasbourg: Reinhard Beck, 1519**

Hentenius, Johannes

Enarrationes vetustissimorum Theologorum, in Acta quidem Apostolorum et in omnes D. Pauli ac Catholicas epistolas ab Oecumenio: in Apocalypsim uerò, ab Aretha Cæsareæ Cappadociæ episcopo magna cura collectæ. Iohanne Hentenio interprete. Paris: Roigny, 1545

Hesychius of Alexandria

Lexicon • ***Hesychiu Lexikon.* Hagenoae: Thomas Anshelm, 1521** • *Sammlung griechischer und lateinischer Grammatiker.* Berlin: de Gruyter, 2009

Hilary of Poitiers (Hilarius Pictaviensis)

Collected works • ***Lvcvbrationes Qvotqvot Extant Olim Per Des. Erasmvm Roterod. haud mediocribus sudoribus emendatae, nunc denuò uigilantissimè & ad plura exemplaria per D. Martinum Lypsium collatae & recognitae.* Basel: Episcopius, 1570** (PL 9–10)

Contra Constantium • *Liber ad Constantium* (PL 10) • *Hilary of Poitiers: Conflicts of Conscience and Law in the Fourth-Century Church: "Against Valens and Ursacius," the Extant Fragments, Together with His "Letter to the Emperor Constantius."* Translated by Lionel R. Wickham. TTH 25. Liverpool: Liverpool University Press, 1997

De Trinitate (CCSL 62, 62A) • *On the Trinity* (NPNF² 9)

Psalms • *Commentarii in Psalmos* (CSEL 22) • *Commentary on the Psalms* (abridged; NPNF² 9)

Histor. tripart.

***Tripertite historie ex Socrate Sozomeno et Theodorico in unum collecte et . . . de greco in latinum translate libri numero duodecim.* Augsburg: Johann Schüßler, 1472**

Homer

Collected works • ***Omnia Quae Quidem Extant Opera, Graece, Adiecta Versione Latina Ad Verbum.* Basel: Nikolaus Brylinger & Bartholomäus Stähelin, 1551**

Iliad. • *Ἰλιάδος* (LCL 170–71) • *The Iliad* (LCL 170–71)

Odyss. • *Ὀδύσσεια* (LCL 104–5) • *The Odyssey* (LCL 104–5)

Hunnius, Aegidius

Collected works • ***Tomvs Primus [–Quintus] Opervm Latinorvm.* Wittenberg: Georg Müller, 1607**

Tract. de lege et evang. • *Articuli Christianae Religionis, De Lege Et Evangelio, Ex Scripturae sacrae fundamentis extructi, & forma Quæstionum ac Responsionum pertractati, Confvtatis Etiam Pontificiorvm, Antinomorvm, Calvinianorum, aliorumqq[ue] novatorum erroribus, [et], quibus eos palliant, rationibus [et] argumentis.* Wittenberg: Porsius, 1606

Ignatius of Antioch

Ad Magnesianos • (Joseph Barber Lightfoot and J. R. Harmer, eds. *The Apostolic Fathers.* London: Macmillan, 1893) • *Epistle to the Magnesians* (ACW 1)

Ad Philadelphianos • (Joseph Barber Lightfoot and J. R. Harmer, eds. *The Apostolic Fathers.* London: Macmillan, 1893) • "Epistle to the Philadelphians." In *The Apostolic Fathers: Greek Texts and English Translations.* Translated by Michael W. Holmes. Grand Rapids: Baker, 2008

Irenaeus

Advers. haereses • ***Libri quinque Aduersus portentosas haereses Valentini & aliorum, accuratius quàm antehac emendati, additis Graecis quae reperiri potuerunt.* Geneva: Jean LePreux & Jean Petit, 1570;** *Adversus haereses* (PG 7) • *Against Heresies* (ANF 1)

Isidore of Pelusium (Isidorus Pelusiota)

Letters • ***Εἰς τὴν ἑρμενείαν τῆς θείας γραφῆς Ἐπιστολων Βιβλια Τεσσαρα . . . De interpretatione diuinae Scripturae Epistolarum Libri IV.* Ed. Konrad Rittershausen. [Heidelberg]: Commelinus, 1606** (PG 78, 84)

Ius canonicum

Friedberg edition • Aemilius Friedberg, ed. *Corpus Iuris Canonici, editio Lipsiensis secunda.* 2 volumes. Graz: Akademische Druck- u. Verlagsanstalt, 1959

Gregorian edition • *Decretvm Gratiani Emendatvm Et Notationibvs Illvstratvm Vnà cum glossis, Gregorii XIII. Pont. Max. iussu editum.* Romae: In Aedibus Populi Romani, 1582; *Decretales D. Gregorii Papae IX. Svae Integritati Vna Cvm Glossis Restitvtae. Cum priuilegio Gregorii XIII. Pont. Max. & aliorum Principum.* Romae: In aedibus Populi Romani, 1582

Decretum Gratiani • Aemilius Friedberg, ed. *Corpus Iuris Canonici, editio Lipsiensis secunda.* Volume 1. Graz: Akademische Druck- u. Verlagsanstalt, 1959

Jerome (Sophronius Eusebius Hieronymus)

Collected works • ***Opera omnia, quae extant.* Cologne: Anton Hierat, 1616; *Operum, tomi I. II. III. continentes . . . epistolas, et libros contra haereticos; ex antiqvissimis exemplaribvs, opera, ac stvdio Mariani Victorii . . . emendati, argvmentis et scholiis illvstrati.* Cologne: Anton Hierat, 1616** (PL 22–30)

1 Timothy • *See* Pauline Epistles

2 Timothy • *See* Pauline Epistles

Adversus Jovinianum (PL 23) • *Against Jovinianus* (NPNF[2] 6)

Catalog. • *De viris inlustribus.* Edited by E. Richardson. Leipzig, 1896 • *Lives of Illustrious Men* (NPNF[2] 3)

Contra Jovinian. • See *Adversus Jovinianum*

Contra Pelag. • See *Dial. contra Pelag.*

De scriptor. eccles. • [Eusebius, *Chronicon* (GCS 23) ?]

Jerome (Sophronius Eusebius Hieronymus), cont'd.

Dial. contra Pelag. • *Dialogi contra Pelagianos libri iii* (PL 23) • *Against the Pelagians* (NPNF² 6)

Ecclesiastes • *Commentarius in Ecclesiasten* (CCSL 72)

Ephesians • *See* Pauline Epistles

Galatians • *See* Pauline Epistles

Hebraicorum nominum interpretatione • See *Liber de Nominibus Hebraicis*

Letters • *Epistolae* (CSEL 54–56) • *The Letters of St. Jerome* (NPNF² 6)

Liber de Nominibus Hebraicis (PL 23)

Minor Prophets • *Commentarii in Prophetas minores* (PL 25)

Pauline Epistles • *Commentarii in IV epistulas Paulinas (ad Galatas, ad Ephesios, ad Titum, ad Philemonem)* (CCSL 77C) • *The Commentaries of Origen and Jerome on St. Paul's Epistle to the Ephesians*. Translated by Ronald E. Heine. New York: Oxford University Press, 2002

Philemon • *See* Pauline Epistles

Titus • *See* Pauline Epistles

Zechariah • *See* Minor Prophets

Justin Martyr

Collected works • ***Τα Ευρισκομενα . . . Opera Qvae Vndeqvaque Inveniri Potvervnt.*** **[Heidelberg]: Hieronymus Commelinus, 1593**

Dial. cum Tryphone • *Dialogus cum Tryphone* (Georges Archambault, ed. *Dialogue avec Tryphon*. Paris, 1909) • *Dialogue with Trypho* (ANF 1)

q. 125 • Pseudo-Justin, *Quaestiones Graecorum ad Christianos* (PG 6). Or Pseudo-Justin, *Quaestiones Christianorum ad Graecos* (PG 6)

Justinianus, Benedict (Giustiniani, Benedetto)

1 Timothy • *See* Pauline Epistles

Pauline Epistles • *In omnes B. Pauli Apost. Epistolas Explanationes*. Lvgdvni: Cardon, 1612–13

Juvenal (Decimus Iunius Iuvenalis)

Satires • *Saturae* (LCL 91) • *Satires* (LCL 91)

Lapide, Cornelius à (Cornelius van den Steen)

Pauline Epistles • ***Commentaria In Acta Apostolorvm, Epistolas Canonicas, Et Apocalypsin*. Antwerpiae: Martinus Nutius, 1627**

Romans • *See* Pauline Epistles

Leo the Great (pope)

Collected works • ***Opera omnia*. Paris: Jérôme Drouart, 1614**

Letters • *Epistolae* (PL 54) • *Letters* (selection) (FC 34; NPNF² 12)

Sermon 10 *in natal. Domini* • See *Sermones*

Sermones In Praecupuis Totius Anni Festivitatibus Ad Romanam Plebem Habiti (PL 54)) • *Sermons* (FC 93; NPNF² 12)

Lombard. *See* Peter Lombard

Lusitanus, Amandus (Amatus)

Curationum Medicinalium Amati Lusitani centuriae duae Quinta videlicet ac Sexta. Venitiis: Valgrisi, 1560

Luther, Martin

Collected works (Jena edition) • ***Der Erste [–achte] Teil aller Bücher vnd Schrifften des thewren, seligen Mans Doct. Mart. Lutheri.* Jena: Donatus Richtzenhain, 1560–62; Tobias Steinmann, 1598–1615; *Tomvs Primvs [–Qvartvs] Omnivm Opervm Reverendi Patris D. M. L.* Jena: Donatus Richtzenhain, 1564–70; Tobias Steinmann, 1600–1611**

Collected works (Wittenberg edition) • ***Der ander [–Fünffte, Siebend] Teil der Bücher des . . . Martini Lutheri.* Wittenberg: Hans Lufft, 1548–54; *Tomus primus [–septimus] omnium operum reverendi Domini Martini Lutheri, Doctoris Theologiae.* Witebergae, 1545–58**

Bible • ***Biblia Das ist: Die gantze heilige Schrifft.* Wittenberg: Johann Schwertel, 1575** (WA DB 6–12)

De captivitate Babylonica ecclesiae praeludium, 1520 (WA 6) • *The Babylonian Captivity of the Church* (AE 36)

Judgment on Monastic Vows • *De votis monasticis M. Lutheri iudicium*, 1521 (WA 8) • *The Judgment of Martin Luther on Monastic Vows* (AE 44)

marginal notes on the Bible, 1545 (cf. WA DB 8:37)

Lyranus (Nicolaus of Lyra)

Bible • ***Textus biblie: Cum glosa ordinaria, Cum Nicolai de lyra postilla, Cum moralitatibus eiusdem, Cum Pauli Burgensis additionibus, Cum Matthie Thoring replicis Prima [–Sexta] pars.* [Basel: Johann Amerbach, 1508]**

Magalianus, Cosmas

1 Timothy • *See* Pauline Epistles

2 Timothy • *See* Pauline Epistles

preface • *See* Pauline Epistles

preface to *Oper. hierarch.* • *See* Pauline Epistles

Pauline Epistles • *Opus hierarchicus sive De ecclesiastico principatu Libri III: in quibus epist. b. Pauli apostoli, quae pontificiae vocari solent, commentariis illustrantur.* Lyon: Cardon, 1609

Maldonatus, Ioannes (Juan de Maldonado)

Gospels • ***Commentarii in quatuor evangelistas.* Pont-à-Mousson: Étienne Marchant, 1596**

Matthew • *See* Gospels

Mantuanus, Baptista *See* Baptista Mantuanus, Johannes

Metaphrastes, Simeon

Sermo de Petro et Paulo Apostolis • *Vita Sanctorum Mensis 06 Junius* (PG 115)

Mornaeus (Philippe de Mornay)

***De veritate religionis Christianae liber; adversus Christian. Atheos, Epicureós, Ethnicos, Judaeos, Mahume distas, & caeteros Infideles.* Herborn: Christoph Corvinus, 1602**

Nazianzen, Gregory (Gregory of Nazianzus)

Collected works • ***Sancti Gregorii Nazianzeni . . . Opera . . . Graecè & Latinè coniunctim edita . . . Jac. Billivs . . . contulit, emendauit, interpretatus est, una cum doctißimis Graecorum Nicetae Serronij, Pselli, Nonij, & Eliae Cretensis commentariis. Aucta est haec editio aliquammultis . . . Gregorij Epistolis . . . ex interpretatione Fed. Morelli.* Paris: Claude Morel, 1609**

Nicephorus Callistos Xanthopulus

Eccl. hist. • ***Ecclesiasticae historiae.* Frankfurt am Main: Sigmund Feyerabend, 1588** (PG 145–47)

Hist. • See *Eccl. hist.*

Novatian

De Trinit. • *De Trinitate* (PL 3) • *Concerning the Trinity* (ANF 5)

Numenius of Apamea

Περὶ Τἀγαθοῦ • *The Neoplatonic Writings of Numenius*. Collated and translated by K. Guthrie. Lawrence, KS: Selene Books, 1987

Oecumenius

1 Timothy • *See* Pauline Epistles

2 Timothy • *See* Pauline Epistles

Pauline Epistles • *Commentarium in Epistolas Pauli* (PG 118–19; *Oecumenii Graecii vetustique Scriptoris in omnes S. Pauli Epistolas absolutissimi Commentarii: Maximo Florentino interprete*. Basil, 1554)

Ostorodus, Christophorus (Christoph Ostorodt)

Instit. • ***Unterrichtung von den vornemsten Hauptpuncten der christlichen Religion, in welcher begriffen ist fast die gantze Confession oder Bekentnis der Gemeinen im Königreich Polen, Grossfürstenthumb Littawen und anderen zu der Kron Polen gehörenden Landschafften.* Rakow: Sebastian Sternacki, 1604**

Palladius of Galatia

Vita Macarii • *Historia ad Lausum* (PG 34)

Pelagius

commentary • *Appendix Augustiniana, In Qua Sunt S. Prosperi Carmen De Ingratis, Cum Notis Lovaniensis Theologi, Johannis Garnerii Societas Jesu Presbyteri Dissertationes Pertinentes Ad Hostoriam Pelagianam; Pelagii Britanni Commentarii In Epistolas S. Pauli, Ac Denique Des. Erasmi, Joan. Lud. Vivis, Jacobi Sirmondi, Henrici Norisii, Johannis Phereponi Et Aliorum Praefationes, Censurae, Notae, & Animadversiones In Omnia S. Augustini Opera Tomus XII*. Antwerpiae: Societatis, 1703

Pererius (Benito Pereyra)

Romans • ***Secvndvs Tomvs Selectarvm Dispvtationvm In Sacram Scriptvram, Continens Centvm Octoginta octo Disputationes super Epistolam beati Pauli ad Romanos.* Lyons: Horace Cardon, 1610**

Peter Lombard (Petrus Lombardus)

***Magistri sententiarum, libri IIII.* Lyon: Pierre Landry, 1593** (PL 192) • *The Sentences*. Translated by Giulio Silano. Toronto: Pontifical Institute of Mediaeval Studies, 2007–10

Phavorinus. *See* Varinus (Guarinus Phavorinus)

Philo of Alexandria

Collected works • ***Operum . . . Tomvs Prior [–Alter]*. Lyon, 1561**

Piscator, Johannes

1 Timothy • *See* Pauline Epistles

2 Timothy • *See* Pauline Epistles

Piscator, Johannes, cont'd.

New Testament • ***Commentarii In Omnes Libros Novi Testamenti*. Herborn: [Christoph Corvinus], 1613**

Pauline Epistles • *Analysis logica quinque postremarum epistolarum Pauli: videlicet epistolae ad Timotheum prioris. Timotheum posterioris. Titum. Philemonem. Hebraeos.* Herbornae: Christophorus Corvinus, 1592

Pistorius, Johann

Hodeget. • ***Wegweisser vor alle verführte Christen*. Vienna: Franz Kolb, 1600**

Plautus, Titus Maccius

Trinummus (LCL 328) • *Three-Dollar Day* (LCL 328)

Pliny the Elder (Gaius Plinius Secundus)

Naturalis historia (LCL 330, 352–353, 370–371, 392–394, 418–419) • *Natural History* (LCL 330, 352–353, 370–371, 392–394, 418–419)

Primasius of Hadrumetum

1 Timothy • *See* Pauline Epistles

2 Timothy • *See* Pauline Epistles

Pauline Epistles • ***In Omnes D. Pauli epistolas commentarij perbreues ac docti*. Cologne: Johann Gymnich, 1538** (spurious)

Prosper of Aquitaine

De vocat. gent. • *De vocatione omnium gentium* (PL 51) • *On the Calling of All Nations* (ACW 15)

Epigrammatum Ex Sententiis Sancti Augustini Liber Unus (PL 51)

Resp. objectionum Vincentianarum • *Pro Augustini Doctrina Responsiones Ad Capitula Objectionum Vincentianarum* (PL 45:1679, 1843–50)

Ravenspergerus (Hermann Ravensperger)

Decad. 3. globor sacror. • *Globus sacer, hoc est Quæsitorum [et] Responsorum Theologicorum Silva.* Groningae: Johannes Sassius, 1618

Salmeron, Alfonsus (Alfonso Salmerón)

1 Timothy • *See* Pauline Epistles

2 Timothy • *See* Pauline Epistles

Pauline Epistles • ***Commentarii in omnes epistolas B. Pauli, & Canonicas; in quatuor tomos distributi . . . quorum hic est primus, in ordine autem Tomus decimus tertius*. Cologne: Anton Hierat & Johann Gymnich IV, 1604**

Scaliger, Joseph Juste

Notis ad N. T. • *Τῆς Καινες Διαθήκης ἁπάντα. Novum Iesu Christi D.N. Testamentum: Cum notis Iosephi Scaligeri in locos aliquot difficiliores.* Coloniae Allobrogum: Rovière, 1619

Scotus Hyberniensis, Sedulius

1 Timothy • *See* Pauline Epistles

2 Timothy • *See* Pauline Epistles

Pauline Epistles • *In Omnes D. Pauli epistolas annotationes.* Basel: Heinrich Petri, 1538

Sedulius. *See* Scotus Hyberniensis, Sedulius

Socrates

Hist. eccl. • ***Tripertite historie ex Socrate Sozomeno et Theodorico in unum collecte et . . . de greco in latinum translate libri numero duodecim*. Augsburg: Johann Schüßler, 1472** • *The Ecclesiastical History of Socrates Scholasticus* (NPNF[2] 2)

Stapulensis. *See* Faber Stapulensis, Jacobus

Stephanus, Robertus

1 Timothy • *See* New Testament

New Testament • *Tês Kainês Diathêkês Hapanta: Euangelion Kata Matthaion. Kata Markon. Kata Lukan. Kata Iôannu. Praxeis Tôn Apostolôn: Nouum Iesu Christi Dn. nostri Testamentum*, Vt ex Bibliotheca Regia Anno M.D.L. per Robertvm Stephanvm excusum fuit. Francofurti: Marnius & Aubrius, 1601

Strabo

***Geographicorvm Lib. XVII. . . . Item, Epitomae eorundem decem & septem de Geographia librorum*. Basel: Johann Waldner, 1539** (LCL 49, 50, 182, 196, 211, 223, 241, 267) • *The Geography* (LCL 49, 50, 182, 196, 211, 223, 241, 267)

Suavis, Petrus

Historiae Concilii Tridentini Libri Octo: Ex Italicis summa fide et accuratione Latini facti. Augustae Trinobantum: [Bill], 1620

Suidas

Suidae lexicon: Graece et Lat. Osnabrück: Biblio-Verl., 1986

Syriac paraphrase

***N. T. versia Syriaca, edita cum interpret. Lat. Jmman. Tremellij*. Paris: Henr. Steph., 1569**

Talmud

Tract. de oblationibus • תלמוד בבלי מסכת זבחים • *Hebrew-English Edition of the Babylonian Talmud: Zebahim*. Translated by H. Freedman. London: Soncino, 1988

In Sanhedrin • תלמוד בבלי מסכת סנהדרין • *Hebrew-English Edition of the Babylonian Talmud: Sanhedrin*. Translated by J. Shachter and H. Freedman. London: Soncino, 1987

Tertullian (Quintus Septimus Florens Tertullianus)

Collected works • ***In Q. Septimii Florentis Tertvlliani Opera, Qvae Ad Manvs Ipsivs Pervenerant, Et Cvra Ipsivs Fverant In Lvcem Edita, Annotationes . . . His Svbiectae Svnt Censvrae Inqvisitionis Hispanicae In B. Rhenani Annotationes Ad Tertvllianvm, Provt editae sunt in Indice librorum expurgatorum*. [Heidelberg: Hieronymus Commelinus,] 1597; *Opera omnia*. [Heidelberg]: Commelinus, 1608**

Adversus Hermogenem (CCSL 1) • *Against Hermogenes* (ANF 3)

Apologeticum (CCSL 1) • *Apology* (ANF 3; FC 10)

Contra Marcion. • *Adversus Marcionem* (CCSL 1) • *Against Marcion* (ANF 3)

De praescript. adv. haeriticos • *De praescriptione haereticorum* (CCSL 1) • *The Prescription of Heretics* (ANF 3)

De pudicitia (CSEL 20) • *On Modesty* (ANF 4)

De resurr. carnis • *De resurrectione mortuorum* (CCSL 2) • *The Resurrection of the Flesh* (ANF 3)

De Trinit. • Novatian, *De Trinitate* (PL 3) ? • Novatian, *On the Trinity* (ANF 5) ?

Theodoret of Cyrus (Theodoretus Cyrrhensis)

Collected works • ***Operum . . . tomus secundus*. Paris: Michel Sonnius II., 1608**

1 Timothy • *See* Pauline Epistles

2 Timothy • *See* Pauline Epistles

Pauline Epistles • *Interpretatio in quatuordecim epistolas S. Pauli* (PG 82) • *Commentary on the Letters of St. Paul*. Translated by R. C. Hill. Brookline, MA: Holy Cross Orthodox Press, 2001

preface to the Pauline Epistles • *See* Pauline Epistles

Theophylact (Theophylactus de Achrida)

1 Timothy • *See* Pauline Epistles

2 Timothy • *See* Pauline Epistles

Pauline Epistles • *Theophylacti Archiepiscopi Bvlgariae, in omnes diui Pauli Epistulas Enarrationes, luculentae ac prorsus diuinae, ex multis approbatis exemplaribus . . . recognitae . . . Christophoro Porsena Romano Interprete*. Cologne: Peter Quentel, 1542; *Commentarius In Omnes Divi Pauli Epistolas* (PG 124–125)

Thomas Aquinas

Collected works • ***Opera omnia*. Rome: Antonio Blado, Giovanni Gigliotti, & Giulio Accolti, 1569–71**

1 Timothy • *See* Pauline Epistles

2 Timothy • *See* Pauline Epistles

Pauline Epistles • *In omnes beati Pauli Apostoli epistolas commentaria*. Parisiis: Johannes De Roigny, 1563 • *Commentaries on St. Paul's Epistles to Timothy, Titus, and Philemon*. South Bend, IN: St. Augustine's Press, 2007

Tossanus, Paul

1 Timothy • See *Biblia*

2 Timothy • See *Biblia*

Biblia Das ist/ Die gantze H. Schrifft/ Durch D. Martin Luther Verteutscht . . . Sonst sind auch Vorreden/ Summarien . . . und underschiedliche Register . . . beygefügt Durch Paulum Tossanum. Franckfurt: Tampach; Heydelberg: Lancellot, 1617

Ulpian

[*Demosthenis et Aeschinis Principum Graeciae Oratorum Opera / Cum utriusque autoris Vita et Ulpiani Commentariis, novisq[ue] Scholiis*. Francofurti: Marnius, 1604]

Varinus (Guarinus Phavorinus)

***Λεξικον Βαρινου Φαβωρινου Καμηρτος του της Νυκαιριας Επισκοπου, το Μεγα και Παννωφελιμον, Dictionarium Phavorini Camertis, Nucerini Episcopi, Magnum Illud ac Perutile*. Basel: Robert Winter, 1538**

Vatablus, Franciscus

***Sacra Biblia, Hebraice, Graece, et Latine. Cum annotationibus Francisci Vatabli . . . cui . . . acceßit . . . Novum Testamentum Graecolatinum Ben. Ariae*. [Heidelberg:] Hieronymus Commelinus Erben, 1616**

Vincent of Lérins

Adversus profanas heresium novitates • *Tractatus pro catholicae fidei antiquitate et universitate adversus profanas omnium haereticorum novitates (Commonitorium)* (PL 50) • *The Commonitory of Vincent of Lérins, for the Antiquity and Universality of the Catholic Faith against the Profane Novelties of All Heresies* (FC 6)

Weller, Hieronymus

***De Officio Ecclesiastico, Politico, Et Oeconomico, Libellvs Pivs Et Ervditvs*. Nürnberg: Johann vom Berg, Ulrich Neuber, [1552]**

Whitaker, William (Witakerus)

De script. • ***Disputatio De Sacra Scriptura; Contra Huius Temporis Papistas, inprimis Robertum Bellarminum . . . & Thomam Stapletonum*. Herbornae Nassoviorum: Corvinus, 1600**

Windeck, Johann Paul

De efficacia mortis Christi • *Controversiae De Mortis Christi Efficacia, Inter Catholicos Et Calvinistas Hoc Tempore Disputatae: In Quibus CCLXXXVI. Argumentis, Calvinistarum errore destructo, confirmatur Veritas Catholica, contra quam, Christum Non Pro Omnium Hominum Salute Mortuum Esse, horribiliter blasphemant Professores Calvinismi Genevenses, Basileenses, Heidelbergenses, Tigurini, Bernenses.* Coloniae Agrippinae: Quentelius, 1603

Xenophon

Paed. • *Cyropaedia* (LCL 51–52) • *Cyropaedia* (LCL 51–52)

Zosimus

Historiae novae libri VI. Basileae: Perna, 1576